Open Architecture Curricular Design in World Language Education

OPEN ARCHITECTURE CURRICULAR DESIGN IN WORLD LANGUAGE EDUCATION

Andrew R. Corin, Betty Lou Leaver,
and Christine Campbell, Editors

Georgetown University Press / Washington, DC

©2025 Georgetown University Press. All rights reserved. No part of this book may be reproduced or utilized in any form or by any means, electronic or mechanical, including photocopying and recording, or by any information storage and retrieval system, without permission in writing from the publisher.

The publisher is not responsible for third-party websites or their content. URL links were active at time of publication.

Library of Congress Cataloging-in-Publication Data

Names: Corin, Andrew R., editor. | Leaver, Betty Lou, editor. | Campbell, Christine (Language consultant), editor.
Title: Open architecture curricular design in world language education / Andrew Corin, Betty Lou Leaver, and Christine Campbell, editors.
Description: Washington, DC : Georgetown University Press, [2025] | Includes bibliographical references and index.
Identifiers: LCCN 2024035526 (print) | LCCN 2024035527 (ebook) | ISBN 9781647125981 (hardcover) | ISBN 9781647125998 (paperback) | ISBN 9781647126001 (ebook)
Subjects: LCSH: Language and languages—Study and teaching.
Classification: LCC P53 .O64 2025 (print) | LCC P53 (ebook) | DDC 407.1—dc23/eng/20250128
LC record available at https://lccn.loc.gov/2024035526
LC ebook record available at https://lccn.loc.gov/2024035527

♾ This paper meets the requirements of ANSI/NISO Z39.48-1992 (Permanence of Paper).

26 25   9 8 7 6 5 4 3 2   First printing

Printed in the United States of America

Cover design by Jason Alejandro
Interior design by Westchester Publishing Services

Table of Contents

Foreword by Karin C. Ryding — vii
A Note to the Reader — ix
Acknowledgments — xiii
Abbreviations — xv

PART 1: THE OACD FRAMEWORK

1. An Introduction to Open Architecture Curricular Design: Concept, Origins, and Range of Applicability
   ANDREW CORIN, BETTY LOU LEAVER, AND CHRISTINE CAMPBELL — 3

PART 2: OACD IN US GOVERNMENT LANGUAGE INSTITUTES: PROGRAMS AT THE DEFENSE LANGUAGE INSTITUTE FOREIGN LANGUAGE CENTER

2. Open Architecture Curricular Design as an Enabler for Transformative Learning in a Korean Course
   JAE SUN LEE — 29

3. Preparing Novice Learners for Open Architecture Learning: The Gradual Release of Responsibility Model
   IRENE KRASNER — 41

4. OACD-Based Immersion Events Outside the Classroom in an Intensive Chinese Mandarin Program
   KUEILAN CHEN — 53

5. Introducing Open Architecture Curricular Design in an Egyptian Dialect Program
   KASSEMA JONES — 67

6. The Use of Project-Based OACD Modules in an Intermediate and Advanced Chinese Mandarin Program
   DANIEL WANG — 79

PART 3: OACD IN US MILITARY SERVICE ACADEMIES: PROGRAMS AT THE US MILITARY ACADEMY (WEST POINT)

7 Emulating Proficiency-Increasing Features of the Semester Abroad Experience through Open Architecture Curricular Design
E. John Gregory — 97

8 Optimizing Flexibility in a Distance Learning Immersion Course at West Point: Three Examples of Open Architecture Curricular Design
Sherry A. Maggin, Zachary F. Miller, Joshua Enslen, John Pendergast, and Olga Dobrunoff — 107

PART 4: OACD IN ACADEME

9 Using OACD and Macrostrategies Frameworks to Enable the Practical Application of Sociocultural Theory in a College Russian Course
Jeff R. Watson — 119

10 Inter-Institutional Collaboration in Curriculum Development: The Design of Flexible Modules in the Less Commonly Taught Languages Partnership
Koen Van Gorp, Emily Heidrich Uebel, and Luca Giupponi — 139

11 From Reading the News to Performing the News: Using Oral Presentations as the Key Component of an OACD-Enabled Course
Rossina Soyan — 151

12 Integrating Open Architecture Curricular Design in a Proficiency-Oriented, Content-Based Instruction Course in Korean
Sang Yee Cheon — 165

13 Spiral-Like Design for Teaching Inflectional Languages at Novice Level in an OACD-Enabled Content-Based Instruction Course
Maria Bondarenko — 177

PART 5: LEARNING ASSESSMENT, PROGRAM EVALUATION, AND PROGRAM MANAGEMENT IN AN OACD CONTEXT

14 Open Architecture Curricular Design as an Enabler of Diagnostic Instruction
Reem Dababneh and Rong Yuan — 193

15 An Open Architecture Approach to Program Evaluation in a Language Learning Setting
Wendy Ashby — 207

16 Implementing Open Architecture Curricular Design at the Classroom and Department Level: Lessons from a Ten-Year Experience
Yaniv Oded and Ilknur Oded — 221

Contributors — 233
Index — 237

Foreword

> "May our ... models for the years ahead combine the richness of the past with the excitement of the new. One must not only hope, but also do."
> Edward Said, presidential address to the MLA 1999,
> PMLA 115 (2000) no. 3: 285–91, p. 291

I HAVE ALWAYS LIKED Edward Said's closing words in his presidential address to the Modern Language Association (MLA) because they stood not only for emphasizing his remarks but also for alerting us to powerful future directions for new ideas and new actions built on the "richness of the past." In a lively progression that extends at least back to the 1970s work on L2 acquisition, methodologies of teaching, assessment, learner psychology, and learning styles including (for example) counseling-learning/community language learning (CL/CLL), the silent way, content-based instruction, and the natural approach, the authors and editors of OACD bring the power of past insights to new applications and new theoretical constructs that incorporate a rich and wide range of options in a coherent, systematic approach to theme-based curriculum development and to classroom praxis.

This volume is notable not only for its pioneering conceptualization of curriculum development and application but also for the rigor and clarity of its presentation, the illustrations of applied theoretical constructs, and the good will and creativity mounted by instructors, scholars, and students in bringing change and innovation into mainstream language and culture learning. Drawn from years of experience in a range of institutional settings, the chapters in this book form both a map and a narrative vision of how to conceptualize, organize, implement, and assess a powerful curricular philosophy that distinguishes OACD not just as an enabler of task-based and genre-based pedagogy but also as an experiment in development of a wide and flexible range of key learning experiences.

These chapters go a long way in providing guidelines, rationales, and analysis of non-text-based but well-organized learning situations. Clearly non-text-based does not mean total lack of an anchoring textbook. It means that the textbook is not the course. A textbook may be one resource in a well-designed, comprehensive curriculum that aims at using and understanding the foreign language in a wide and realistic range of communicative contexts built on OACD principles. Open architecture provides an overarching theoretical framework for the practice and development of valid alternative approaches to language teaching and learning that incorporate ambitious learning goals and capture the creativity of both teachers and students.

One of the key strengths of this book is the quality and extent of contributions by experienced classroom teachers who have applied and evaluated the effectiveness of a wide variety of approaches, combining and assessing the impact of various curricular designs, activities, and assignments. Each chapter features study questions as well as a detailed bibliography that will serve readers well as resources for current and future reexamination of the many options offered by OACD. Moreover many of the contributions focus on the less commonly taught languages (LCTLs), which have had far fewer resources at both the academic and governmental institutional levels. These chapters provide explicit ideas, blueprints, and outlines for further development and implementation of "open" curricula that lead to significant and measurable gains in proficiency. These are not just handy recipes for classroom activities but clearly formulated and well-articulated discussions of why and how to implement the open architecture model of curriculum design, with teacher and administrator buy-in and clear and careful assessment of and by the learners themselves, including development of learner autonomy and the power of their own voices, moving and modulating in accordance with situational needs and appropriateness.

The usefulness of this book for teacher training, curriculum discussion and building, and designing thoughtful institutional learning experiments cannot be overstressed. Its particular strengths lie in its presentation of theory, its rich resources for classroom research, its explanatory clarity, and the detailed reporting on new designs for different organizational contexts. It represents the best of collaboration between and among academic and governmental institutional organizations that deal with language learning and content, between scholarship and practice, and it will certainly stimulate an open dialogue among language professionals based on the rigor, openness, and vitality of emergent curricular frameworks.

Karin C. Ryding, Georgetown University

A Note to the Reader

THE VOLUME BEFORE YOU introduces *open architecture curricular design* (OACD), a textbook-free curricular design framework for world language learning. For more than three decades the editors of this volume have observed and fostered the practice and potential of OACD through its employment in numerous and varied learning situations. These have included high-stakes episodes of immediate, sometimes critical need to achieve rapid language acquisition but also more typical nonintensive learning settings. Repeatedly over this period OACD has proven its potential to yield proficiency outcomes beyond those typically expected for a given timeframe and learning context, a number of them documented in this volume.

In the chapters that follow the editors will first define OACD and explain its conceptual framework, origins, and range of applicability (Chapter 1: An Introduction to Open Architecture Curricular Design). The follow-on chapters by author-practitioners will illustrate OACD in action across a variety of languages and learning settings.[1] First, though, a few words about the volume's objective, intended audience, and organization are in order.

Objective of This Volume

The primary purpose of this volume is to introduce OACD to a broad readership of language learning professionals and interested language learners, many of whom may be unfamiliar or only marginally familiar with it. It is our hope that this will encourage more language learning professionals and learners alike to experiment with OACD, explore its potential and, ultimately, to come to view the attainment of professional-level, even near-native proficiency in a non-native language as a realistic goal over a course of study.

Intended Audience

This volume is directed toward all language-learning professionals, including teachers, professors, program managers or coordinators, language teacher education programs, and language learning researchers. Additionally language learners seeking ways to "supercharge" their learning efficiency may also find grist for organizing their study efforts.

Organization of the Volume

Part 1, "The OACD Framework," sets the stage for the following practically oriented chapters that will provide instantiation of the principles and common features of OACD, alongside features unique to individual programs. Part 1 is comprised of Chapter 1, "An Introduction to Open Architecture Curricular Design: Concept, Origins, and Range of Applicability" by Corin, Leaver, and Campbell. Chapter 1 begins by defining OACD. It then lays out its conceptual background, including how OACD fits into the broader picture of language learning concepts and practices, while exploring certain theoretical ramifications, especially those related to learner variation. The chapter then turns to a survey of the origins and development of OACD in both governmental and nongovernmental programs, especially over the past four decades, culminating with the defining of OACD as a distinct curricular design framework in 2015 at the Defense Language Institute Foreign Language Center (DLIFLC). Within the survey of OACD's origins, the authors highlight noteworthy learning outcomes achieved through OACD. Finally the chapter explores the wide range of applicability of OACD, addressing both real and apparent challenges to its implementation in a variety of learning settings.

Wherever possible, the authors of this and subsequent chapters cite actual proficiency outcomes and other beneficial outcomes achieved through OACD. In some cases those data cannot be made available because of privacy regulations or security concerns. The rapid operational pace of government programs is another limiting factor. Much of the data reported from US government programs was preserved because it was used to prepare unpublished quarterly or annual internal reports. For many nongovernment programs, including those in colleges and universities described in Part 4, pre-course and exit proficiency testing data are only infrequently available.

Part 2 contains descriptions of OACD in US government programs, represented by courses at DLIFLC. Lee (Chapter 2) describes the North Korean component of an advanced OACD Korean language course, focusing on OACD's role as an enabler for *transformative language learning and teaching* (defined in Chapter 1). Krasner (Chapter 3) describes the use of the *gradual release of responsibility* model for accustoming Novice-level (ILR 0/0+) learners to OACD-based learning in a Russian basic language acquisition program. Chen (Chapter 4) illustrates the exploitation of OACD immersion events in a Chinese Mandarin basic language acquisition program that is otherwise textbook-based. Jones (Chapter 5) demonstrates how an otherwise textbook-based basic language acquisition program in Egyptian dialect can be modified in the direction of OACD. Finally Wang (Chapter 6) demonstrates an advanced modular OACD Chinese Mandarin course that can be delivered in classroom, technology-mediated, and hybrid modes. These chapters thus reflect a range of levels (from novices to more advanced), languages, and modes of instruction (classroom, technology-mediated, hybrid, and immersion events).

Part 3 describes service academy programs, represented by the US Military Academy (West Point). The language programs at West Point combine aspects of

Note to the Reader

governmental and nongovernmental programs. While their instructors interact occasionally with those from other government language institutes, these programs are nevertheless organized and function more along the lines of university programs and thus can present fruitful terrain for cross-fertilization. Gregory (Chapter 7) presents a Mandarin Chinese course that exploits OACD to maintain and build upon the proficiency gains of recent returnees from study abroad. Maggin et al. (Chapter 8) describe a unique OACD course for Portuguese, Russian, and Spanish learners while on study abroad, managed by instructors at the home institution.

Part 4 describes OACD programs in academe. These descriptions are drawn from a wide variety of instructional contexts and span an equally wide variety of languages. Watson (Chapter 9) demonstrates the use of the OACD and macrostrategies frameworks to enable the practical application of sociocultural theory in a second-year Russian course. In Chapter 10 Van Gorp, Heidrich Uebel, and Giupponi share the approach of an academic alliance of less commonly taught language (LCTL) programs that draws upon OACD to address the special challenges that they face, highlighting the use of open educational resources in a Swahili and a Hindi program. In Chapter 11 Soyan describes an advanced open-architecture Russian media course in Portland State University's Russian Language Flagship Program focused on "performing the news," while in Chapter 12 Cheon describes an open-architecture advanced Korean film course in the University of Hawai'i at Mānoa's Korean Language Flagship Program. Finally in Chapter 13 Bondarenko presents an intensive OACD Russian course for beginning Novice (ILR 0) learners at the Middlebury School of International Studies that employs content-based learning from the second week of instruction.

Part 5 explores the critical metatopics of learning and learner assessment, program evaluation, and program management in an OACD context. Dababneh and Yuan (Chapter 14) describe the formalized and informal processes of formative assessment that inform the holistic process of *diagnostic instruction* (instruction oriented toward learners' zone of proximal development). OACD-enabled diagnostic instruction has been a key contributor to achieving outstanding proficiency outcomes at DLIFLC. Ashby (Chapter 15) describes *open architecture program evaluation*, locating it in the historical development of evaluation concepts and processes, drawing on her work at DLIFLC. Finally Oded and Oded (Chapter 16) address the challenges and successes language programs can experience through establishing and fostering OACD at the classroom and department level. The authors draw on the metaphor of fractals to describe the similarity of processes that occur at the various levels from that of individual learners up through their instructors and on to higher levels of program management.

A unique feature of this volume is that the descriptive chapters are all written by author-practitioners who have driven innovation on the front lines of instructional practice and instructional support—designing, delivering, and assessing OACD-based courses across many languages and instructional contexts. Here these author-practitioners take the lead role in reporting their experiences. Together they provide language learning professionals and learners with examples of a unifying curricular framework that can promote creativity and enhance learning.

The editors have endeavored to include, to the extent possible, a range of both commonly and less commonly taught languages. Attention has been paid to documenting the generalizability of OACD to programs across the teaching spectrum: intensive government programs and more traditional academic environments (service academies and universities), in a range of formats (short and long, classroom, technology mediated, hybrid, and immersion/study abroad). While the primary purpose of Parts 2–4 is to describe full-fledged OACD instruction, several chapters demonstrate how instructors have endeavored to adapt more traditional curricula in the direction of OACD, primarily through modular approaches. A largely unexplored and no doubt rich area remaining for future examination is the application of OACD with younger (K-12 and preschool) learners, though some applications of OACD at these levels are noted in Chapter 1.

The large representation of US government language programs described in this volume reflects the circumstances within which OACD first took shape as a distinct curricular design framework. This is explained in greater detail in Chapter 1.

References to Language Learning

Throughout this volume authors refer to language or world language learning/education rather than distinguishing categories of language learning (second language, world, language, English as a second language, L2, and similar). This choice is based on the understanding that OACD is equally amenable to any of these settings. Generally the contributions to this volume fall into the category of world language learning, but examples could be cited from various other contexts as well.

Language Proficiency Levels

Language proficiency levels will be presented in the two most common proficiency scales currently in use in the United States. The ACTFL American Council on the Teaching of Foreign Languages) scale (ACTFL Proficiency Guidelines; www.actfl.org/educator-resources/actfl-proficiency-guidelines) is most familiar to language professionals operating within academe. US government agencies utilize the Interagency Language Roundtable (ILR) scale (ILR Skill Level Descriptions; www.govtilr.org/). Base proficiency levels in the two scales are coordinated, as the ACTFL scale is a derivation from the ILR Scale. See Corin 2020c, cited in Chapter 1, for a brief account of the origin and history of these scales. In this volume all proficiency levels will be presented in the form "ACTFL (ILR)," for example, "Superior (ILR 3)."

Study Questions

At the conclusion of each chapter study questions are provided. These can be used by individual readers to personalize the information in the chapter or by groups of students as a supplemental text in a teaching methods course.

Note

1. Program descriptions in this volume reflect their status of the time of writing. The nature of some of the programs, particularly those supported by grant funds and those conducted by government institutions, may differ in small or large details at the time of book release. Readers interested in one or another program's current details should query the authors for an update.

Acknowledgments

THE EDITORS WISH TO thank all of those who have made the completion of this book possible. First and foremost we are indebted to Georgetown University Press for taking on a project of this seminal nature, presenting applications shared by teacher-practitioners, in whom most of the experience of OACD lies, in advance of the scholar-researchers, most of whom have yet to add OACD concepts and applications to their research agendas. We especially thank Hope LeGro, acquisitions editor at Georgetown University Press, as well as the GUP production and marketing staffs, who supported us from start to finish, together with the insightful and perspicacious reviewers with whom she shared our proposal and early chapters; all of these individuals provided us with important feedback, helping us to gradually frame the book into its final form.

The concept of OACD as a curricular design framework is new not just to teaching world languages but also to teaching in general. There is not a body of research that we can acknowledge as being a springboard to current practice; however, there is indeed a body of individuals who provided the wherewithal for the early explorations shared in this volume. We would like to acknowledge colleagues in the field who have contributed to our understanding of OACD, such as Natalia Lord and the late Boris Shekhtman, whose advanced course at the Foreign Service Institute (FSI) (1984–90) may have been the first instance of OACD; a number of colleagues teaching English as a foreign language in programs around the world, especially in the late 1990s and early 2000s, who had no access to textbooks and shared their OACD-enabling archives with each other and with us (e.g., those working in the American Council for Collaboration and Education in language study programs in Uzbekistan, Kazakhstan, Turkmenistan, and Moldova); and colleagues whose work informed this volume—Dr. Roni Abusaad, Dr. Rita Deyoe-Chiullán, Dr. Jack Franke, Dr. Vatche Ghazarian, Dr. Ghada Omer Attia, Dr. Diana Ruggiero, Dr. Steven Sacco, Dr. Farid Saydee, and Dr. Anjel Tozcu. Given that all three editors spent a large portion of their language careers at the Defense Language Institute Foreign Language Center, we recognize an indebtedness to the institutional leadership who allowed us the opportunity for exploration and supported us as we worked through the implications and worked out the implementation of OACD in various DLIFLC programs, namely, COL Donald C. Fischer Jr., PhD (USA, ret.), former DLIFLC provost and commandant, as well as COL Tucker Mansager (USA, ret.), COL Sue Ann Sandusky, PhD (USA, ret.), and COL Danial Pick (USA, ret.), former DLIFLC commandants. Additionally BG Gregory Ebner, PhD (USA, ret.), former department head for the Department of Foreign Languages at the US Military Academy (West Point), provided similar support, as did Ambassador Jack Mendelssohn at FSI.

We would be remiss not to mention the dozens upon dozens of language teachers in many different languages from many different language families who tested the concepts in their classrooms and who shared their results and lessons learned with us (beyond the ones represented in this book). We learned from them all—the students in the classes, the teachers of the classes, and the administrators of programs where OACD was implemented.

Several colleagues served as readers for the various chapters in this book, and we are grateful to them for their insights and for catching leaps in logic, infelicitous expressions, and even typographical errors. Their efforts have proven indispensable for ensuring quality and accuracy in the final product. We therefore thank the following individuals for their generous assistance: Dr. Mowafiq Alanazi (US Naval Postgraduate School), Dr. Evgeny Dengub (University of Southern California), Dr. Grazyna Dudney (DLIFLC) who read every chapter in detail, Dr. Gregory Ebner (US Military Academy at West Point), Dr. Thomas Jesús Garza (University of Texas at Austin), Dr. Hyunsoo Hur (US Naval Postgraduate School), Dr. Stacey Johnson (Vanderbilt University), Dr. Mina Lee (DLIFLC), Natalia Lord (US State Department Foreign Service Institute), Elena Litvinenko Patterson (DLIFLC, ret.), Dr. Surinder Rana (DLIFLC), Jane Shuffelton (Brighton High School), and Michael Vezilich (DLIFLC). Dr. Susan Kresin (University of California Los Angeles) provided valuable feedback in the early review process. We would not have been able to complete this book without their kind and able assistance.

We are also indebted to two leaders in the field who anonymously vetted the original proposals for book chapters. The guidance they provided in the early development and initial conceptualization of this project was critical in allowing us to move forward with making a formal proposal for publication.

Abbreviations

ACTFL: American Council on the Teaching of Foreign Languages
DLIFLC: Defense Language Institute Foreign Language Center
E&L: Ehrman and Leaver (of the *E&L Cognitive Style Construct*)
FSI: Foreign Service Institute
ILR: Interagency Language Roundtable
L: listening
OACD: open architecture curricular design
OAPE: open architecture program evaluation
OER: open educational resource
Q&A: questions and answers
R: reading
SCT: sociocultural theory
SCT-L2: sociocultural theory in relation to L2 (second language [learning])
S: speaking
SLD: spiral-like design
SLDP: spiral-like design principle
STEPS: subtopics/themes essential to progress

Part 1
The OACD Framework

1

An Introduction to Open Architecture Curricular Design
Concept, Origins, and Range of Applicability

ANDREW R. CORIN, BETTY LOU LEAVER, AND CHRISTINE CAMPBELL

THE PRESENT VOLUME INTRODUCES readers to *open architecture curricular design* (OACD), a textbook-free curricular design framework for learning world languages that enables the integrated application of best practices in world language education to enhance the efficiency of learning. First formally defined in 2015 at the Defense Language Institute Foreign Language Center (DLIFLC) as part of the Advanced Language Academy for senior leaders at DLIFLC and other US government agencies (DLIFLC 2015), OACD has since been gaining a growing number of practitioners across a range of language learning communities (Bondarenko and Kogan 2019; Derderian 2017; Leaver, Davidson, and Campbell 2021a, as well as presentations at a growing number of conferences and symposia[1]). A parallel developmental trend in general education is discussed later in this chapter.

Open Architecture Curricular Design: What It Is

OACD is a curricular design framework in which instruction proceeds independently of a textbook, either eschewing it entirely or relegating it to a supporting role. Instead learning is organized around a theme-based syllabus that integrates interchangeable unadapted authentic texts, tasks, and other activities, often organized into modules. The term *open architecture* is borrowed from the field of information technology, in which it similarly designates systems designed to enable the free interchangeability of components.

Independence from a textbook ensures compatibility with most, and likely all, learner-centered techniques and models at both micro and macro levels of course organization (task-based instruction, scenario- and content-based instruction, community-based learning, etc.) and modes of instruction (face-to-face, technology-mediated, and hybrid). Because the instructional process is not dependent on a textbook, OACD maximizes the potential to exploit and respond to individual and cohort variation. The flexible curricular design framework also empowers teachers to modify or change themes, texts, tasks, and activities between iterations or on the spot in response to emerging needs and opportunities.

While a theme-based syllabus rather than a textbook is an essential principle of OACD, the role, if any, of a textbook can vary according to circumstances. Teachers can (preferably) forgo it entirely or use it as a support resource at lower levels, through the American Council on the Teaching of Foreign Languages (ACTFL) Intermediate Low and Mid (ILR 1). A second core principle of OACD enabled by its independence from a textbook is ongoing learner involvement in the selection and delivery of content, as well as in the design or directing of activities as feasible. Choice of themes, texts, tasks, and activities is based in part on teacher-learner negotiation, with all parties contributing to the drafting and ongoing revision of aspects of the curriculum. A third is continual and systematic (versus occasional) tailoring to learner and cohort needs. A fourth principle of OACD—one that it shares with transformative language learning and teaching (which we introduce in the following section)—is the evolution of the instructor's role from that of a facilitator to that of a mentor, coach, or advisor.

The first of these four principles thus defines OACD's distinctness from traditional, textbook-based instruction. The remaining three are key affordances that this approach enables to a greater degree than is possible in a textbook-based course, in order to maximize learner-centeredness of the instructional process.

The Conceptual Background of OACD: Where It Fits In

Practices in world language education have shifted profoundly from the 1960s to the present. Changing educational philosophies, new curricular and syllabus designs, and advances in instructional approaches have all contributed to transforming the landscape of language learning. Among the most striking developments of this period have been:

- proficiency-oriented learner-centered instructional approaches such as content-, project-, and scenario-based instruction, task-based instruction, community-based learning, service learning, and others;
- instructional support constructs such as the scaling and testing of language proficiency and the *World-Readiness Standards for Learning Languages* (The National Standards Collaborative Board 2015); and
- performance- and proficiency-based formative assessment integrated into the learning process.

These and other developments in instruction, program design, and learning support have been further informed by a recent paradigm shift in the philosophy of language education—*transformative language learning and teaching* (TLLT), an approach that focuses on developing bilingual/bicultural competence and learner autonomy (Leaver, Davidson, and Campbell 2021b). TLLT borrows from the transformative education construct (Mezirow 1991) that has gained traction over the past thirty years in other areas of education. Mezirow posited ten steps in the process of transformation, initiated by a disorienting dilemma—a learning experience that causes a learner to question his or her assumptions—and culminating in a reframing of previously held beliefs.

This entire chain of developments reflects a broader paradigm shift in the understanding of learning that began to take shape in the late 1940s—a shift away from top-down, one-size-fits-all models in favor of approaches that place learners themselves at the center of the learning process, a corollary of which was the recognition of the individuality of each learner. The title of Klein and Schlesinger's 1949 article about the most elementary level of learning—"Where Is the Perceiver in Perceptual Theory?" (Klein and Schlesinger 1949)—broadcast a clarion call for this shift. A multidimensional exploration of individual variation began to develop out of this shift, one major aspect of which came to be termed *cognitive style*, referring to deep-seated preferences in cognitive functioning. Over subsequent decades the exploration of individual variation expanded into a number of applied fields including education and, in particular, language learning, where focus on learners and learner differences began to be incorporated in teaching, counseling, and curricular development.

By the late 1970s a reaction to this trend began to set in among some observers, who questioned the utility of recognizing individual learner variation in education, including language education. This reaction focused on the concept of *learning style*, that is, cognitive style and other dimensions of deep-seated individual variation as applied to learning. Paradoxically one major contributing factor to this trend was the very wealth and complexity of the factors involved rather than their absence. Gradually a style denial literature gained prominence, including occasional highly subjective opinion pieces that rue the continuing "myth" of learning styles (e.g., Kirschner 2017, albeit not focused on language learning). These often present strawman arguments that wrongly understand learning style to be solely or primarily concerned with accommodating learners' preferred approaches to learning, while noting the limitations of existing cognitive style constructs. (For a broader overview of this entire course of developments with further documentation and a pointed critique of the style denial movement, see Corin and Leaver, forthcoming.)

Alongside this style denial literature, work on the development of cognitive and learning style theory has continued to advance. Moreover, despite the claims of style deniers (see Newton et al. 2021 on the "neuromyth of Learning Styles" in medical education), neuroscience research into the reality of cognitive style has in fact yielded results that support the existence of biological and psychological variations among learners (Bendall et al. 2019; Kozhevnikov, Evans, and Kosslyn 2014; Kraemer, Rosenberg, and Thompson-Schill 2009).

In the end what matters is whether cognizance of learner variation can be brought to bear in a way that enhances learning outcomes. Despite the difficulty inherent in documenting the answer, in the experience of some of the authors in this volume as well as the extensive experience of the three editors with thousands of learners, it is unequivocally affirmative. This has been demonstrated most notably within certain US government language programs, in which recognition of learner variation has been exploited systematically through OACD that is informed by continuous formative assessment (Corin and Entis 2022; Dababneh and Yuan, this volume). When applied consistently, this approach has resulted in noteworthy learning outcomes (some described subsequently).

Just as striking as the changes listed previously in language learning philosophy, design, and practice has been the revolutionary reshaping over the past thirty years of the informational context in which learning occurs. Almost universal access to the internet combined with efficient search applications allows today's learners to find, compare, select, and exploit current authentic materials in real time on almost any subject from a range of sources and viewpoints. Along with this access comes previously undreamed-of electronic interactivity among learners, between them and their instructors, and the possibility for them to interact directly, without mediation, with the target culture.

This combined expansion of expertise, access, and connectivity creates a plethora of opportunities and affordances for today's world language learners and their instructors—teachers, lecturers, and professors alike. Opportunities for group work, projects, research, and engagement of higher-order cognitive skills are essentially unlimited, and it is only natural that such a complex and dynamic course of developments would also lead to innovation in frameworks for course design.

OACD is born out of this cornucopia of opportunity, informed by the World-Readiness Standards for Learning Languages and impelled by the demand for learner-centeredness, development of multicultural competencies, and overall learning efficiency[2] in world language education. The coalescence of the practices that comprise OACD into a distinct, unifying framework has occurred perhaps most notably in certain US government language institutes and service academy programs including West Point. It can also be observed, though, and to an increasing extent, across a range of nongovernmental (though in some instances government-supported) academic programs, including several described in this volume, typically not using use the term OACD in describing their instructional approaches.

OACD may be therefore viewed as an intersection of leading trends in the design of language learning curricula that have arisen in recent decades out of constructivist and sociocultural approaches to language learning. Its purpose is in fact to serve as a unifying curricular framework that enables the integrated exploitation of the many recent innovations in world language learning, including but not limited to those listed previously, reflecting both transactive[3] and transformative educational philosophy in a way that affords maximal flexibility to exploit the expanded connectivity and access to current information from target-culture milieus. Simply stated, OACD is a force multiplier[4] that enhances efficiency of learning.

Exploiting these innovations in an integrated manner leads to a fundamental shift in the role of the textbook as the traditional course anchor, as expressed through OACD's core principles outlined previously. While textbooks provide structure and standardization of the learning process and support monitoring for accountability, they can also limit creativity—of instructors and learners alike—in responding to learner and cohort needs, exploiting emerging opportunities in the target-culture environment, and generally tracking developments in the target-language society in real time. Institutional and course requirements emphasizing traditional summative testing, especially when anchored to a textbook, can further confine creativity, resulting in over-testing and under-teaching. OACD's flexible framework supports the integration of learning with ongoing performance- and proficiency-based formative assessments, with occasional summative ones, all embedded organically into the learning process (Dababneh and Yuan, this volume).

Once the learning process is freed from dependence on a textbook, the remaining three core principles of OACD become available as key affordances. Learners can become involved more centrally in the selection and delivery of content and, based on their level of preparedness, can also take on a more central role in the design or even in the directing of activities. This in turn removes some of this burden from the instructor. Teachers, for their part, gain greater freedom to switch out, shift, or adapt activities in real time in response to need or opportunity. In such a context, continual and systematic (versus occasional) tailoring to ever-changing learner and cohort needs also becomes feasible.

Another benefit of this fundamental shift in the role of teachers is that it increases their freedom to serve as a mentor, coach, or advisor in each learner's journey toward proficiency in the target language. This is a feature that OACD shares with transformative language learning and teaching. OACD is in fact a core feature of transformative language learning, though it functions equally well in nontransformative programs. The OACD-transformative learning connection is explained and illustrated in several contributions to the recent edited volume by Leaver, Davidson, and Campbell (2021a) that describe DLIFLC programs (Campbell 2021; Corin 2021), study abroad programs (Collin 2021; Farraj 2021), and language courses at the French War College (Cleret 2021) as well as three chapters in the present volume (Lee; Maggin et al.; Oded and Oded). The distinct yet related concepts of OACD and transformative language learning are disambiguated in Corin (2020a).

OACD provides today's language learning practitioners, who are often challenged by conflicting demands imposed by the needs of learners, administrators, and external stakeholders, with a proven option for enhancing language learning while maintaining flexibility and enabling creativity (see the outcomes cited subsequently). We return to the question of the practical feasibility of OACD in a later section.

Definition, Principles, and Common Practices of OACD in World Language Learning

A more elaborated practical definition of OACD in relation to language learning incorporates the four core principles specified previously:

1. Courses structured around a theme-based syllabus rather than a textbook
2. Ongoing learner involvement in the selection and delivery of content and design or directing of activities
3. Continual and systematic (versus occasional) tailoring to learner and cohort needs
4. Evolution of the role of the teacher from facilitator of learning toward that of mentor/coach/advisor, who provides resources and informed guidance to individuals and groups of learners in support of their short- and long-term activities and projects, and who consistently supports the development of learner autonomy

Through its adherence to these four principles, OACD provides a non-textbook-based alternative to traditional fixed curricula. OACD courses are structured to allow ongoing real-time modification of all content, both during and between course iterations, to meet emerging need without resource-intensive substantive revision processes. This is achieved in part by eliminating restrictive linear scope and sequence of target-language elements and functions. Modules or their elements can thus be freely switched out, modified, or reordered as desired, promoting learner empowerment and both transactive and transformative learning effects. Gregory (this volume) provides one striking example of how an OACD course's content was modified in real time to exploit an emerging development in the target-language society.

In addition to these core principles, experience has shown that the following features play a critical role in OACD courses (Campbell 2021; Corin 2020b; Derderian 2017; and Leaver and Campbell 2015, prior to the published use of the term OACD):

- Uses performance- and proficiency-based formative assessments integrated into the learning process (though some more traditional summative assessments may also be used) to free learners to the greatest possible extent from test preparation and enable them to focus more fully on learning the language and free teachers to be maximally creative in lesson preparation
- Operates within a context grounded in the World-Readiness Standards for Learning Languages and proficiency-oriented learner-centered instructional approaches such as content-, project-, and scenario-based instruction, task-based instruction, community-based learning, service learning, and others
- Integrates the following features commonly considered desirable for language learning. Some can be employed daily from day one of instruction, while others are addressed holistically over the course of learning:
  - Use of unadapted authentic materials from day one
  - Deliberate, continual use of the target language
  - Incorporation of collaborative learning such as group presentations and projects based on learner research
  - Development and use of critical reflection and higher-order cognitive skills
  - Integration of formal, colloquial, and nonstandard language
  - Use of a wide variety of listening and reading genres across a broad spectrum of social media platforms
  - Systematic defossilization
  - Focus on discourse analysis and stylistics, including use of register
  - Incorporation of language spoken by two or more people with ambient noise, grammatical mistakes, fillers, etc.
  - Top-down and bottom-up processing of information, especially for high-level presentations on topical domains such as politics, economics, and history by native speaker experts

To reiterate, what is new in all of this is not the practices that comprise or characterize OACD or even their combined application, as they are largely accepted as best practices in world language education. Rather, it is the recognition that eliminating the textbook as course anchor facilitates their combined and integrated application, enabling a force multiplication effect to enhance learning efficiency.

Origins of OACD

No doubt most current language programs and instructors strive to incorporate most or all of the practices associated with the principles and features identified previously, whether individually or in some combination. Moreover, well before the emergence of OACD as a distinct framework for course design, some language instructors and programs combined these principles and features in course designs that are now recognizable as OACD. Some early reformed approaches to language instruction (the direct method, for example) in fact "cried out" for an open approach to course design, as did many content-based programs, some of them dating back at least to 1911 in Russia; Nikonova (1968/1994) details proceedings of an all-union conference in Moscow that year on the topic of content-based language instruction. There have also been instances of teaching language without a textbook in de facto content-based learning situations such as Peter I's early eighteenth-century shipbuilders learning Dutch as a by-product of instruction in shipbuilding from visiting Dutch specialists who spoke no Russian. Similar undocumented language learning experiences have undoubtedly occurred over the centuries in worldwide locations.

That being said, OACD's rise as a defined framework can be tied more directly to the reaction that began to take hold in the late 1940s against behaviorist-based and teacher-centered approaches to learning in favor of constructivist and learner-centered approaches. This sea change in instructional philosophy gradually gathered steam in the 1950s and 1960s before unleashing a veritable torrent of conceptual and practical innovation from the 1970s onward.

The optimism created by the tremendous advances in concepts and methodology beginning in the late 1970s and early 1980s generated expectations of improved learning outcomes (Higgs 1984)—namely that more learners would achieve significantly higher levels of target-language proficiency than with "traditional" (e.g., at the time, audiolingual) approaches. Some academic programs, perhaps most notably The Language Flagship since 2003, have achieved significant success, to the extent that their participants can now realistically expect to reach the initial professional level of proficiency (Superior, ILR 3) during a four-year university program if they spend their final year in the Language Flagship's Capstone year abroad programs, some components of which have an open architecture (Eisen 2020; Murphy et al. 2016).

Viewed globally, however, since the publication of Carroll's (1967) well-known study, the number of university students in the United States reaching Superior (ILR 3) proficiency has remained low (Corin 2020c), creating the impression that this is simply an unrealistic objective for most university and K-12 students.

In the late 1970s specialists from US government language institutes established a model and graphic representation of the so-called inverted pyramid to explain this seemingly universal difficulty in achieving higher levels of language proficiency. According to this model, the difficulty of reaching the next level becomes greater the higher the initial level, since each subsequent level contains a greater amount of knowledge and skills than the previous level. The growth rate of difficulty is, moreover, exponential, so it is much harder to progress from Advanced (ILR 2) to Superior (ILR 3) than from Intermediate (ILR 1) to Advanced (ILR 2), and so on (Corin 2020c).

There is, however, another explanation for the stagnation experienced by many learners in their progress through successive proficiency levels. The depth and breadth of advances in instructional approaches over recent decades suggests that something at the level of organization of instruction may not be fully aligned with those approaches, thus limiting their effect and preventing learners from achieving rapid proficiency growth at successive levels (Corin 2020c, 2021).

It is instructive to look at exceptions—programs in which learners have, with greater consistency, attained unexpectedly high proficiency levels in light of the broader picture. These programs appear to share one common feature—abandoning the dependence on textbooks and resorting to alternatives referred to by various terms such as modular course or theme-based syllabi (Evans-Romaine and Murphy 2021; Leaver and Campbell 2015, 2020; Shekhtman et al. 2002; Stryker and Leaver 1997) but which fall generally within the definition of OACD.

It is equally instructive to view exceptions from the point of view of learners who have achieved exceptional results. Leaver and Atwell (2002) determined that of speakers rated at Distinguished (ILR 4), those without direct instruction aimed at attaining Distinguished (ILR 4) required 17 years to reach the goal, whereas those in an OACD program at the Foreign Service Institute were able to reach the goal in 5 years (or less), which included 1,400 hours of beginning study, much of it conducted in OACD format, three years of working in country, and a six-month OACD advanced course.

Early OACD at the Foreign Service Institute

It was against the backdrop of the global picture described previously that a number of language programs began to adopt curricula identifiable as OACD, though not yet using that label, with US government language institutes playing a leading role. Most notable initially was the Language School of the US Department of State's Foreign Service Institute (FSI). In 1979 OACD formed the basis of FSI's Familiarization and Short-Term Course in multiple languages that responded to an urgent requirement for filling US Embassy support positions (e.g., plumbers and electricians) with language-enhanced personnel (Natalia Lord, personal communication, November 21, 2023).

In the mid-1980s, in an attempt to "dismantle classroom walls" (Leaver 1989), FSI introduced into its basic courses from nearly the beginning of study multiple textbook-free modular activities. These included the Monolingual Language Training Program (MOLT) comprised of standalone scenarios related to diplomats' future job duties that were introduced as supplements at the end of each textbook unit (Leaver 1997); today they would be considered scenario-based instruction (Corin 2021). While that term was not used with MOLT, the concept of scenario-based instruction entered the sphere of world language learning (particularly in relation to content-based instruction on political topics and translation studies) at approximately the same time (Brecht et al. 1984).

Another FSI basic-course component introduced at this time was an "internship" program pairing each learner with a native speaker in the local Russian community

INTRODUCTION TO OPEN ARCHITECTURE CURRICULAR DESIGN

who spoke little to no English. This was an early form of service learning (Farraj 2021; Van Deusen-Scholl and Charitos 2021). As described in Leaver (1989), every Friday learners would meet with their native-speaker partner and assist as needed with living, parenting, medical, and other needs.

Yet another innovation at this time (circa 1983) in all FSI basic courses was language/area integration weekly seminars. Every week a guest-speaker content specialist would make a presentation in English on a topic related to the culture and politics of the learners' country of assignment. The next day, language teachers would replicate that information in the target language using such tools as presentations, debates, interviews, and panel discussions. During early weeks of the course, learners had to stretch to handle these professional topics with low levels of proficiency; they were aided by the fact that the content was already known and just the words and grammar were new. The overall effect of these various programs was to reduce the dependence on textbooks, especially in the more advanced phases of the basic courses (Ryding and Stowasser 1997).

FSI also instituted a six-month open architecture advanced Russian curriculum in 1984. This course was composed of 50 possible topics and 50 possible instructional techniques offered as choices to groups of learners who had tested at Superior (ILR 3). Learners used these choices to design their own highly individualized programs with the aim of achieving Distinguished (ILR 4) proficiency in reading, listening, and speaking (Leaver 1997; Leaver and Campbell 2015). Not one student who met the entry requirement in the six years that the course was taught (1984–1990) failed to achieve Distinguished (ILR 4). Following the success of this program, FSI added similar programs in Spanish and French during that same period. These courses developed over time into the Beyond Three Program that still has OACD as its basic design framework.

Early OACD at the Defense Language Institute Foreign Language Center

The early 1990s saw highly effective OACD innovations in the basic Czech and Russian programs at DLIFLC. In 1991 the DLIFLC Basic Czech Program adopted OACD. The first half of the forty-seven-week intensive course was task-based, using exclusively authentic materials and no textbook. During the second half of the course learners explored work-related and culturally prompted themes, focusing on the content of subject-matter textbooks from elementary and secondary schools in Czechoslovakia (e.g., physics, history). At graduation, every learner surpassed the proficiency objective of that time: Intermediate High (ILR 1+) in reading and listening. Two thirds of the class reached Superior (ILR 3), highly unusual in a basic program (Duri 1992; Leaver and Kaplan 2004). Some of the Russian basic programs followed this same pattern with similar results (DLIFLC 1992).

In 1993 so-called "Turbo-Serbian" immersion-conversion courses were initiated that "converted" learners' proficiency from Czech, Russian, or another Slavic language to Serbian/Croatian. These intensive elementary OACD courses used only unadapted authentic materials from day one, with a content-, project-, and scenario-based structure (Corin 1997). One of the first iterations (summer 1993) relied on eight instructors, most of whom had no language teaching experience and none of whom had experience teaching in an open-architecture environment. A one-week crash course by skilled trainers and ongoing support by a skilled instructor-coordinator were sufficient to enable success. In eleventh-week testing, the forty learners achieved levels from Intermediate (ILR 1) to Superior (ILR 3) in speaking, from Intermediate (ILR 1) to Advanced High (ILR 2+) in reading, and from Novice High (ILR 0+) to Advanced High (ILR 2+) in listening.

These same principles were used to create a highly successful Ukrainian course. This beginning conversion course for learners who had earlier acquired Russian to Advanced (ILR 2) or Superior (ILR 3) was conducted exclusively in Ukrainian with authentic materials from day one. Its objective was to bring learners from no proficiency to Superior (ILR 3) in 12 weeks of half-day study with a content-based, task-based OACD curriculum that took into account similarities between Russian and Ukrainian. Individualization and course adaptation resulted in part from faculty analysis of learners' daily diaries in Ukrainian. Remarkably, for a videoteletraining course that predated online learning, 88 percent of the learners tested at Superior (ILR 3) in reading and listening after 12 weeks (Leaver and Kaplan 2004).

Early OACD in Academe
In the nongovernmental academic sphere, many of the early *content-based instruction* courses also had an open architecture (Crandall and Tucker 1989; Stryker and Leaver 1997). Later, *languages across the curriculum* programs (Kecht and von Hammerstein 2000; Shaw 1997; Straight 1998), partly analogous to today's *content and language integrated learning* (CLIL; Commission of the European Communities 2003), reflected many of the OACD principles identified previously, though differing in their definitional strategy for taking language learning out of the traditional language classroom.

The "Turbo-Serbian" experience at DLIFLC provided the impetus for later experiments by Corin (2022) at the University of California, Los Angeles. One of these, building on an earlier innovation by Froelich at Pomona College (Froelich 1988), was a second-year Serbian/Croatian course in 1998–99 centered on same-language subtitling of target-language films. This OACD course was content-based at three levels, involving learners developing proficiency in:

- same-language subtitling using the technology of that time,
- analyzing the film's language and meaning to enable competent transcripts, and
- literary analysis of the film.

While proficiency outcomes were not measured, the course generated intense learner engagement and satisfaction. Analogous experiences of open-architecture language learning designed by innovative instructors could doubtless be enumerated from other academic programs at around this time.

Emergence of the OACD Framework at DLIFLC
In 2006 DLIFLC adopted OACD (though not yet using this term) as the framework for all intermediate, advanced, and "refresher" language courses in all languages. This resulted in a striking improvement in proficiency outcomes. Between

2008 and 2013 attainment of graduation proficiency requirements rose from 50 percent to just over 80 percent for 850 intermediate- and advanced-course students (Leaver and Campbell 2015; Dababneh and Yuan, this volume), with almost 60 percent exceeding requirements, though many had not met stated entrance requirements. In 2013 one of every fifteen exit-test results (listening, reading, or speaking) was a 3+ or 4.

The striking success of these OACD courses led to the expansion of OACD between 2012 and 2014 into contexts requiring short but high-impact courses that could be launched on short notice and continually modified in real time.

One of these consisted of short (four to eight week) remedial courses designed to enable learners who initially failed to achieve required proficiency levels on a basic program's exit proficiency tests to attain those levels. These courses often needed to be designed and launched in several days, yet gains of a half or even full proficiency level were typical, though not universal. In one example for which documentation remains available, Persian/Farsi learners who had achieved Intermediate High (ILR 1+) in reading, listening, or both in the textbook-based basic program were "recycled" for six weeks of remedial instruction. Because of basic-program staff shortages, OACD-experienced teachers from the intermediate/advanced program were assigned. Six weeks later, following a hastily prepared OACD course with no textbook, all achieved Advanced (ILR 2); several attained Advanced High (ILR 2+) and/or Superior (ILR 3) in at least one skill. The senior student in the group commented that "this is the way all courses should be taught" (Corin 2021).

Another such context was initial acquisition courses of three months or less taught at distant venues for personnel readying to deploy to field operations. These courses often produced results as high as Intermediate High (ILR 1+) and Advanced (ILR 2) in less than half the duration of the typical basic program (Mowafiq Alanazi, personal communication, May 16, 2022), though the learners were not language professionals.

A third was the transition in 2014 to short, high-impact intermediate and advanced courses intended to achieve the same proficiency outcomes as those previously achieved in courses two or three times their length. The initial intermediate and advanced "short courses" needed to be designed in months, even weeks in some cases (Corin 2021).

Yet another success of OACD in short programs was achieved in the two-to-four-week study abroad immersions for intermediate- and advanced-course learners (Leaver and Campbell 2015), in which participants engaged with native-speaker content-area specialists at local universities and had no language classes *per se*. In the advanced Arabic immersion, for example, learners gained as much as one full proficiency level in four weeks (Farraj 2021). Analogous proficiency outcomes were common in other intermediate/advanced overseas immersion programs for which statistical evidence is less readily available today.

In 2015 in response to a requirement for enhanced proficiency outcomes, an intensive effort was launched to encourage the introduction of OACD in advanced phases of DLIFLC basic language acquisition programs. As part of that effort, the aforementioned Advanced Language Academy (ALA) was organized, together with a series of symposia and other gatherings for exchange of experiences in applying OACD. It was at that time, in connection with planning and implementation of the ALA, that the phrases *open architecture* (OA) and *open architecture curricular design* (OACD) were introduced as a formal designation.[5]

This whirlwind of ALA-related activities provided the impetus to define, articulate, and theoretically ground OACD as a distinct curricular framework for world language instruction that was then elaborated in a series of publications and presentations by authors from DLIFLC and other institutions. The guiding idea throughout this process was that the openness or flexibility ensured by OACD is not an end unto itself but rather a tool—a framework enabling integration of the full range of principles of effective and efficient world language learning and best practices deriving from them. Eliminating reliance on a textbook enabled instructors and learners to develop and apply course organization and language acquisition strategies, respectively, that enabled superior outcomes (Corin 2020b).

OACD in General Education

Considering the developmental trend in learning-related concepts outlined previously, it is only natural that OACD, with or without that specific term, would be applied in other areas of education beyond world language learning. In postsecondary education, organizations like the International Society for Exploring Teaching Alternatives (ISETA; since 2003 known as the International Society for Exploring Teaching and Learning, or ISETL; ISETA 2002) have been promoting open architecture-based learning and teaching in practice, though not in name, for decades. Created at Purdue University in the 1970s, ISETL is dedicated to the study and implementation of nonlecture, generally textbook-free, instructional approaches. One such approach that gained a following in the 1980s and 1990s at Purdue University, the University of Windsor, West Virginia University, and elsewhere is *guided design*. A guided design curriculum consists of a series of well-designed, discipline-specific problems taken from real life that learners spend one to two weeks solving in groups. The textbook, if used, provides supplementary material. While instructional approaches rooted in problem solving are commonplace today, they were relatively rare in the early 1980s. In one such example from 1983, Campbell (1989) successfully implemented guided design in a language learning setting at Purdue University.

In relation to K-12 education, Travitzki and Keilan (2019) presented a broadly envisioned concept of *open architecture curriculum* that also ties in with the literature on transformative education. The authors argued that teachers should be transformative intellectuals functioning in communities of practice and innovation, with the responsibility, among others, to listen to student voices. For them,

> [a]n architecture is "open" if it can not only be inhabited but also be transformed by its inhabitants though always maintaining some structure. It must be permeable to elements external to itself, it must allow and facilitate adaptations and changes, eventually in the very foundations of the architecture. (Travitzki and Keilan 2019, 97)

Travitzki and Keilan put forward their model in response to a new national curriculum then under development in Brazil:

that imitates the US *Common Core* curriculum and aims to guide the details of educational activities, such as textbook production, standard assessments, and everyday life in the classroom. The idea behind the curriculum design is that educators need more information about what to teach and how to teach, and also more "incentives" (or pressure) to do a good job. (Travitzki and Keilan 2019, 94)

They noted that according to some authors (citing Giroux and McLaren 1986), this can lead to a situation in which:

the curriculum is not influenced by teachers anymore but is mainly in the hands of administrative experts. In more extreme cases, Giroux and McLaren claim, the curriculum is pre-packaged and designed to be "teacher-proof," to be applied in any classroom regardless the sociocultural context." (Travitzki and Keilan 2019, 96)

In their approach to open architecture curriculum for entire K-12 educational systems, Travitzki and Keilan are not opposed to the use of textbooks, as long as they are continually updated. In other respects, the purpose and mechanisms of their proposal are in broad agreement with the more narrowly defined concept of OACD for world language learning proposed in this volume.

Travitzki and Keilan cite Wrigley (2005) as the earliest example they encountered of the term *open architecture* in relation to general education. Wrigley, similar to Travitzki and Keilan, proposed his concept of *open architectures for learning* in opposition to primarily "transmission teaching" imposed by administrators on teachers, and in turn by teachers on learners, thus limiting learners' agency and voice. Wrigley's *open architectures* involve techniques such as *project method*, *problem-based learning*, *storyline*, and *design challenges* that are closely analogous to the project-based, scenario-based, content-based, and similar approaches that figure prominently in OACD for world language education.

Range of Applicability (Generalizability) of OACD Across Diverse Learning Settings

Experience to date has amply demonstrated the applicability of OACD to languages of all typological classes, including those with complex synthetic morphology (e.g., Russian: Bondarenko, Krasner, Soyan, and Watson, this volume). For those languages to which it has been applied, OACD has enabled effective and efficient learning, as measured by proficiency outcomes (see previous discussion). Often OACD has enabled substantial gains in proficiency over shorter time frames than would typically be expected, as examples cited previously indicate.

The majority of the programs described in this volume are US government intensive (multi-hour per day) programs, government-supported programs (The Language Flagship at the university level), or nongovernment intensive programs. This preponderance of government, government-supported, and other intensive programs is understandable, given that the OACD concept was first articulated and applied within US government language institutes and naturally spread most directly to other programs that communicated closely with them or were similarly structured. The nature of these institutes positioned them uniquely to take curricular risks at a scale sufficient for the development of a new framework, thanks to having large aggregate numbers of learners distributed in small cohorts in both lengthy and short intensive programs in many languages, as well as instructional support divisions dedicated to faculty professional development and curriculum development. Proficiency outcomes, moreover, were measured for almost all learners. A further stimulus to these institutes was imparted by intense internal and external pressures to achieve ever higher proficiency outcomes that have no analog in most nongovernmental academic institutions.

The question therefore arises as to the applicability of OACD in environments not forming the core of this volume. These might include more typical university classes, learning programs for younger learners (both K-12 and nonacademic opportunities in a wide variety of formats), and language training for business purposes. The contributions in Part 4 of this volume provide an affirmative answer in regard to university programs. More generally OACD has begun to make inroads in all of these environments, but there are challenges that teachers and administrators may need to address in each case. These are addressed in the following subsections.

OACD and Learner Variation

The ease with which learners become accustomed to OACD depends on individual characteristics, including motivations, personality type, sensory preferences, and cognitive style. In a simplified formulation, learners with a *synoptic* orientation as defined within the E&L Cognitive Style Construct (Dabbs and Leaver 2019; Ehrman and Leaver 2003; Leaver and Ehrman in press) exhibit greater comfort with holistic approaches to learning, including learning from context, and do not feel the need for a high degree of control over the material. Generally, synoptic learners adapt easily to OACD learning. The analogy would be to "chasing a frog into the water" (referencing a South Slav proverb; "chasing" a frog into the water is easy because frogs like being in water). Other learners may be characterized within the E&L construct as *ectenic*. Such learners seek conscious control over the learning process and are reluctant to extract knowledge from context. They can sometimes feel disoriented when first confronted with an OACD learning context. The analogy might be to "chasing a cat into the water." After a short time, however, such learners almost always become accustomed to OACD and achieve satisfactory results. Nevertheless it is best, especially for ectenic learners, if initial OACD modules, tasks, projects, and scenarios are less demanding (Dababneh 2018). Furthermore learners accustomed from previous education to OACD or, generally, learner-centered approaches, whether for world language learning or other subjects, will have a higher level of comfort at the beginning of an OACD course, while those with little or no such previous experience may at first be less comfortable, so a less challenging introduction to OACD is also useful for them.

OACD in Multisection versus Single-Section Courses

In recent literature and presentations OACD has been discussed primarily in relation to smaller, typically single-section, courses in which requirements for coordination and uniformity do not present obstacles to experimentation. At DLIFLC the expansion of OACD to the advanced segments of basic language acquisition programs beginning in 2015 (bearing in mind that some instructors and teams had applied OACD earlier and at lower levels) did involve large multisection programs in several languages. It might

INTRODUCTION TO OPEN ARCHITECTURE CURRICULAR DESIGN

have been expected that a need for coordination and comparability among parallel student sections would present obstacles to a shift to OACD, especially on account of achievement-type in-course summative tests that were standardized across multiple sections and iterations during this time period.

In fact coordination among sections proved not to be an impediment to OACD, at least in and of itself. After all the grade that mattered the most, that determined whether a student would graduate, was the level achieved on exit proficiency tests in listening, reading, and speaking, to which coordination among sections was irrelevant. The highly successful and fully OACD Hebrew Basic Program (Oded and Oded, this volume) was also multisectional. To be sure it was smaller than most DLIFLC basic programs, which perhaps made it easier to support any professional development needed for a shift to OACD.

In the end the most important factors affecting successful application of OACD in these programs (Chen, this volume; Oded and Oded, this volume)—and the same can be anticipated for larger university and K-12 programs—are threefold.

The first is alignment between learning objectives and the metrics (assessments) that determine their attainment. When learning objectives are framed in terms of performance or proficiency, and when learning objectives and assessments are aligned, OACD can function as smoothly in multisection courses as in single-section ones (Oded and Oded, this volume). As an example of how this can be structured, Clifford (2021, 232) describes a three-level testing model aligning instructional goals and testing such that "proficiency tests are used to assess learners' *far transfer* of unrehearsed, internalized abilities across a range of real-world abilities," "performance tests are used to assess the *near transfer* of rehearsed abilities in familiar settings," and "achievement tests are used to assess the direct application of low-level knowledge [i.e. no transfer and no transformation]." Naturally this conclusion speaks to possibility and does not address local academic culture within institutions or departments concerning testing or the necessity of course textbooks.

The second factor—one that affects smaller programs as well—is the culture shift required of many instructors accustomed to highly regimented courses dependent on standardized materials and processes. The same goes for managers or coordinators of such programs.

The third factor—one that can disproportionately affect large university programs—is the level of instructional skills of teaching faculty. A dependence on insufficiently trained teaching assistants can indeed limit the successful application of OACD. Yet the amount of initial familiarization, mentoring, and support required for its effective implementation is not great, and it is precisely in larger universities that the potential for such support is greatest. There is, therefore, every reason to expect that in coming years open-architecture approaches to instruction will be implemented to a greater extent in larger university programs, especially those that employ skilled instructional support personnel.

OACD at Upper versus Lower Levels of Proficiency

Learners' incoming proficiency level can affect the application of OACD. Learning at Advanced (ILR 2) and above is a natural environment for OACD because of the requirement at that level for constructivist and sociocultural approaches that OACD supports, including engagement of higher-order cognitive skills, learner autonomy, and other instructional characteristics critical to achieving Superior (ILR 3) and higher levels of proficiency (Leaver and Shekhtman 2002). Novice-level courses, in contrast, are problematic due to the proportionately greater demand they place on learners' cognitive resources (Bondarenko, this volume; Krasner, this volume), typically leading elementary course developers to resort to approaches based on cognitive models of learning, especially at the initial stages. This is traditionally expressed through various models of gradual, programmed linear or spiraled introduction of specific linguistic elements (vocabulary, grammatical categories and forms, etc.) according to frequency, complexity, or other criteria. This is especially true of languages with complex synthetic syntax and morphology, such as Russian, in which individual noun and verb paradigms may contain many forms (Bondarenko, this volume; Krasner, this volume). However, fixed linear introduction of linguistic elements is incompatible with OACD.

For these reasons OACD has commonly been considered applicable beginning at approximately Intermediate High (ILR 1+), and most publications and conference presentations on OACD to date describe learning beginning at that level (Campbell 2021; several chapters in this volume). Nevertheless there is increasing evidence of the successful introduction of OACD at much lower levels, including the very beginning of study, with examples (described previously) reported beginning even from the mid-1980s at FSI and from the 1990s at DLIFLC. A parallel trend toward replacing language textbooks at lower proficiency levels with authentic materials and experiences can also be noted in both K-12 and university programs, particularly online and especially outside the United States. These too date even from the 1980s and early 1990s (e.g., Allwright 1981; Billah 2014; Littlejohn and Windeatt 1989; Rossner and Bolitho 1990).

Three approaches to applying OACD at low proficiency levels are described in this book. Krasner proposes application of the *gradual release of responsibility* model (GRR), a form of assisted learning that envisages a gradual transition over the course of a module from activities under the control of the instructor to those in which learners take on increasing autonomy. This process is repeated cyclically. GRR, which the author illustrates with examples from the DLIFLC Russian Basic Program, can also be imagined as a gradual transition of responsibility from the first day of the course, when the instructor controls most of the learning process, to later stages of the course, which gradually approach OACD.

A second approach has been demonstrated by a Russian course at the Middlebury Institute of International Studies (Bondarenko, this volume), which introduced content-based instruction conducted in the target language from the second week of instruction. Enablers included:

- direct method technique;
- reliance on international and other cognate words (i.e., those immediately recognizable to learners) as the initial basis for the construction of vocabulary and grammar;
- the gradual release of responsibility model;

- a unique form of spiral, in which content-based activities are occasionally interrupted for "inter-tasks"—discussions on grammatical, lexical-phraseological, or cultural issues of importance for performing the activity; and
- authentic (mostly internet) materials, aided by target-language slides that connect graphic representations with linguistic correlates to illustrate and contrast concepts and categories.

A third approach is delineated by Chen—the use of OACD immersion events for learners with proficiency as low as Intermediate Low (ILR 1).

OACD in Intensive versus Non-Intensive Courses

Given the large proportion of intensive programs represented in this volume, another significant question concerns the applicability of OACD across more typical non-intensive learning environments, in which classes may meet for one hour three or five times per week. This would include multi-section university or K-12 programs as well as the smaller courses typical of less commonly taught languages that may be staffed by a single instructor responsible for the entire program. Each of these situations faces its own set of challenges in applying OACD.

The first apparent challenge is the amount of time available in a single class session for the critical interactive task-, project-, or scenario-type activities that provide opportunities for higher-order cognition and result in innovative target-language production. While this may be viewed as a limitation for applying OACD, there are also counterbalancing benefits. The non-intensive learning schedule allows more processing time between interactive class activities for reflection and intake of new learning, while avoiding the challenge of "diminishing returns" that can result from activities whose length exceeds learners' attention span and processing capabilities. The less intensive class schedule, in which contact hours are more spread out, thus creates additional opportunities for "flipped" learning (Cheon, this volume; Lee, this volume), as there is proportionally more out-of-class time available for independent research, reflection, target-language community contacts, and innovative written target-language production.

OACD at Various Levels of Learning

Finally while in literature and conference presentations to date OACD has been discussed predominantly in relation to post-secondary instruction, its application in the K-12 context has also been, and continues to be, noted and discussed. One example is from the government-funded STARTALK Program (National Foreign Language Center 2023). Saydee (2023) describes four STARTALK programs where OACD has proven effective with K-12 learners of Hindi and Urdu. For decades, Concordia Language Villages have been implementing OACD in all but name, with flexible, theme-based curricula, content-based/project-based instruction, and formative assessment adjusted according to K-12 learner needs, interests, and proficiency levels.

Aubrey and Zmarzly (2023) describe another case where OACD is being applied in practice (but not in name) at the K-12 level. These elementary school teachers have set aside the textbook, creating instead learning centers or stations in the classroom with different themes and resources that learners visit, according to their interests. Using authentic materials, content-based/project-based instruction, and formative assessment, their goal is to "de-center" the teacher in the learning process and encourage learners to forge their own "proficiency journeys through collaboration, culturally-responsive teaching, and social-emotional learning" (Aubrey and Zmarzly 2023, conference *Guidebook*, Session 282).

Other OACD programs at the middle school and high school levels were described in an American Council of Teachers of Russian webinar on March 25, 2022. Though the presenters used the term *project-based instruction* in reference to their programs, some had distinctly OACD structures, particularly the programs described by John Rook at Smith Middle School and Kateryna Ratushnyuk at Staten Island Technical High School. In the middle school program, in one example, all learning activities centered around the theme of *nash gorodskoĭ t͡sentr* (our city center); used task-based activities including student interviews, peer reviews, and authentic materials; and evinced a wide range of flexibility not tied to any one textbook or preordained curriculum, Similarly in the high school program, in one course, learners brainstormed with the teacher what would be included in the curriculum, using "can do" statements as a guide.

Examples of non-textbook-based learning can be cited even at the preschool and early elementary levels, at which learners cannot be expected to use language textbooks even if they are available (though their teachers could, in principle, direct learning by following a textbook). To cite just two of the many examples that could likely be noted, the Aronoff Preschool at the Merage Jewish Community Center in Irvine, California, offers immersion programs in a variety of languages (for 2022–23 this included Spanish, Italian, Chinese Mandarin, and Hebrew), while the K-8 Irvine Hebrew Day School overlaps its Hebrew language and Jewish studies curricula to provide what is effectively a form of content-based OACD instruction in Hebrew beginning in kindergarten.

OACD and Instructor Workload

Beyond questions related to the applicability of OACD in diverse learning contexts, a more general issue of feasibility (more apparent than real) has often been voiced by instructors not experienced in its use. This is the perception that OACD requires instructors to spend considerably more time preparing courses and lessons than would be the case with a textbook. Experienced practitioners of OACD recognize that the opposite is true (Corin 2020b, 2021).

First OACD eschews the type of noncontextualized exercises that are genuinely time-consuming to prepare and correct. There is no need for them when the repetition of target-language elements and structures needed for intake (versus input) arises naturally during spiraled repetition through contextualized meaningful activities that occurs naturally in content-based, task-based, scenario-based, and project-based instructional contexts (Bondarenko, this volume; Wang, this volume).

Second it is by no means overly time-consuming for instructors to find and prepare current authentic materials necessary for OACD-based learning, especially at higher levels, including for individualized or small group work with different learners or groups working on different materials. Ongoing learner involvement in the selection and delivery of content and design or directing of activities is a core principle of OACD. Instructors may prepare and utilize slides, especially for Novice (ILR 0/0+) learners (Bondarenko, this volume) or at higher levels occasional formal presentations (Cheon, this volume). They also typically provide initial reading and listening texts for introducing topics before learners begin to seek their own materials.

Based on the successful application of OACD in many languages across the full range of proficiency levels, when instructors feel overwhelmed by course preparation they are typically missing opportunities to support learner autonomy and application of higher-order cognitive skills through learning that occurs while addressing actual or simulated real-world needs. In such instances, it is important that instructors be prepared to relinquish control sufficiently to enable learners to take on the bulk of the effort, with the instructor supporting that work. There is, to be sure, an initial workload required for laying out course and module structure. Yet as noted previously the structure of highly effective four- to eight-week intensive nonspecialized courses can, in a pinch, be laid out in as little as several days, since some of the structure of each module should best be rounded out through learner-teacher negotiation (see, for example, Wang, this volume).

OACD and Institutional Culture

One caveat is in order for large programs with a culture of strong hierarchical organization and inclination toward uniformity. OACD flourishes in environments in which faculty are given free rein to develop their own courses, and administrators support them with the needed resources. No two courses and no two iterations of the same course will look alike in an OACD program. Leaders in this environment understand how to manage and embrace the lack of uniformity; more importantly, they understand how individualization leads to greater proficiency in learning and teaching. In their relationships with faculty they serve as models (cf. the "fractals" analogy in Oded and Oded, this volume) for a teacher-learner relationship founded on mentoring (teacher) and realized autonomy (learner).

Limitations

The outcomes of OACD-based learning enumerated previously are noteworthy but reflect statistical compilations over small, specialized populations and anecdotal experiences. While the potential of OACD is well known to the experienced practitioners who have achieved those outcomes, only a few years have passed since OACD was defined as a distinct unifying curricular framework. There are as yet no large-scale empirical studies of its effects and potential. It is the editors' hope that this volume will stimulate practitioners and researchers alike to further explore and experience OACD's potential, so that such studies can soon become feasible.

It has not been possible here to examine all theoretical ramifications of OACD. As just one example OACD raises questions about application (and scope of application) of the *comprehensible input hypothesis* (Krashen 1981) and associated $i + 1$ rule.

As noted OACD is incompatible with predetermined linear scope and sequence. It utilizes unadapted authentic texts from day one, and both materials and activities are subject to constant on-the-spot change. Such a learning context requires a nuanced understanding of the *i + 1* rule, at the very least, and further research is clearly needed.

Finally, in both this chapter and this volume, the amount of space devoted to US government language programs is disproportionate relative to the overall numbers of programs and learners in various learning settings in the United States and likely in most countries. As noted previously, this circumstance reflects the historical reality of how OACD arose and where it first gained a compact following of practitioners. The far greater potential for OACD, however, lies in the nongovernmental realm, with its far greater numbers and variety of programs and learners. One of the purposes of this volume is to increase awareness among nongovernmental readers concerning the opportunities afforded by OACD in most if not all language learning settings.

Conclusions

The purpose of OACD is to provide a unifying framework that acts as a force multiplier to enhance the efficiency of learning. It accomplishes this by creating the flexibility needed to support the integrated application of the full panoply of principles and best practices of learner-centered world language education. As such its application is not limited to one or a few instructional contexts. As the contributions to this volume illustrate, OACD can be applied equally well in intensive US government language courses and five-hour-per-week university courses, large multisection courses taught by several instructors and small less commonly taught language programs staffed by a single instructor, and so forth.

While the practices that comprise OACD have emerged gradually, crystalizing into a distinct curricular framework beginning in the 1980s, this framework was recognized as such, named, and defined in 2015 at DLIFLC. The literature on OACD that began to appear at about that time is still young, and the exploration of OACD in some instructional contexts—notably early childhood—remains a desideratum.

Notes

1. Venues include the Tenth International Conference on Language Teacher Education (UCLA, 2017), CATESOL 2018, AATSP 2019, ASEEES 2019, CARLA 2019, AATSEEL 2020, ACTFL 2020, FLANC 2020, TESOL 2020, AATSP 2021, NSSUVD 2021, and AATSP 2022.
2. The concept of learning efficiency has been defined in various ways. Here it refers to proficiency gain per hours of class instruction or per some other measure of learning activity.
3. Miller and Seller (1985) identify three educational philosophies, in terms of increasing levels of learner involvement in the learning process: transmission (learner remembers presented information), transaction (learner acquires skills for accomplishing tasks), and transformation (learner interacts with course content such that the learner is affected or even changes in some way).
4. While the term "force multiplier" has become commonplace in numerous civilian contexts, it is defined in the Joint Chiefs of Staff Joint Publication 3–05 (as of version 26 April 2007, later deleted) as "[a] capability that, when added to and employed by a combat force, significantly increases the combat potential of that force and thus enhances the probability of successful mission accomplishment" (Joint Chiefs of Staff 2007, GL 11).

INTRODUCTION TO OPEN ARCHITECTURE CURRICULAR DESIGN

5. While the term OACD was intentionally used in faculty and administrator training, curriculum development, program evaluation, and cross-institutional discussions beginning in 2015, its informal use in reference to curricular design began as early as 2007 (Richard Brecht, personal communication, 2020, as documented in the Minutes of the DLIFLC Board of Visitors of December 12–13, 2007 (DLIFLC 2007).

References

Allwright, Richard L. 1981. "What Do We Want Teaching Materials for?" *English Language Teaching Journal* 36, no. 1: 1–17.

Aubrey, Rebecca, and Joshua Zmarzly. 2023. "'Centering' Student Independence, Collaboration, and SEL Skills with Centers." In *American Association of the Teachers of Spanish and Portuguese Annual Conference*. Salamanca, Spain.

Bendall, Robert C. A., Adam Galpin, Lynne P. Marrow, and Simon Cassidy. 2019. "Cognitive Style: Time to Experiment." *Frontiers in Psychology* 7: 1786.https://doi.org/10.3389/fpsyg.2016.01786 Billah, Masum. 2014. "Teaching Language without Textbook." Accessed August 14, 2023. https://bdeduarticle.com/teaching-language-without-textbook/.

Bondarenko, Maria, and Vita Kogan. 2019. "Open Architecture Curricular Design (OACD) Meeting Cognitive Architecture: Spiral-like Design Model for Teaching Inflectional Languages at Elementary Levels." Preprint for project, Cognitive Pedagogy for Language Learning: International Research Group, Université de Montréal.

Brecht, Richard, Robert C. Noel, and Jonathan Wilkenfeld. 1984. "Computer Simulation in the Teaching of Translation and International Studies." *Foreign Language Annals* 17, no. 6: 575–84.

Campbell, Christine. 1989. "The Guided Design Model and Methodology: Emphasizing Critical Thinking and Proficiency in the University Foreign Language Classroom." In *Thinking Across Cultures*, edited by Donald M. Topping, Doris C. Crowell, and Victor N. Kobayashi, 445–544. Hillsdale: Lawrence Erlbaum Associates Inc.

Campbell, Christine. 2021. "Open Architecture Curricular Design: A Fundamental Principle of Transformative Language Learning and Teaching." In *Transformative Language Learning and Teaching*, edited by Betty Lou Leaver, Dan E. Davidson, and Christine Campbell, 43–50. Cambridge: Cambridge University Press.

Carroll, John B. 1967. *The Foreign Language Attainments of Language Majors in the Senior Year: A Survey Conducted in U.S. Colleges and Universities*. Cambridge: Harvard University.

Cleret, Emilie. 2021. "The Challenges of Implementing Transformative Pedagogy." In *Transformative Language Learning and Teaching*, edited by Betty Lou Leaver, Dan E. Davidson, and Christine Campbell, 61–68. Cambridge: Cambridge University Press.

Clifford, Ray. 2021. "Testing and Transformative Language Learning." In *Transformative Language Learning and Teaching*, edited by Betty Lou Leaver, Dan E. Davidson, and Christine Campbell, 227–37. Cambridge: Cambridge University Press.

Collin, Jérôme. 2021. "Immersion and Transformative Pedagogy in the French Language Department of the French War College." In *Transformative Language Learning and Teaching*, edited by Betty Lou Leaver, Dan E. Davidson, and Christine Campbell, 129–36. Cambridge: Cambridge University Press.

Commission of the European Communities. 2003. *Communication from the Commission to the Council, the European Parliament, and the Economic and Social Committee, and the Committee of the Regions: Promotion of Language Learning and Linguistic Diversity, An Action Plan 2004–2006*. Brussels: COM (2003) 449 final.

Corin, Andrew R. 1997. "A Course to Convert Czech Proficiency to Proficiency in Croatian and Serbian." In *Content-Based Instruction in Foreign Language Education: Models and Methods*, edited by Stephen B. Stryker and Betty Lou Leaver, 78–104. Washington: Georgetown University Press.

Corin, Andrew R. 2020a. "Open Architecture Curriculum and Transformative Language Learning Revisited. Part 1. The Relationship between Open Architecture Curricular Design and Transformative Language Learning." *ACTR Letter* 46, no. 3–4: 1–2, 4–5.

Corin, Andrew R. 2020b. "Open Architecture Curriculum and Transformative Language Learning Revisited. Part 2. Toward a Constrained Definition of OACD." *ACTR Letter* 47, no. 1: 1–2, 4.

Corin, Andrew R. 2020c. "The Challenge of the Inverted Pyramid in Attaining Distinguished-Level Proficiency." *Journal for Distinguished Language Studies* 7: 107–37.

Corin, Andrew R. 2021. "Foreign Language Learning Efficiency: Transformative Learning in an Outcomes-Based Environment." In *Transformative Language Learning and Teaching*, edited by Betty Lou Leaver, Dan E. Davidson, and Christine Campbell, 51–60. Cambridge: Cambridge University Press.

Corin, Andrew. 2022. "Kurikulum sa otvorenom arhitekturom za učenje srpskog i drugih jezika u SAD." *Naučni sastanak slavista u Vukove dane* 51: 17–27.

Corin, Andrew, and Sergey Entis. 2022. "Protocol-Based Formative Assessment: Evolution and Revolution at the Defense Language Institute Foreign Language Center." *Journal of Distinguished Language Studies* 8: 95–115.

Corin, Andrew R., and Betty Lou Leaver. Forthcoming. *Fields of the Mind: History, Theory, and Application of Cognitive Field Concepts to Language Learning*. Hollister, CA: MSI Press.

Crandall, JoAnn, and G. Richard Tucker. 1989. *Content-Based Instruction in Second and Foreign Languages*. ERIC Number: ED312895.

Dababneh, Reem. 2018. "The Scenario-Based Syllabus for the Post-Basic Arabic Program." *Dialog on Language Instruction* 28, no. 1: 13–26.

Dabbs, Laura, and Betty Lou Leaver. 2019. *The Invisible Foreign Language Classroom: Bringing Hidden Dynamics to Light for Individual and Group Harmony and Success*. Hollister: MSI Press LLC.

Derderian, Ani. 2017. "Designing for Teaching and Learning in an Open World: Task-Supported Open Architecture Language Instruction." *International Journal of Adult Vocational Education and Technology* 8, no. 3: 55–67.

DLIFLC (Defense Language Institute Foreign Language Center). 1992. *Russian Program Curriculum Review*. Presidio of Monterey: The Defense Language Institute Foreign Language Center.

DLIFLC. 2007. *Defense Language Institute Foreign Language Center Board of Visitors (BoV) Minutes. December 12–13, 2007*. Unpublished manuscript.

DLIFLC. 2015. *Advanced Language Academy Syllabus*. Unpublished manuscript.

Duri, Jayne. 1992. "Content-Based Instruction: Keeping DLI on the Cutting Edge." *The Globe* 15, no. 3: 4–5.

Ehrman, Madeline E., and Betty Lou Leaver. 2003. "Cognitive Styles in the Service of Language Learning." *System* 31, no. 3: 393–415.

Eisen, Samuel. 2020. "The Language Flagship Program and Multilingualism in Overseas Language Immersion." *Russian Language Journal / Русский язык* 70: 7–22.

Evans-Romaine, Karen, and Dianna Murphy. 2021. "Designing Learning Environments to Facilitate Transformative Language and Culture Learning in a US Language Flagship Program." In *Transformative Language Learning and Teaching*, edited by Betty Lou Leaver, Dan E. Davidson, and Christine Campbell, 98–106. Cambridge: Cambridge University Press.

Farraj, Amer. 2021. "Transformative Dimensions of Community Engagement and Service Learning during In-Country Immersion." In *Transformative Language Learning and Teaching*, edited by Betty Lou Leaver, Dan E. Davidson, and Christine Campbell, 120–28. Cambridge: Cambridge University Press.

Froelich, Jürgen. 1988. "German Videos with German Subtitles: A New Approach to Listening Comprehension Development." *Die Unterrichtspraxis / Teaching German* 21, no. 2: 199–203.

Giroux, Henry, and Peter McLaren. 1986. "Teacher Education and the Politics of Engagement: The Case for Democratic Schooling. *Harvard Educational Review* 56, no. 3: 213–39. Higgs, Theodore, ed. 1984. *Teaching for Proficiency, the Organizing Principle*. Lincolnwood: National Textbook Company.

ISETA (International Society for Exploring Teaching Alternatives). 2002. *Proceedings: The Thirty-Second Annual Conference of ISETA, Point Park College. October 24–27, 2002*. Pittsburgh.

Joint Chiefs of Staff [of the Armed Forces of the United States]. 2007. *Joint Publication 3–05.1. Joint Special Operations Task Force Operations*.

Kecht, Regina, and Katharina von Hammerstein. 2000. *Languages across the Curriculum. Interdisciplinary Structures and Internationalized Education*. Columbus: The Ohio State University Press.

Kirschner, Paul A. 2017. "Stop Propagating the Learning Styles Myth." *Computers & Education* 106: 166–71. https://doi.org/10.1016/j.compedu.2016.12.006.

Klein, George S., and Herbert Schlesinger. 1949. "Where Is the Perceiver in Perceptual Theory?" *Journal of Personality* 18, no. 1: 32–47.

Kozhevnikov, Maria, Carol Evans, and Stephen M. Kosslyn. 2014. "Cognitive Style as Environmentally Sensitive Individual Differences in Cognition: A Modern Synthesis and Applications in Education, Business, and Management." *Psychological Science in the Public Interest* 15, no. 1: 3–33.

Kraemer, David J. M., Lauren M. Rosenberg, and Sharon L. Thompson-Schill. 2009. "The Neural Correlates of Visual and Verbal Cognitive Styles." *Journal of Neuroscience* 29, no. 12: 3792–8.Krashen, Stephen. 1981. *Second Language Acquisition and Second Language Learning*. Oxford: Pergamon.

Leaver, B. L. 1989. "Dismantling Classroom Walls for Increased Foreign Language Proficiency." *Foreign Language Annals* 22, no. 1: 67–74.

Leaver, Betty Lou. 1997. "Content-Based Instruction in a Basic Russian Program." In *Content-Based Instruction in Foreign Language Education: Models and Methods*, edited by Stephen B. Stryker and Betty Lou Leaver, 30–54. Washington, DC: Georgetown University Press.

Leaver, Betty Lou, and Boris Shekhtman. 2002. *Developing Professional-Level Language Proficiency*. Cambridge: Cambridge University Press. Leaver, Betty Lou, and Christine Campbell. 2015. "Experience with Higher Levels of Proficiency." In *To Advanced Proficiency and Beyond: Theory and Methods for Developing Superior Second Language Ability*, edited by Tony Brown and Jennifer Bown, 3–22. Washington, DC: Georgetown University Press.

Leaver, Betty Lou, and Christine Campbell. 2020. "The Shifting Paradigm in Russian Language Pedagogy: From Communicative Language Teaching to Transformative Language Learning and Teaching." In *The Art of Teaching Russian*, edited by Evgeny Dengub, Irina Dubinina, and Jason Merrill, 147–62. Washington, DC: Georgetown University Press.

Leaver, Betty Lou, Dan E. Davidson, and Christine Campbell, eds. 2021a. *Transformative Language Learning and Teaching*. Cambridge: Cambridge University Press.

Leaver, Betty Lou, Dan E. Davidson, and Christine Campbell. 2021b. "Introduction." In *Transformative Language Learning and Teaching*, edited by Betty Lou Leaver, Dan E. Davidson, and Christine Campbell, 1–9. Cambridge: Cambridge University Press.

Leaver, Betty Lou, and Marsha Kaplan. 2004. "Task-Based Instruction in U.S. Government Slavic Language Programs." In *Task-Based Instruction in Foreign Language Education: Practices and Programs*, edited by Betty Lou Leaver and Jane Willis, 47–66. Washington, DC: Georgetown University Press.

Leaver, Betty Lou, and Sabine Atwell. 2002. "Preliminary Qualitative Findings from a Study of the Processes Leading to Advanced Professional Proficiency Level (ILR4)." In *Developing Professional Level Language Proficiency*, edited by Betty Lou Leaver and Boris S. Shekhtman, 260–95. Cambridge: Cambridge University Press.

Littlejohn, Andrew, and Scott Windeatt. 1989. "Beyond Language Learning: Perspectives on Materials Design." In *The Second Language Curriculum*, edited by Robert Keith Johnson, 155–75. Cambridge: Cambridge University Press.

Mezirow, J. 1991. *Transformative Dimensions of Adult Learning*. San Francisco: Jossey-Bass.

Miller, John P., and Wayne Seller. 1985. *Curriculum: Perspectives and Practice*. Boston, MA: Addison-Wesley.

Murphy, Dianna, Karen Evans-Romaine, Valerie Anishchenkova, and Zhuo Jing-Schmidt. 2016. "Laying the Groundwork: Programmatic Models in US Language Flagship Programs." In *Exploring the US Language Flagship Program: Professional Competence in a Second Language by Graduation*, edited by Dianna Murphy and Karen Evans-Romaine, 29–50. Bristol: Multilingual Matters.

National Foreign Language Center. 2023. "STARTALK Principles for Effective Teaching and Learning." Accessed August 14, 2023. https://nflc.umd.edu/resources/startalk-principles-effective-teaching-learning.

Newton, Philip M., Hannah Farukh Najabat-Lattif, Gabriella Santiago, and Atharva Salvi. 2021. "The Learning Styles Neuromyth Is Still Thriving in Medical Education." *Frontiers in Human Neuroscience* 15: Article 708540. https://doi.org/10.3389/fnhum.2021.708540.

Nikonova (Thompson), Sofia M. 1968/1994. *U istokov sovetskoĭ metodiki obucheniia inostrannym iazykam*. Moscow: Vysshaya shkola. Reprint 1994, Salinas, CA: AGSI Press.

Rossner, Richard, and Rod Bolitho, eds. 1990. *Currents of Change in English Language Teaching*. Oxford: Oxford University Press.

Ryding, Karin, and Barbara Stowasser. 1997. "Text Development for Content-Based Instruction in Arabic." In *Content-Based Instruction in Foreign Language Education: Models and Methods*, edited by Stephen B. Stryker and Betty Lou Leaver, 107–17. Washington, DC: Georgetown University Press.

Saydee, Farid. 2023. *Open Architecture Curricular Design in Four STARTALK Hindi and Urdu Programs*. Unpublished manuscript.

Shaw, Peter. 1997. "With One Stone." In *Content-Based Instruction in Foreign Language Education: Models and Methods*, edited by Stephen B. Stryker and Betty Lou Leaver, 282–310. Washington, DC: Georgetown University Press.

Shekhtman, Boris, and Betty Lou Leaver, with Natalia Lord, Ekaterina Kuznetsova, and Elena Ovtcharenko. 2002. "Developing Professional-Level Oral Proficiency: The Shekhtman Method of Communicative Teaching." In *Developing Professional-Level Language Proficiency*, edited by Betty Lou Leaver, and Boris S. Shekhtman, 119–40. Cambridge: Cambridge University Press.

Straight, Stephen. 1998. *Languages across the Curriculum*. Washington, DC: Educational Resources Information Center: Clearinghouse on Languages and Literatures.

Stryker, Stephen, and Betty Lou Leaver, eds. 1997. *Content-Based Instruction in Foreign Language Education*. Washington, DC: Georgetown University Press.

The National Standards Collaborative Board. 2015. *World-Readiness Standards for Learning Languages*, 4th ed. Alexandria: Author.

Travitzki, Rodrigo, and Lilian L'Abbate Kelian. 2019. "Open Architecture Curriculum: Towards an Education Committed to Pluralistic Democracy." *International Education Journal* 18, no. 1: 93–110.

Van Deusen-Scholl, Nelleke, and Stephane Charitos. 2021. "The Community as Transformative Classroom." In *Transformative Language Learning and Teaching*, edited by Betty Lou Leaver, Dan E. Davidson, and Christine Campbell, 80–88. Cambridge: Cambridge University Press.

Wrigley, Terry. 2005. "Inclusive Pedagogies—Restoring Agency and Voice to the Learner." *REICE. Revista Iberoamericana sobre Calidad, Eficacia y Cambio en Educación* 3, no. 1: 297–315. https://www.redalyc.org/articulo.oa?id=55130132.

Part 2
OACD in US Government Language Institutes
Programs at the Defense Language Institute Foreign Language Center

2

Open Architecture Curricular Design as an Enabler for Transformative Learning in a Korean Course[1]

JAE SUN LEE

THIS CHAPTER DESCRIBES OACD in the context of a Korean language course as an enabler of *transformative learning*, the educational philosophy in adult education that asserts that one way learning occurs is when the learner's perspective is transformed through a disorienting dilemma followed by critical reflection and reframing of one's perspectives. In 1978 Mezirow (Mezirow 1978) introduced the transformative learning concept in his study of women who returned to community college to continue their education, defining it as follows:

> Transformative learning refers to the process by which we transform our taken-for-granted frames of reference (meaning perspectives, habits of mind, mind-sets) to make them more inclusive, discriminating, open, emotionally capable of change, and reflective so that they may generate beliefs and opinions that will prove more true or justified to guide action. (Mezirow 2012, p. 76)

Transformative learning so described is a humanistic approach to learning based in part on critical social theory (Cranton and Taylor 2012), which promotes the critical examination of ideology.

Transformative learning applied to language learning—*transformative language learning and teaching* (Leaver, Davidson, and Campbell 2021)—has as its primary goals bilingual and bicultural competence and the development of learner autonomy, both of which are connected to learner personal transformation. OACD is a key principle of transformative language learning and teaching.[2]

Transformative language learning and teaching have largely been applied within two contexts: cultural awareness education (Johnson and Nelson 2010) and learner-centered instruction (multiple contributions in Leaver, Davidson, and Campbell 2021). These instructional approaches, especially in combination and informed by the

World-Readiness Standards for Learning Languages (The National Standards Collaborative Board, 2015), can contribute to enabling change in learner perspective.

OACD has been discussed as a unifying curricular design framework that can enhance transformative learning in the context of adult world language education. According to language learning professionals who have led the promotion of OACD (Campbell 2021; Corin 2020; Leaver 2021), it is a flexible, textbook-free framework structured around a theme-based syllabus that integrates interchangeable unadapted authentic texts, tasks, and other activities, often organized into modules. It ensures ongoing learner involvement in the selection, processing, and delivery of course content and design or directing of activities. It fosters continual and systematic (vs. occasional and limited) tailoring to learner and cohort needs and the evolution of the role of the teacher from facilitator of learning toward that of mentor/coach/advisor, who provides resources and informed guidance.

The Relevance of Transformative Language Learning and Teaching for Native English-Speaking Learners of North Korean

OACD can be applied to learning any world language but is particularly valuable to learning North Korean because of the special relevance of transformative language learning and teaching in relation to North Korean. North Korea has long been isolated and framed negatively by Western and South Korean news coverage, with the framing often based on inaccurate information. This author has observed two main perceptions about North Korea by US learners. First, some learners are indifferent to and/or have almost no knowledge of North Korea, yet they have a vague negative impression about the society due to US media coverage of negative aspects of the society. Second, learners may have some degree of knowledge about the society, but it is associated with just its dark side. Most professionals working with North Korean subject matter in the United States would agree that, in general, US learners have negative perceptions about North Korea regardless of their level of knowledge about the society.

This one-dimensional view and the dehumanization of the North Korean people associated with it can hinder understanding of North Korean perspectives. This chapter demonstrates how a textbook-free flexible curriculum enables learners to construct a more accurate framework for perceiving the reality of North Korean culture through the use of contemporary authentic texts, which can create disorienting dilemmas between what learners thought they knew and what they are seeing in the texts, thus stimulating subsequent critical reflection about those texts.

The Learning Context of the North Korean Segment of the DLIFLC Korean Course for Learners Who Have Previously Achieved Advanced (ILR 2) Proficiency in Korean

The Korean course described here is conducted at the Defense Language Institute Foreign Language Center (DLIFLC), the largest language learning facility in the United States operated by the US Department of Defense. Most of the learners in this course began learning Korean as a world language after attaining adulthood in

Bloom's Taxonomy

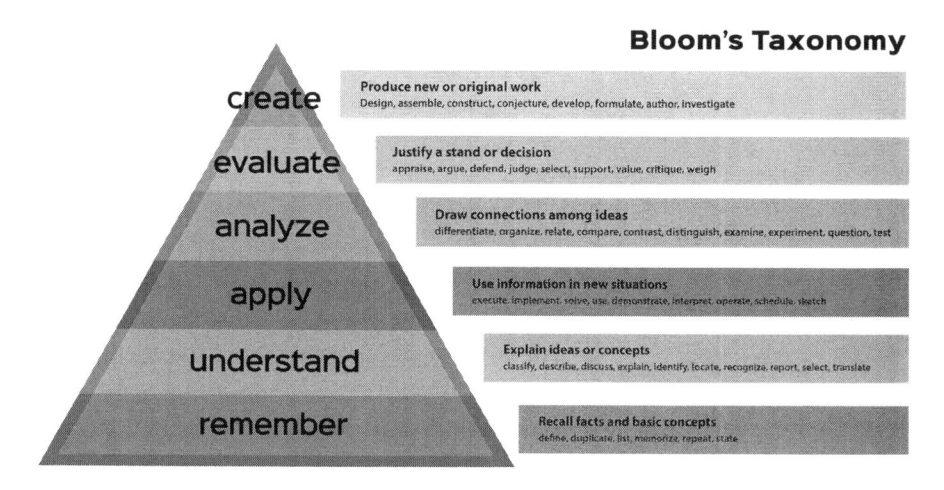

- **create** — Produce new or original work
  Design, assemble, construct, conjecture, develop, formulate, author, investigate
- **evaluate** — Justify a stand or decision
  appraise, argue, defend, judge, select, support, value, critique, weigh
- **analyze** — Draw connections among ideas
  differentiate, organize, relate, compare, contrast, distinguish, examine, experiment, question, test
- **apply** — Use information in new situations
  execute, implement, solve, use, demonstrate, interpret, operate, schedule, sketch
- **understand** — Explain ideas or concepts
  classify, describe, discuss, explain, identify, locate, recognize, report, select, translate
- **remember** — Recall facts and basic concepts
  define, duplicate, list, memorize, repeat, state

Figure 2.1. A hierarchy of thinking skills derived from Bloom's taxonomy (from Armstrong 2010)

the United States and having previously achieved Advanced (ILR 2) (limited working proficiency) or higher in listening and reading. The class size is small, on average about six learners; the teaching team is usually composed of two teachers. The course varies from two to nineteen weeks in length and includes a North Korean segment. The course uses a theme-based syllabus and implements the flipped learning approach.

The Flipped Learning Network (2014) defines this concept as:

> a pedagogical approach in which direct instruction moves from the group learning space to the individual learning space, and the resulting group space is transformed into a dynamic, interactive learning environment where the educator guides students as they apply concepts and engage creatively in the subject matter.

In other words, learners study specific content autonomously at their own pace outside the classroom, while class time is dedicated to collaborative learning activities that engage higher-order thinking, such as analyzing, evaluating, and creating, within a framework adapted from Bloom's taxonomy of learning (Armstrong 2010; see Figure 2.1). The teacher's role consists of mentoring learners based on their professional needs, learning styles, and personal interests. Although diverse applications of the model exist, the main tenets of flipped learning—a flexible learning culture and learner-centeredness—are inherent in transformative learning and OACD. As Van Gorp et al. (this volume) affirm, flipped pedagogies are a key topic explored in the professional development program for instructors who participate in the Less Commonly Taught Languages and Indigenous Languages Partnership Project within the Big Ten Academic Alliance.

How OACD Promotes the Development of Learner Cultural Awareness in the North Korean Segment of a Korean Course

North Korean language and culture provide a unique setting for the US language learner. In general, US learners are not allowed or do not want to visit the target society for security reasons and are therefore limited in their possibilities for interacting with the target culture. North Korean public discourse, which is generally available via the internet, is often used by teachers as the main source of class material. The discourse is mostly transmitted through North Korean state-controlled mass media and is comprised primarily of state ideology-embedded texts.

Fostering learner cultural awareness in North Korean language courses is complicated by the fact that most teachers of North Korean in the United States were raised in South Korea, where they received an intense anticommunist education. The author grew up watching a series of popular anti-North Korean animated movies, as did the majority of children growing up in South Korea in the 1970s. The series focused on North Korean power structures at the time of the South Korean dictatorship during the Cold War era. Some of the movies portrayed the North Korean military as vicious wolves and North Korean leaders as monstrous pigs. Annual anticommunist writing, drawing, and speech contests were commonly conducted in schools across South Korea.

Both the education system and South Korean society as a whole were exposed to the anticommunist campaign organized by the South Korean authoritarian government from 1948 through the end of the 1980s. In general the South Korean public has had very limited access to North Korean texts, including North Korean mass media, due to the South Korean National Security Act of 1948. As a result Korean teachers in the Korean programs in the United States who do not have a high level of subject-matter expertise can have insufficiently informed negative opinions about the target society even though both Koreas share the same language.

As is typical of transformative programs and OACD, the curriculum of the program described here is co-constructed through ongoing communication and negotiation between learner and teacher about aspects of the curriculum. The co-construction can be gradually introduced from the outset of instruction, as both Krasner and Oded and Oded (this volume) attest. The theme of the North Korean segment of the course is North Korean area studies, encompassing politics, economy, education, and family life from a North Korean perspective. The North Korean state ideology, especially the *Juche*[3] (self-reliance) belief, has been characterized as North Korea's unique brand of socialism (King 2007) since the end of the 1960s. Without understanding the ideology, it is difficult to comprehend the North Korean perspective fully. However neither learners nor teachers typically understand the belief in depth. For this reason the *Juche* ideology is incorporated as one fundamental theme.

The majority of learner feedback from the program underscores the value of learning about the ruling ideology of the target country. For example:

> After learning about the state ideology of North Korea, I could connect the ideology and its popular culture, and it was a very interesting experience. (Anonymous student, October 16, 2018, summarized and translated by the author)

In the beginning phase of the North Korean segment of the Korean course, learners research the *Juche* ideology, including the tenets of the belief, historical background, and the influence of the ideology on daily life. Through the flipped learning approach, learners apply critical thinking skills while discussing North Korean state ideology based on their research conducted before class. Through this process, learners explore aspects of the unique North Korean culture such as ethnonationalism, use of expressions of reverence for the state leaders (the Kim family), and vilification of perceived enemies (e.g., the United States) in North Korean public discourses (Lee 2018). The following is one learner's observation:

> Learning about the *Juche* ideology really gave me perspective into how North Koreans think and gives me a better understanding of why they do the things they do. (Anonymous student, October 24, 2020)

Learners develop cultural awareness in the OACD classroom by researching topics, for example, North Korean state ideology, based on their needs and interests. The textbook-free framework of OACD allows learners to explore the newest authentic North Korean mass media texts under the guidance of teachers. When analyzing such texts it is important that learners be aware that because most public discourse reflects the voice of the North Korean government regardless of genre or speaker, it is necessary to read between and beyond the lines in order to analyze the purpose of the texts within the sociopolitical and historical context of the society. Learners also come to understand the value of comparing and contrasting sources of information in determining whether the content of the media is truth, distortion, or misinformation.

Although North Korean media texts are the voice of the ruling power structures of society, learners can gain valuable insights into the society through critical analysis. For instance, in 2019, the year after the summit meeting between North Korea and the United States in Singapore, North Korean media used only a few hostile expressions when referring to the United States. In fact, one of the frequently used key terms was "economy." After analyzing Kim Jong Un's 2019 New Year's Address and learning that the main focus of the North Korean government was economic development based on peace-building, one learner reflected:

> I had thought North Korea would never change no matter what happened [in terms of being a threatening state with its nuclear weapon development]. However, after learning about its new focus on the "economy," I hope the North Korean state will follow this new path in order to improve the lives of the North Korean people. (Anonymous student, October 21, 2020, summarized and translated by the author)

This reflection shows how learners become aware of changes in North Korea such as this focus on the economy and are able to break away from fixed assumptions about a target society, which allows them to adopt a more realistic perspective on the society. This kind of analysis of lexical items is often conducted in class, enabling learners to develop a better understanding of the agenda of the power base of society. Without the flexible framework of OACD, it would be difficult to stay abreast of such dynamic changes in US-North Korea relations as well as inter-Korean relations.

Critical thinking skills play a crucial role in text analysis. These skills are especially effective when examining North Korean texts produced by the government, as shown by the example in the previous paragraph. Reading between and/or beyond the lines is an important part of *critical discourse analysis* (see Gregory, this volume). Critical discourse analysis is generally considered a combination of approaches that seek to examine how language is used as an ideological tool. As Machin and Mayr (2012) explain, critical discourse analysis focuses on why and how linguistic features are produced and what possible ideological goals they might serve rather than on the linguistic features themselves. The meaning of "critical" in critical discourse analysis is defined as the notion of analyzing linguistic elements to reveal connections between language, power, and ideology (Fairclough, 1989). The critical discourse analysis approach is relevant to teaching North Korean language because learners deal mainly with state-controlled public discourse. Through this approach, learners can increase their critical thinking skills as well as their sociolinguistic and sociocultural competence, both of which are critical for perspective transformation.

Awareness of the perspectives of the target culture should thus be a key learning objective. To this end, the following process is employed to support learner transformative learning:

1. Learners examine their assumptions about the theme, analyze why these assumptions were created, and write down the assumptions.
2. Learners research their selected theme, including the cultural perspectives of the target society on the theme, through authentic materials. They explore why and how people in the target society express those cultural perspectives.
3. Learners develop a new, more inclusive perspective through reframing of the theme based on their research and collaborative learning in class.

This process can be applied to making a presentation, writing an essay, and authoring a reflective journal. For example when learners select the theme "the political leadership of North Korea," they first write down their assumptions on this theme as framed by the US and/or South Korean media. Second, they research the practices and perspectives of the political leadership through authentic North Korean texts, including movies and TV dramas. During this process they can examine the North Korean perspective in the context of public discourse about North Korea. The critical discourse analysis approach encourages learners to ask and answer questions related to cultural awareness such as why North Koreans typically use, in public discourse, extreme honorific forms for their state leaders. Through Critical Discourse Analysis, learners can gain a new perspective on a theme (e.g., the role of the political leadership in North Korea, the self-reliance [Juche] ideology, or attaining nuclear deterrence) while engaging in collaborative learning activities.

Regarding learner participation in the selection, processing, and delivery of course content and design or directing of activities, in the beginning phase of the Korean course a variety of surveys are conducted in order to obtain valuable information about each learner, such as needs, learning goals and plans, interests, learning style, personality type, and sensory preferences, as well as personal background related to learning. For example one learner wrote the following about his learning plan on the first day of the course:

> I am currently weak in listening and speaking skills but strong in reading skills. I think it is very helpful to have a lot of listening practice, especially through dramas or movies. I enjoy listening to K-pop and watching K-dramas as a way to help with study, but I also enjoy political discussions. I hope to have meaningful discussion in class. . . . I know that I make a lot of mistakes. But I am very open to criticism, so please let me know how I can improve. (Anonymous student, January 6, 2020)

Based on this and more in-depth data, the teaching team was able to glean information about the learner's perceptions of his linguistic weaknesses and strengths; realize his interest in Korean pop culture, TV dramas, and politics; better understand his motivation to learn the language; and become aware of his positive attitude toward collaborative learning and critical feedback. In addition, from his personality type survey and face-to-face individual consultation with the teaching team, other valuable information was added to his profile. He had low confidence in public speaking due to his introverted personality, and his speaking level was low (1+/Intermediate High). His speaking and writing samples revealed a considerable number of fossilized errors although his reading level was beyond Advanced (ILR 2).

To help this learner and others like him, the teaching team conducted one-on-one speaking sessions and asked teachers outside the team to hold such sessions on an almost daily basis during the entire course. The curriculum included a variety of projects to promote public speaking, such as *learning by teaching*, where the learner presents the course content to classmates after research and then leads discussion. In order to defossilize errors, daily writing in a reflective learning journal proved very helpful. Learners receive feedback on their journal entries as well as their speaking in one-on-one speaking sessions.

In terms of content, learners are invited to select topics of interest—for instance a political and/or cultural theme—for projects such as learning by teaching or writing an essay. When dealing with the theme "the modern history of North Korea," a learner who was interested in politics chose to research and present on one of the major political figures of North Korea. This practice is one of the learner-centered strategies for empowering learner decision-making. In the author's experience, when learners have ownership over the learning process motivation, responsibility, and achievement increase, which contributes to enhanced learning in all domains, including transformative learning.

When learners are involved in learning by teaching, they engage in peer teaching activities with one leading the discussion based on questions generated by classmates. The teacher should assist learners as needed to produce questions that promote critical thinking, such as by providing examples of such questions and helping frame open-ended and provocative ones. This process can also encourage transformative as well as autonomous learning. When a learner has an advanced proficiency level and is independent in their learning, such as the learner described earlier, peer teaching activities are very efficient.

In peer-teaching activities, the teacher offers step-by-step mentoring to the learner about how to prepare class material following activity rubrics or guidelines. These activities include ample opportunities for peers and teachers to provide feedback, thus enabling them to serve as a tool for formative assessment.

In flipped learning, learners use time out of the classroom to research and prepare for class activities such as in-class peer teaching. Class time can be four hours per day or every other day. Learners and teachers interact during the noncontact day when needed, utilizing online learning management systems such as Blackboard or Microsoft Teams. The every-other-day class structure provides more time for learners to engage in self-directed learning before coming to class. In general learners evaluate this every-other-day class structure positively, citing the added time factor. The learning-by-teaching activity can occur every class, weekly, biweekly, or monthly, depending on the class environment. For example the higher the learners' proficiency level, the more frequently the activity can be implemented. Similarly the content level of this activity can also vary according to level of learner proficiency, experience with self-directed learning, and more. However the common denominator in this practice is the learner-centered instructional approach as it functions within flipped learning, which enhances transformative learning.

The flexibility that OACD fosters encourages teachers to change themes, texts, tasks, and activities based on learner voice, according to their needs and interests. For example if learners need to increase the level of their writing, they should be able to choose a writing task, such as writing an essay, individually or collaboratively, about their research on the target society. Once the writing activity is completed, it can be used as a point of departure for a speaking activity.

While the foregoing process promotes the development of learner cultural awareness, it does not automatically generate transformative learning. The next section will explain how writing a reflective learning journal can promote perspective change, the ultimate goal of transformative learning.

Reflective Learning Journals: A Practical Tool for Changing Learner Perspectives about the Target Language, Culture, and the Learners Themselves

As part of their homework, learners in this course practice writing through a daily reflective learning journal in the target language. They write at least one three-paragraph-length daily journal entry. The reflective learning journal, which can be used as both a learning and assessment tool, is beneficial in three ways. First, it is a language production tool through which learners can review and reflect on both the linguistic and cultural content of the course. Second, the act of reflecting, when writing one's opinions on a topic, is a meaningful process for connecting learning objectives to learner experiences, which promotes perspective shift (Crane 2019). Third, the reflective learning journal is a useful formative assessment tool for the teaching team to evaluate and monitor learning in relation to learning objectives. This formative assessment function helps the teaching team to modify course content and activities to improve learning in the context of the OACD framework.

The process for writing a reflective learning journal is as follows. Learners write and submit the journal daily, and the teacher provides feedback on both the linguistic form and content of the journal entry. The learner, reflecting on teacher feedback, then revises the journal and resubmits it. The teacher then provides final feedback on the revised journal. Before learners revise journal entries, the teacher helps them if they have questions regarding the initial feedback. The entire process of writing, feedback, and revision is done in the target language.

For example after studying the address-reference terms, which reveal the nature of human relationships among language users in both Koreas, a learner wrote:

> One topic that highlights the similarities between North and South Korean society is the terms of address. Learning these address forms was challenging, so it was a relief to discover that the terms used in North and South Korea have not really changed. Of course, there are some differences in the words that are

used, but despite 70 years of division, many of the same address forms are still used in both North and South Korea. For example, it is common to use familial terms to address people who may not be related to you. Even the terms used among couples like "darling" or "child father/mother" are the same. The address term "comrade" is one of the major differences.

To me, it seems that a society that has [systemic] terms of address is one that puts great emphasis on how people relate to each other within that society. By using terms of address, it removes any sense of ambiguity in societal relationships. In the US there are far fewer forms of address that are used like this in modern society, so learning them for the first time felt awkward. But on the other hand, I imagine that for someone who is used to them, coming to a place like the US where there is more emphasis on word choice and tone [rather than address terms] must be challenging for them as well. (Anonymous student, May 10, 2021)[4]

This journal entry reveals that, first, the learner produced linguistic and cultural content that she learned on that day. Second, she pointed out the main content of the theme and connected the content to her opinions and experiences. Through the process of reflection and her study of authentic texts, she began a shift in her perspective regarding the linguistic divergence between the two Koreas. She realized that the two Koreas share similar address terms, although a strikingly different term, *comrade*, is commonly used in North Korea as a result of its socialist ideology. The learner examined the cultural characteristics of the two Koreas through the use of the address/reference terms as social practice and compared the Korean culture with her native language culture. One question to stimulate learners' further reflection might be: What sociocultural assumptions underlie the use of certain address/reference terms depending on the relationship between the interlocutors?

The preceding example illustrates how the process of reflection promotes learner cultural awareness. The journal also serves the function of formative assessment. The teaching team was better able to discern learning effects by analyzing the journal input. For example the teaching team examined whether learners appropriately reproduced key terms and grammatical forms that they had learned on the given day as well as the cultural content of the topic. About journal writing, a learner reflected:

The journal was a good way to internalize not only the content of the lessons from each day, but also to practice the grammar and vocabulary that we learned. I know that I wasn't able to memorize everything, but I feel like the things that I did learn I will never forget because I was able to put them into practice thanks to writing a journal. (Anonymous student, May 11, 2020)

The reflective learning journal is also a useful resource for the learner to defossilize errors by receiving teacher feedback and then revising work. In addition when learners write about their weaknesses, learning strategies, or learning plans in the journal, the teaching team can then tailor the curriculum and/or activities to accommodate their needs. For instance if a learner writes that they want to explore a specific topic or improve a linguistic skill such as some aspect of speaking, the teaching team can then modify the curriculum to accommodate their needs and interests.

In essence, changes in perspective about the target language, culture, and even learners themselves can be observed in the reflective learning journal. The following is one learner's testimony:

> I enjoyed being able to sort out my thoughts in a logical manner. . . . Normally in any other class I would have to think of a way to say what I was thinking in Korean right on the spot. Or I would have to reply candidly throughout the class. No reflection was available. So, writing out my thoughts, new things learned and what I already knew was very beneficial for me. I wish that I was encouraged to keep a journal a long time ago, even if it was just one or two sentences. (Anonymous student, October 24, 2020)

Conclusions

Learners can experience a change in perspective—transformative learning—about the target language, culture, and even themselves if:

- They are able to learn in an environment that encourages such change through the use of dynamic discussions, presentations, and reflective learning journals.
- These activities respond to their particular needs and interests.
- They reflect the current reality of the target society.

OACD enables this change in perspective.

One learner noted he had come to view North Koreans as human beings rather than dehumanized objects after his research on the target society. This change in perspective can even lead to a change in behavior. The following learner comment speaks to progress made toward achieving the primary goals of transformative language learning and teaching—bilingual and bicultural competence and learner autonomy:

> At the beginning of this course, I wanted to improve my test scores and speaking, but throughout this course I have improved my global proficiency immensely. This course not only gave me the confidence I needed in the language, but has also cultivated a deeper appreciation and understanding of the culture. My new goals go much farther than the test. I want to focus on my global proficiency and maintaining my language. Before this class, I was unsure if this is what I wanted to do as a career, but now I know I want to continue using Korean in my everyday life because I have gained the confidence that I needed to continue to improve and build upon what I know. (Anonymous student, May 10, 2020)

OACD, especially the emphasis on ongoing learner involvement in the selection, processing, and delivery of course content and design or directing of activities, encourages learners to engage in research and reflective practices such as critical discourse analysis. Its implementation can thus contribute to personal transformation in learner perspective, the ultimate aim of transformative learning.

Study Questions

1. Armstrong (2010) adapted Bloom's taxonomy of learning objectives, opting to include "creating" as the ultimate learning objective. How might creation lead to a transformation in learners' cultural perceptions? Have your own cultural learning activities changed learners' frames of reference, bringing greater cultural understanding and acceptance? If they do not lead to creation and transformation, how might you change them?

2. The author uses critical discourse analysis to guide learners to understand ideological orientation in North Korean authentic materials. How might you use critical discourse analysis in your teaching context?
3. Transformative learning, critical discourse analysis, and OACD are not easy concepts for new instructors, many of whom have not heard of any of these terms before. As an experienced instructor, how might you help a new colleague? If you are a new instructor, where might you go for help?

Notes

1. This chapter has been approved for public release by the Defense Language Institute Foreign Language Center's Public Affairs Office. For verification please email mpao@dliflc.edu. Contents of this chapter are not necessarily the official views of the Defense Language Institute Foreign Language Center, nor are they endorsed by the Department of the Army, the Department of Defense, or the US government. All third-party products or materials featured in the chapter remain the intellectual property of their respective authors or originators. Use of outside materials is done under the fair use copyright principle, for educational purposes only. The content of this chapter is the sole responsibility of the author(s).
2. OACD can be applied equally well in transactional and transformative learning environments but is essential for optimizing transformative learning.
3. Whenever available the author has followed North Korean convention in romanizing the names of well-known North Korean ideological terms and persons, e.g. *Juche* and *Kim Jong Un*.
4. This journal entry was translated into English by the same student.

References

Armstrong, P. 2010. *Bloom's Taxonomy*. Vanderbilt University Center for Teaching. Retrieved August 11, 2023. https://cft.vanderbilt.edu/guides-sub-pages/blooms-taxonomy/.

Campbell, Christine. 2021. "Open Architecture Curricular Design: A Fundamental Principle of Transformative Language Learning and Teaching." In *Transformative Language Learning and Teaching*, edited by Betty Lou Leaver, Dan Davidson, and Christine Campbell, 43–50. Cambridge: Cambridge University Press.

Corin, Andrew R. 2020. "Open Architecture Curriculum and Transformative Language Learning Revisited. Part 2. Toward a Constrained Definition of OACD." *ACTR Letter* 47, no. 1 (Fall): 1–2, 4.

Crane, C. 2019. "Shifting Perspectives in Language (Teacher) Education: Transformative Learning Theory for L2 Learning and Teaching." In *11th International Language Teacher Education Conference*. https://carla.umn.edu/conferences/lte2019/docs/Crane_LTE2019.pdf.

Cranton, P., and E. W. Taylor. 2012. "Transformative Learning Theory: Seeking a More Unified Theory." In *The Handbook of Transformative Learning. Theory, Research, and Practice*, edited by E. W. Taylor, P. Cranton, and Associates, 3–20. San Francisco: Jossey-Bass.

Fairclough, N. 1989. *Language and Power*. London: Longman.

Flipped Learning Network. 2014. "Definition of Flipped Learning." https://flippedlearning.org/definition-of-flipped-learning/.

Johnson, S. M., and B. M. Nelson. 2010. "Above and Beyond the Syllabus: Transformation in an Adult Foreign Language Classroom." *Language Awareness* 19, no. 1: 35–50.

King, R. 2007. "North and South Korea." In *Language and National Identity in Asia*, edited by A. Simpson, 200–35. New York: Oxford University Press.

Leaver, Betty Lou. 2021. "Transformative Language Learning and Teaching: The Next Paradigm Shift and Its Historical Context." In *Transformative Language Learning and Teaching*, edited by Betty Lou Leaver, Dan Davidson, and Christine Campbell, 13–22. Cambridge: Cambridge University Press.

Leaver, Betty Lou, Dan Davidson, and Christine Campbell, eds. 2021. *Transformative Language Learning and Teaching*. Cambridge: Cambridge University Press.

Lee, Jae Sun. 2018. "State Ideology and Language Policy in North Korea: An Analysis of North Korea's Public Discourse." PhD diss., University of Hawaiʻi at Mānoa.

Machin, David, and Andrea Mayr. 2012. *How to Do Discourse Analysis: A Multimodal Introduction*. Los Angeles: Sage.

Mezirow, J. 1978. "Perspective Transformation." *Adult Education* 28, no. 2: 100–10. https://doi.org/10.1177/074171367802800202.

Mezirow, J. 2012. "Learning to Think Like an Adult: Core Concepts of Transformation Theory." In *The Handbook of Transformative Learning. Theory, Research, and Practice*, edited by E. W. Taylor, P. Cranton, and Associates, 73–95. San Francisco: Jossey-Bass.

The National Standards Collaborative Board. 2015. *World-Readiness Standards for Learning Languages*, 4th ed. Alexandria: Author. www.actfl.org/sites/default/files/publications/standards/World-ReadinessStandardsforLearningLanguages.pdf.

3

Preparing Novice Learners for Open Architecture Learning[1]
The Gradual Release of Responsibility Model

IRENE KRASNER

THIS CHAPTER WILL EXPLORE the author's experience of applying features of OACD in the Russian language classroom at the Defense Language Institute Foreign Language Center (DLIFLC), focusing on the early stages of an elementary course. It will demonstrate that the *gradual release of responsibility* model presents an attractive response to the unique challenges faced by novice-level learners in an OACD environment, especially for languages with complex inflectional systems like Russian.

Context for the Development of OACD and Its Introduction at the Defense Language Institute Foreign Language Center (DLIFLC)

DLIFLC is the largest language learning institution in the United States and one of the most important language facilities of the US government. The institute currently offers instruction in a dozen languages to over 2,500 learners in basic programs lasting from thirty-six to sixty-four weeks, depending on the language and the degree of difficulty it poses for native speakers of English. The large majority of learners are aspiring military language professionals who learn their language as preparation for assignments related to some aspect of national security.

OACD has been in use at DLIFLC since it was first implemented in the Directorate of Continuing Education (at that time DLIFLC's directorate for intermediate, advanced, and nonresident instructional programs) in 2006 by Continuing Education Associate Provost Betty Lou Leaver. In the 1980s, Leaver had applied OACD (though not yet using this nomenclature) with considerable success in the Advanced Russian Course at the Foreign Service Institute (FSI) in Washington, DC, another of the US government's premier language training facilities (Leaver and Campbell 2015). The course objective was to take learners to near-native levels of linguistic and cultural proficiency—Levels 3+ and 4 on the Interagency Language Roundtable (ILR) scale[2]—in as little as six months of intensive study (thirty hours a week), depending on the language. The course involved a contract system between learner and teacher, where both collaborated on the choice of topics to be studied and learning activities. This collaboration facilitated adaptation to learner individual differences—learning styles, zone of proximal development, language learning strategies, strengths and deficiencies in the language, future work assignments, and interest in opportunities such as making target-language presentations to émigré communities and participating in émigré professional and social activities.

The excellent results achieved in the FSI Advanced Russian Course over a six-year period led Leaver to introduce OACD at DLIFLC, initially in the Directorate of Continuing Education, and subsequently (beginning in 2015) at advanced stages of the much larger basic programs. OACD's flexible, textbook-free framework fostered creativity in the faculty, who were empowered to involve learners directly in the selection and delivery of content and design or directing of activities. Content, continually and systematically tailored to individual learner/cohort needs, consisted of interchangeable, unadapted authentic texts, tasks, and other activities, often organized into modules. In the majority of languages, OACD was introduced initially in the second and/or third semester of the three-semester basic program sequence, when learners had attained or were approaching ILR Level 1+. Its application stimulated inquiry into whether and how OACD could be beneficially applied at lower levels of proficiency, and how novice learners could be most effectively prepared for study in an OACD environment.

The Special Challenge of Applying OACD at the Novice Level for Languages with Complex Inflectional Systems Like Russian

Over the past several years, the implementation of OACD at all levels of proficiency has been discussed in the literature on L2 learning and teaching (Dababneh 2018; Krasner 2018; Leaver and Campbell 2020; Campbell 2021; Corin 2020a, 2020b, 2021a, 2021b). A considerable number of examples in the context of learning at higher proficiency levels (ILR 1+ through 4) have been presented. At the lower levels (ILR 0+/1), the practice of OACD presents a special challenge, given that OACD requires an abundant input of authentic materials followed by ample learner output. In addition to their limited vocabulary, learners have generally not yet attained the control of structural forms that allows for easy processing of authentic materials arranged in interchangeable, thematically organized blocks of instruction, an OACD feature. In addition in cases where no textbook is used, learners who are directly involved in the selection and delivery of content might not know what their needs are at the beginning of an elementary course. Thus designing a curriculum at the lower levels that does not employ a textbook or some alternate form of fixed, linear scope and sequence of target language structure, lexicon, and functions poses a distinct challenge.

Some might argue that applying OACD at lower proficiency levels in highly inflected languages like Russian is impractical due to the complexity of the morphological system. In Russian this pertains to both its nominal and verbal systems. "Nouns, adjectives, and certain pronouns are specified for gender, number, and case. Modifiers agree with the head nouns; thus, words in these grammatical categories can have up to 24 different word forms" (Rozovskaya and Roth 2019, 3). Typical imperfective verb paradigms include almost two dozen forms, and that number can be greatly increased if one considers that participles are declined as adjectives. Since multiple verbs may be derived from a single root or stem and differ only in passive/reflexive versus active voice, or in aspect or related categories (e.g., unidirectional vs. non-unidirectional verbs of motion), the number of related verbal forms that learners must master can be (ideally) as high as 160, according to Lyashevskaya (2013). In addition, numerals in Russian also have their own inflectional paradigms. While syncretism of two or more categories reduces the number of actual forms in some paradigms, the challenge faced by learners is nevertheless considerable.

Morphological variation can affect the form of stems as well as endings, rendering even high-frequency words incomprehensible to beginners. For instance, "друг" (*drug*, friend) in the nominative singular form becomes "друзьями" (*druz'jam'i*, friends) in the instrumental plural. A learner who has not yet been sufficiently exposed to the noun paradigms in Russian might have difficulty recognizing the latter and its relationship to the "basic" (nominative singular) form of the word, as they look and sound quite different. Thus, a simple phrase like "Я недавно виделся с друзьями" (I recently met with my friends) might present a challenge for novice learners even if they know the nominative singular form of the word "друг" and all the other words in the sentence. The morphological complexity of Russian can thus potentially lead to cognitive overload if learners are exposed to authentic materials when they do not yet know the basics of grammar or possess learning strategies for dealing with authentic materials, which makes the application of OACD especially challenging at the beginning of learning Russian.

One Response to This Challenge: Gradual Transition from a Fixed, Linear Scope and Sequence to OACD through the Gradual Release of Responsibility Model

Despite the morphological complexity of the Russian language, it is nevertheless possible to start the acculturation of learners to the OACD framework at the outset of instruction. One of the available strategies is a gradual transition from a fixed, linear scope and sequence to OACD using gradual release of responsibility. Gradual release of responsibility is a model that gradually, through stages, transfers control of learning and practice from an instructor to learners, progressing from a teacher-dependent mode of instruction to an autonomous learning environment in which learners can co-create curriculum with teachers and transfer their learning to new situations. Applying gradual release of responsibility from the outset of instruction thus lays a foundation for the transition to fully implemented OACD at later stages of learning.

The term *gradual release of responsibility* was first applied in the work of Pearson and Gallagher (1983). As described in Pearson, McVee, and Shanahan (2019), the gradual release of responsibility concept drew in part on the rediscovered work of Vygotsky with its concept of the zone of proximal development. From its inception a variety of gradual release of responsibility schemes have been defined. Figure 3.1 describes the stages of gradual release of responsibility as formulated by Fisher and Frey (2011, 2021).

```
                    TEACHER RESPONSIBILITY
                    ╱╲
                   ╱  ╲  Focused Instruction       "I do it"
                  ╱────╲
                 ╱      ╲ Guided Instruction       "We do it"
                ╱────────╲
               ╱          ╲ Collaborative Learning  "You do it together"
              ╱────────────╲
             ╱              ╲ Independent Learning  "You do it alone"
            ╱────────────────╲
                    STUDENT RESPONSIBILITY
```

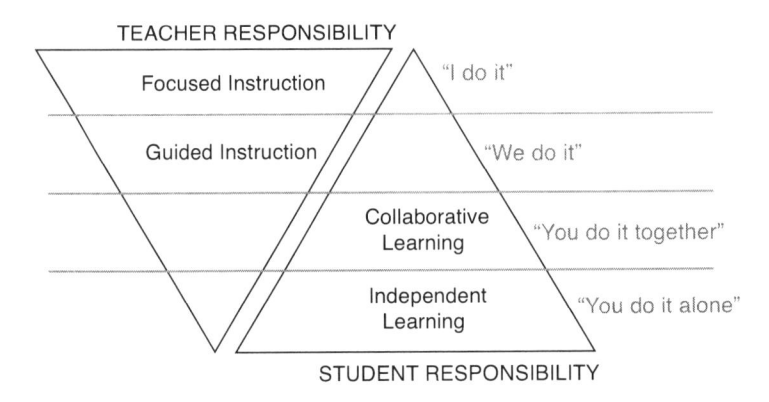

Figure 3.1. Gradual release of responsibility (Fisher and Frey 2021, reproduced with permission)

According to their formulation (2011, 2³), there are four components (stages) of the gradual release of responsibility model:

- "Focus lessons in which the teacher establishes the purpose of the lesson and models his or her thinking
- Guided instruction in which the teacher questions, prompts, and cues students to facilitate their thinking about the topic
- Collaborative learning in which students work together, using academic language, to complete a task
- Independent learning in which students apply what they have learned individually"

Historically, the gradual release of responsibility model has been used mostly at the lesson level (i.e., within individual lessons or units). However its application can be expanded to the program level, which allows faculty to co-create the content of the course with learners to a progressively greater extent and ever more directly over the course of study. This approach requires that teachers deviate systematically from the prescribed "closed" curriculum (typically based on a textbook) and open learner horizons gradually through exploration of authentic language and experimentation with the real world. As expressed by Clifford (2021, 234):

> To maintain an expansive view of learning and create an environment where learners are striving to enhance their learning, teachers must consciously work to counteract the institutionalized pressures that otherwise result in a step-by-step reduction in learning opportunities — a reduction that shrinks both the quantity of the knowledge that can be acquired and the development of students' cognitive abilities.

In other words teachers should use every opportunity to expand the existing course beyond the textbook from day one of instruction.

These OACD-type practices, in which students select their own materials and create highly personalized real-life products, should be well planned and systematic. Among other considerations, they should be within learners' zone of proximal development, that is, within "the distance between the actual developmental level as determined by independent problem solving and the level of potential development as determined through problem solving under adult guidance, or in collaboration with more capable peers" (Vygotsky 1978, 86).

In the initial stages of learning Russian, application of gradual release of responsibility may emphasize receptive skills (listening and reading comprehension) over productive ones (speaking and writing). It can be argued, moreover, that gradual acculturation to the structure of Russian is easier if the exposure to authentic materials initially emphasizes reading comprehension, as inflections are typically easier to discern in the written form.

Gradual Release of Responsibility Techniques for Introducing Features of OACD in a Russian Classroom from the Start of an Elementary Course

This section illustrates techniques based on the gradual release of responsibility model, primarily at the lesson level, for introducing aspects of OACD from the beginning of novice-level instruction in Russian.

Teaching the Sound Representations of Cyrillic Letters

Comer and Murphy-Lee (2004) draw attention to the importance of learning the sound representations of Cyrillic letters as early as possible. Their research found that the earlier learners acquire letter-sound knowledge, the better they will perform later in the Russian course. Among other concerns, autonomous experimentation with authentic Russian texts from day one of instruction, through which learners can begin their acculturation to the OACD environment, depends on them rapidly achieving at least passive familiarity with the letters.

According to Leaver (1984), the Russian alphabet can in fact be introduced in less than one hour. Through Leaver's technique, which is based on mnemonic research and Piagetan learning theory, alphabet acquisition is "achieved rapidly, enjoyably, and successfully" (Leaver 1984). The approach emphasizes similarities between English and Russian writing and sound systems rather than their differences. Accordingly the Russian alphabet is introduced via audiovisual aids using cognates[4] or borrowings which are similar in Russian and English.

In the first phase students access the materials through audiovisual aids. This is done initially under a teacher's guidance, corresponding to the guided instruction stage of gradual release of responsibility, after which learners can transition to a collaborative learning process and finally to independent or semi-independent learning through homework assignments.

Under one such procedure (among the many possibilities), the audiovisual aids used to be two 8-inch × 10-inch index cards taped together; today, they appear on computer/mobile device screens. On the top card/screen, the letter appears; on the bottom, a word containing the letter. The word must be a Russian language cognate of an English word or borrowed word similar to English in its graphic representation of sounds. Table 3.1 presents a sampling of possible words.

For the full alphabet list, see Leaver (1984). Since the words are cognates of English words, the material becomes instantly familiar. Every letter in the list is reused on multiple occasions, "thus, the material is 'spiraled,' with students reviewing while they

Table 3.1. Adapted from Leaver (1984)

Russian word	English cognate	Russian letter	English letter
Мама	Mama	м, а	m, a
Папа	Papa	п, а	p, a
Парк	Park	р, к	r, k
Танк	Tank	н	n

move forward. If they were to move forward in a linear fashion, as opposed to a spiral, they would quickly forget the first letters presented" (Leaver 1984, 216).

The technique may be used in a variety of ways depending on teacher preferences. After the initial introduction of the alphabet, the review of the letters based on cognates might be turned into a game in a homework assignment that learners carry out independently. Alternatively one might introduce the Russian alphabet using online resources. Sites such as russianlessons.net or masterrussian.com provide a concise overview of the Russian alphabet. Note that at this stage learners are not yet practicing writing or learning cursive script. A similar technique for rapid introduction of the alphabet is employed in some textbooks published in Russia. For instance, in Esmantova (2008) the Russian letters are introduced on the basis of geographical names of countries and their capitals, e.g., А а [a] Анкара (Ankara), Б б [b] Берн (Bern), В в [v], Вена (Vienna), and so on.

Teaching Effective Strategies to Recognize Cognates

After the quick introduction of the Russian alphabet, a next step is to teach learners strategies for recognizing cognates. At this stage, the teacher shows learners multiple sets of cognates (up to 200), using comparative linguistic analysis (patterns of comparison of suffixes, prefixes, and roots) to aid word recognition. This phase of instruction can engage the "focus lesson" and "guided instruction" stages of the gradual release of responsibility model. Showing learners the similarities between the Russian and English alphabets and helping them recognize cognates from the start of instruction alleviates some of the anxiety that learners might experience when beginning to learn a language with a different writing system from that of their native language.

Familiarizing learners with strategies for recognizing cognates, including word formation (e.g., that the suffix—ция in Russian is normally rendered in English cognates as—tion), is a critical step before asking learners to decipher and read them independently. Some novice teachers assume that cognates are self-evident and omit this cross-linguistic preparatory stage in the sequence of activities. Cognates in Russian, especially in listening, might sound completely different from their counterparts in English; thus thoughtful scaffolding is needed to prepare learners to recognize them.

Introducing Features of OACD at Level 0/0+

After practicing deciphering sets of cognates, one can proceed to collaborative and semi-independent learning stages in combination and ask learners to select a number of cognates by category (e.g., economics, culture, politics) and find on the internet three titles of articles on those topics. Using this technique, learners can start reading some titles and subtitles of articles from day one, which is highly motivational. The following example from Aleinikov and Krasner (2014) illustrates the abovementioned procedure:

> Структурные параллели (structural parallels): -ор, -ер, -ёр = -or, -er; Профессии и люди (professions and people): 1. Профессор (professor); 2. Инспектор (inspector); 3. Авиатор (aviator); 4. Диспетчер (dispatcher); 5. Дизайнер (designer); 6. Доктор (doctor); 7. Диктатор (dictator); 8. Актёр (actor); 9. Координатор (coordinator); 10. Офицер (officer).
>
> Task based on the previous example: "From the list of cognates, select four to five cognates on a topic of your choice. Find three titles of articles on the internet that you understand. Working in pairs, share in English with your partner your predictions about the main idea of the articles."

In this OACD-preparatory task, if a learner selects the topic "economy," and the following six cognate pairs, кризис-crisis, экономика-economy, программа-program, процесс-process, прогресс-progress, инфляция-inflation, an internet search at the time of writing produced the following results:

- "Тест по экономике на тему 'Инфляция' 11 класс" ("Test on Economics on the Topic of Inflation, 11th grade");
- "Финансовый кризис 2007–2008 годов" ("Financial crisis. Years 2007–2008");
- "Инфляция: ее методы регулирования" ("Inflation: Its Methods of Regulation").

Normally learners are able to discern the meaning of titles they have found on the internet and are excited to be able to understand them so early in the course. However, teacher help may still be needed to guide learners as they work with the titles. For instance, in the first title above, learners might need help with the word "класс" (pronounced like English "class"), which is a false cognate. This word means "a grade" in this context.

It has been the author's experience that quite often learners continue reading the articles, amazed they are able to understand not only the titles but parts of the texts themselves. In fact, it can be difficult to finish the lesson and move to the next task because of learner interest, which leads to a form of what might be considered positive perseveration.

This OACD-preparatory task can thus potentially combine the three active stages of Fisher and Frey's gradual release of responsibility construct: guided instruction, collaborative learning, and independent learning. In addition learners can also work cooperatively on both selecting the categories and searching the internet for the titles of articles. Stages of gradual release of responsibility applied in an OACD-preparatory task should nevertheless depend on learner zones of actual and proximal development; not all stages should necessarily be used in a particular activity.

As mentioned previously, at this stage of the course every task should be carefully designed and tried out by the designer before being given to learners. Sometimes key words need to be changed; sometimes links should be provided. The scaffolding will depend on learner needs. The above-described instructional sequence has been used successfully by the author during a series of introductory lessons even before the official start of the Russian Basic Program.

Work with cognates thus enables the use of authentic materials from the beginning of instruction, a feature of OACD. Use of authentic materials, in turn, can promote incidental vocabulary retention—the assimilation of vocabulary that results from learner exposure to ample amounts of authentic materials. L2 research indicates that second language vocabulary can be learned incidentally while the learner is engaged in reading for meaning, inferring the meaning of unknown words (Krashen 1993; Pigada and Schmitt 2006; Huckin and Coady 1999; Gass 1999). It should be noted that incidental vocabulary retention is mostly a characteristic of learners with a global learning style, who learn osmotically. Their polar opposites, particular[5] learners, focus on discrete items and details and learn quite consciously (Ehrman, Leaver, and Shekhtman 2005, 75). Particular learners, then, need to develop the tolerance of ambiguity that global learners naturally practice as they deal with both the known and unknown while reading or listening to authentic materials. Teachers can help particular learners develop a willingness to tolerate ambiguity through instruction in learning strategies that allow them to disambiguate at least a part of what they are hearing or seeing, such as using context clues, risk taking, and predicting the content of an article from its title.

Providing Learners with a Choice of Materials, Tasks, and Activities

Learners can participate in the design of the curriculum in limited ways from the very start of the course. One way to implement some features of OACD at Levels 0+/1 is to build on the existing authentic materials in textbooks and expand them by adding task-based activities where learners are afforded the opportunity to select their own authentic materials, choose associated tasks and activities, and create their own products. For instance in the current DLIFLC Russian Basic Program textbooks, there are many advertisements about apartments and cars, help wanted sections, business cards, and other materials at Levels 0+, 1, and 1+. Those texts could be expanded to OACD-based tasks. The three following examples illustrate how this may be done at various proficiency levels.

At Level 0+, the instructor can begin with the following activity from the textbook:

Read the business cards below and complete the following table in Russian.

In this activity learners have to read four business cards of Russian professionals and fill out a table which contains columns for first and last names, professions, addresses, and phone numbers.

A task-based activity that augments the foregoing exercise in accordance with OACD principles follows:

> Step 1: Find two or three Russian business cards on the internet. Present them to your classmates in Russian. Indicate the first and last names, professions, and addresses of those individuals.
> Step 2: Design your own business card. Present it to the class.

Learners typically show exceptional creativity when designing their own business cards and talk about their future "dream" professions, normally with a lot of humor. To accomplish this task, learners conduct research, select cards that they like and design their own products, thus exemplifying several features of OACD, including (among others) learner choice, personalization, co-creation of the curriculum with the faculty and fellow learners, and engagement of the higher-order thinking skills of synthesis (Bloom et al. 1956) and creativity (Anderson and Krathwohl 2000). The multitude of choices of business cards on the internet creates a great opportunity for learners to deepen their cultural knowledge and research skills. While the task of selecting materials in this sequence is still (at least initially) a guided instruction, since learners are presented with the models of business cards in the textbook, this assignment leads them toward linguistic self-reliance and learner autonomy. Although the assignment has a low level of overall cognitive complexity, it nevertheless acculturates learners to approach learning tasks as creative opportunities. The final product of the task, learner business cards, is a representation of a real-life, personalized, and culturally loaded artifact.

Moving to Level 1 texts, the following augmentation based on OACD features might be suggested. After reading two "for rent" advertisements from the DLIFLC Russian Basic Program (Lessons 1-6 Review) and filling out a table in the textbook, learners are given a task based on OACD principles in which they are asked to find three apartments on the internet that will fit their family needs in a Russian city. The premise is that they are planning to spend a year in Russia for business. Learners can select the city of their choice, which creates a lot of excitement. Then they research "for rent" advertisements and select three apartments of their choice, after which they present their three top choices to their classmates and ask for advice on which apartment to choose. Alternatively learners can ask Siri in Russian to find them apartments in the selected cities. Using voice recognition software like Siri in real time in the classroom adds to the authenticity of the situation. This task also includes some of the same features of OACD, including learner choice, personalization, and engagement of critical thinking skills. Following the gradual release of responsibility model, this task can approach the stage of independent learning (or independent practice), as learners transfer acquired knowledge to meet a simulated real-life situation.

Similarly at Level 1+, after reading an authentic text from the textbook about a new dress uniform in the Russian military, learners are asked to research on the internet various Russian military uniforms of their particular service (service dress, camouflage, and regular uniforms) and describe them to their classmates as well as to compare Russian and American uniforms of their branch of service. The features of OACD in this task also include learner choice, personalization, and engagement of critical thinking skills such as comparison. In both examples, learner practice can still be carefully guided but highly personalized and open-ended.

Conclusions

The foregoing examples demonstrate how to introduce features of OACD into the Russian classroom beginning even at the earliest stages using the gradual release of responsibility model. It is important to keep in mind that the majority of OACD features are oriented toward meaning versus form and feedback is given to learners holistically, keeping real-life communicative goals in mind. Once learners reach Level 1+/2, are familiar with the basic structural features of the Russian language as well as their own learning preferences, and have developed a range of learning strategies, instruction can move to the full-blown OACD framework. At this point transition to the OACD framework should be smooth, since learners have been gradually acculturated to it from day one of instruction. The author's experience has shown that the incorporation of OACD features into the learning environment enhances the learning experience.

Study Questions

1. This chapter described the use of the gradual release of responsibility model with military learners studying Russian. How might the use of the gradual release of responsibility model differ in other venues (e.g., university classrooms, study abroad programs) and for other languages?
2. What features of the gradual release of responsibility model allow OACD to be applied at very early levels of L2 instruction? How would implementing these features and the gradual release of responsibility model generally require you to modify your program of instruction?
3. Taking responsibility does not come easily to some learners. Can the gradual release of responsibility model help overcome this obstacle? What modifications to the gradual release of responsibility model described in this chapter might benefit such learners in your own environment?

Notes

1. This chapter has been approved for public release by the Defense Language Institute Foreign Language Center's Public Affairs Office. For verification please email mpao@dliflc.edu. Contents of this chapter are not necessarily the official views of the Defense Language Institute Foreign Language Center, nor are they endorsed by the Department of the Army, the Department of Defense, or the US government. All third-party products and materials featured in the chapter remain the intellectual property of their respective authors and originators. Use of outside materials is done under the fair use copyright principle, for educational purposes only. The content of this chapter is the sole responsibility of the author(s).
2. The two American scales of language proficiency, the ILR and ACTFL guidelines, are related, the latter having been developed out of the former. There are clear equivalencies between the two at their base levels. ILR 0/0+, 1, 2, and 3 correspond to ACTFL's Novice, Intermediate, Advanced, and Superior levels, respectively, though the sublevels do not fully correspond. ILR levels 4 and 5 were previously encompassed within ACTFL's Superior level but are now separated out into a Distinguished level (Corin 2021a).
3. A more comprehensive exposition may be found in Fisher and Frey (2021).
4. Here cognates are defined broadly as recognizable borrowings from various languages as well as words with the same recognizable roots.
5. The oft-cited opposition *global* versus *analytic* conflates multiple independent traits, as some learners are both global and analytic in orientation, and is best resolved into a "quadrant" of two independent oppositions: *global* versus *particular* (more properly termed *local*) and *synthetic* versus *analytic* (Leaver and Corin 2019).

References

Aleinikov, Andrei, and Irina Krasner. 2014. *Russian Alphabet through Cognates*. Unpublished manuscript. Monterey: Defense Language Institute Foreign Language Center.

Anderson, Lorin W., and David R. Krathwohl, eds. 2000. *A Taxonomy for Teaching, Learning, and Assessing: A Revision of Bloom's Taxonomy of Educational Objectives*. New York: Longman.

Bloom, Benjamin S., Max D. Engelhart, Edward J. Furst, Walker H. Hill, and David R. Krathwohl. 1956. *Taxonomy of Educational Objectives: The Classification of Educational Goals. Handbook I: Cognitive Domain*. New York: David McKay Co., Inc.

Campbell, Christine. 2021. "Open Architecture Curricular Design." In *Transformative Language Learning and Teaching*, edited by Betty Lou Leaver, Dan Davidson, and Christine Campbell, 43–50. Cambridge: Cambridge University Press.

Clifford, Ray. 2021. "Testing and Transformative Language Learning." In *Transformative Language Learning and Teaching*, edited by Betty Lou Leaver, Dan Davidson, and Christine Campbell, 227–37. Cambridge: Cambridge University Press.

Comer, William J., and Meghan Murphy-Lee. 2004. "Letter-Sound Correspondence Acquisition in First-Semester Russian." *Canadian Slavonic Papers* 46, no. 1–2: 23–35.

Corin, Andrew R. 2020a. "Open Architecture Curriculum and Transformative Language Learning Revisited. Part 1. The Relationship between Open Architecture Curricular Design and Transformative Language Learning." *ACTR Letter* 46, no. 3–4: 1–2, 4–5.

Corin, Andrew R. 2020b. "Open Architecture Curriculum and Transformative Language Learning Revisited. Part 2. Toward a Constrained Definition of OACD." *ACTR Letter* 47, no. 1: 1–2, 4.

Corin, Andrew R. 2021a. "The Challenge of the Inverted Pyramid in Attaining Distinguished-Level Proficiency." *Journal for Distinguished Language Studies* 7: 107–37.

Corin, Andrew R. 2021b. "Foreign Language Learning Efficiency: Transformative Learning in an Outcomes-Based Environment." In *Transformative Language Learning and Teaching*, edited by Betty Lou Leaver, Dan Davidson, and Christine Campbell, 51–60. Cambridge: Cambridge University Press.

Dababneh, R. 2018. "The Scenario-Based Syllabus for the Post-Basic Arabic Program." *Dialog on Language Instruction* 28, no. 1: 13–26.

Ehrman, Madeline, Betty L. Leaver, and Boris Shekhtman. 2005. *Achieving Success in Second Language Acquisition*. Cambridge: Cambridge University Press.

Esmantova, Tatiana. 2008. *Russian Language: 5 Elements: Level A1 (Elementary)*. St. Petersburg: Zlatoust.

Fisher, Douglas, and Nancy Frey. 2011. "Engaging the Adolescent Learner. The First 20 Days: Establishing Productive Group Work in the Classroom." International Reading Association. Accessed July 18, 2020. https://dpi.wi.gov/sites/default/files/imce/ela/resources/Fisher_and_Frey_-_Engaging_the_Adolescent_Learner.pdf.

Fisher, Douglas, and Nancy Frey. 2021. *Better Learning through Structured Teaching: A Framework for the Gradual Release of Responsibility*, 3rd ed. Alexandria: ASCD.

Gass, Susan. 1999. "Discussion: Incidental Vocabulary Learning." *Studies in Second Language Acquisition* 21, no. 2: 319–33. https://doi.org/10.1017/S0272263199002090.

Huckin, Thomas, and James Coady. 1999. "Incidental Vocabulary Acquisition in a Second Language: A Review." *Studies in Second Language Acquisition* 21, no. 2, SPECIAL ISSUE: Incidental L2 Vocabulary Acquisition: Theory, Current Research, and Instructional Implications (June 1999), 181–93. Cambridge: Cambridge University Press.

Krashen, Steven. 1993. *The Power of Reading: Insights from the Research*. Englewood: Libraries Unlimited.

Krasner, Irene. 2018. "Open Architecture Approach to Teaching Russian as a Foreign Language." *ACTR Letter* 45, no. 2: 1–5.

Leaver, Betty Lou. 1984. "Twenty Minutes to Mastery of the Cyrillic Alphabet." *Foreign Language Annals* 17, no. 3: 215–20.

Leaver, Betty Lou, and Andrew R. Corin. 2019. "Fields of the Mind: An Integral Learning Styles Component of the E&L Cognitive Styles Construct." *Russian Language Journal* 69: 61–88

Leaver, Betty Lou, and Christine Campbell. 2015. "Experience with Higher Levels of Proficiency." In *To Advanced Proficiency and Beyond: Theory and Methods for Developing Superior Second Language Ability*, edited by Tony Brown and Jennifer Bown, 3–22. Washington: Georgetown University Press.

Leaver, Betty Lou, and Christine Campbell. 2020. "The Shifting Paradigm in Russian Language Pedagogy: From Communicative Language Teaching to Transformative Language Learning and Teaching." In *The Art of Teaching Russian*, edited by Evgeny Dengub, Irina Dubinina, and Jason Merrill, 147–62. Washington: Georgetown University Press. https://doi.org/10.2307/j.ctv18sqxnd.12.

Lyashevskaya, Olga. 2013. *Frequency Dictionary of Inflectional Paradigms: Core Russian Vocabulary*. Higher School of Economics Research Paper no. WP BRP 35/HUM/2013.

Pearson, P. David, and Margaret C. Gallagher. 1983. "The Instruction of Reading Comprehension." *Contemporary Educational Psychology* 8, no. 3: 317–44.

Pearson, P. David, Mary B. McVee, and Lynn E. Shanahan. 2019. "In the Beginning: The Historical and Conceptual Genesis of the Gradual Release of Responsibility." In *The Gradual Release of Responsibility in Literacy Research and Practice*, edited by Mary B. McVee, Evan Ortlieb, Jennifer Reichenberg, and P. David Pearson, 1–22. Bingley: Emerald Publishing Limited.

Pigada, Maria, and Norbert Schmitt. 2006. "Vocabulary Acquisition from Extensive Reading: A Case Study." *Reading in a Foreign Language* 18: 1–28.

Rozovskaya, Alla, and Dan Roth. 2019. "Grammar Error Correction in Morphologically Rich Languages: The Case of Russian." *Transactions of the Association for Computational Linguistics* 7: 1–17. https://doi.org/10.1162/tacl_a_00251.

Vygotsky, Lev S. 1978. *Mind in Society: The Development of Higher Psychological Processes*. Cambridge: Harvard University Press.

4

OACD-Based Immersion Events Outside the Classroom in an Intensive Chinese Mandarin Program[1]

KUEILAN CHEN

The Challenge of Introducing OACD in a Large Basic Language Acquisition Program at DLIFLC

Beginning in 2006, intermediate and advanced courses at the Defense Language Institute Foreign Language Center (DLIFLC) shifted from textbook-based instruction to reliance on OACD (see also Chapter 1; Lee; Dababneh & Yuan; Wang, this volume). The change was not without its fits, starts, and backsliding, but over time instructional teams developed skill in the approach and achieved notable improvements in proficiency outcomes.

In DLIFLC's much larger basic language acquisition programs (hereafter, basic programs) a similar move in the direction of OACD launched in 2015 proved more difficult despite a concerted effort. Several reasons can be identified beyond the inevitable resistance to abandoning established practices rooted in traditional textbook-based approaches. One major factor is that OACD had previously been applied, at DLIFLC and elsewhere, primarily at proficiency levels beginning with ACTFL Intermediate High (ILR 1+), so it is unsurprising that transitioning to OACD, especially in earlier stages of basic programs with novice-level (ILR 0+) learners, proved challenging. The size and complexity of many basic programs was an exacerbating factor: large numbers of students, teachers, and sections; interplay of the multiple interconnected courses that comprise each program; and the requirement for day-to-day accountability for the progress of each participant (Chapter 1, this volume). Finally, many teachers, team leaders, and managers had limited training and experience in applying OACD. Some teachers, moreover, came from professional backgrounds unrelated to language teaching and had little or no formal training in world language education beyond what they received at DLIFLC.

Various strategies have been adopted to address the challenges of transitioning to OACD, especially for large programs and at low proficiency levels, depending on circumstances in particular programs, departments, and teams. Krasner describes the gradual-release-of-responsibility model adopted by her team in the DLIFLC Russian Basic Program. Oded and Oded discuss the comprehensive adoption of OACD in the smaller DLIFLC Hebrew Basic Program. Bondarenko describes an OACD content-based intensive elementary Russian course at the Middlebury Institute of International Studies.

This chapter describes another approach as applied by DLIFLC's large Chinese Mandarin Basic Program: OACD-based immersion events outside the classroom (hereafter, immersions). Two types of immersions will be described: one- and two-day *iso-immersions*[2] at a local immersion facility and two-week immersions at external institutions. Iso-immersions, generally set up based on open-architecture-type design, have been employed by all DLIFLC basic programs for many years, while opportunities and designs for longer immersions have varied from program to program.[3]

Two core OACD principles inform both the one- and two-day and the two-week immersions:

- Curriculum structured around a theme-based syllabus (rather than a textbook) that integrates interchangeable unadapted authentic texts, tasks, and other activities
- Continual and systematic (vs. occasional) tailoring to learner and cohort needs

The shorter iso-immersions are employed by DLIFLC basic programs for the primary purpose of enhancing learner motivation and confidence in their ability to function autonomously in target-language contexts (see subsequent discussion). Longer immersions in a target-language-speaking country or at external institutions in the United States target proficiency gain (see below), while simultaneously enhancing motivation and confidence. If well designed, immersions (especially longer ones) can act as an initial foray into open architecture learning, providing learners "affordances," which van Lier (2000) describes as learning activities where learners choose from a variety of specifically created interactive and collaborative learning tasks or scenarios that best meet their learning needs. Opportunities to choose allow learners to self-regulate, taking more control of their own learning in various task- or scenario-based contexts.

Currently Chinese Mandarin Basic Program students welcome immersion events, which constitute a change from the eighteen-year-old curriculum. In-course and end-of-course student questionnaires often note the outdated nature of the curriculum and request "any activities that are different from the daily classroom teaching [that] would support students' motivation of learning" (from one questionnaire).

DLIFLC's Textbook-Based Chinese Mandarin Basic Program

The Chinese Mandarin Basic Program is a sixty-three-week intensive program with six class hours and two hours of homework Monday through Friday. Courses are taught by teams of instructors, generally four for a cohort of twelve learners divided into two sections. Proficiency outcome objectives for 2023 were 80% Advanced/Advanced/Intermediate High (ILR 2/2/1+) (listening/reading/speaking), 40% Advanced High/Advanced High/Intermediate High (2+/2+/1+), and 10% Superior/Superior/Intermediate High (3/3/1+). The program is divided into three semesters, and textbooks are used the entire time.

Semester 1 is divided into five units that focus on survival content. Semester 2 is divided into four units devoted to "Family and Society" (Unit 6), "Education and Employment" (Unit 7), "Health and Welfare" (Unit 8), and "Geography" (Unit 9), utilizing 60%–80% of authentic materials. Semester 3 is divided into three units (Units 10-12), during which learners study all ten DLIFLC-mandated area studies domains (enumerated by Wang, this volume) while progressing gradually to 100% utilization of authentic materials.

Achieving the proficiency objectives noted previously has proven difficult but is doable if a transition is made from a highly structured, static curriculum to an OACD one grounded in OACD principles like the two core ones listed previously and features such as a focus on higher-order thinking and learner self-regulation. Such a curriculum can promote learner and teacher creativity and "defeat" the inverted pyramid construct according to which ever greater time is required to achieve successive levels of proficiency (Corin 2020).

One-Day and Two-Day Immersions at DLIFLC's Immersion Facility

DLIFLC basic program iso-immersions last one day (Semester 1) or two days (Semesters 2 and 3) and take place at a local immersion facility that can be decorated according to culturally specific criteria. Most daytime activities are designed as series of scenarios with increasingly more challenging tasks and situations; other cultural activities are also included.

The teaching team and immersion specialist/coordinator meet before each immersion to discuss the scenarios and activities, making changes as needed from previous iterations, swapping out certain activities for others, and so on. After the immersion, they meet again to review what worked and did not work. In this way, the immersions are routinely reviewed and improved.

Semester 1 Iso-Immersion

The theme of the Semester 1 immersion, which occurs in the eighteenth week of a sixty-three-week program and is focused on enhancing learner motivation, revolves around a group of American students who are going to China for several months of immersive studies at a Beijing university. The scenarios are designed for learners at Level 1/1+. Cultural activities such as tai chi, Chinese chess, mahjong, calligraphy, and Chinese paper cutting are also included. All activities are exclusively in Chinese.

The immersion includes four scenarios: (1) at the airport and with the host family, (2) shopping, (3) restaurant, and (4) class field trip. The first involves meeting the host family at the airport and exchanging individual information at their home. The second scenario involves a series of events associated with stations—vegetable-fruit produce market, bank, department store, movie theater, post office, rental house, electronics store. At each station, teams of three learners engage in various tasks and activities from a "passport booklet" they received at the outset, interacting with instructors playing various roles—host family members, bank cashier, sale clerks, and so on. At the "bank," for example, learners fill out the currency exchange form to change US dollars to renminbi, the official currency of the People's Republic of China.

At the "store" they can bargain for price and use Alipay and a QR code or credit card versus cash. If time allows, learners report in small groups about their shopping experience. Afterward, they learn about Chinese regional food specialties and eating etiquette at a restaurant, integrating elements of Chinese culture into the learning experience.

The last scenario, Class Field Trip, involves exploring a Chinese website to find the best place for a class field trip. Working in small groups, with instructors as advisors, learners study, discuss, and select the best scenic points for the class trip. They create sets of slides to explain their chosen location to the class: why it has the best scenic points, where they can stay overnight, and how they will get there from Beijing. After one hour of preparation, learners address the entire class, taking turns to report their finding to persuade the class their selected city is the best place for the class trip. Each group reports for five to seven minutes followed by a three-minute questions-and-answers (Q&A) period.

Semester 2 Iso-Immersion
The Semester 2 immersion theme is "Finding a Job in China," and it involves American university students who have been studying at a Beijing university. It consists of four scenarios designed to deepen cultural understanding for learners at levels Advanced/Advanced High (ILR 2/2+) through the process of finding a job in China. Learners work in large- and small-group activities but also have individual activities. Instructors serve as role-players, observers, motivators, sources of culture, and facilitators.

In the first scenario learners, who are playing the role of students at a Beijing university, go to the university's student counseling center to get advice about how a foreigner can apply for and obtain a job in China. The counselor shares a video where an alumnus discusses how she, as a foreigner, found a job in China. The video has Chinese captions. A team of two to three learners engages with instructors who facilitate discussion about different aspects of job-hunting, for example, comparing how it is done in China versus in the United States.

The second scenario concerns a physical exam at a hospital. Following the alumnus's advice, learners go to a clinic/hospital to get a health certificate for job application. The physical exam involves several steps listed in a "Job Physical Examination Form for Foreigners": check-in, nurse station, otorhinolaryngology, neurology, laboratory, and so on, with instructors as clinic assistant and doctor. Learners can also play the role of physician's assistant.

In the third scenario learners explore linguistic and cultural differences when they write a resume, fill out a "Foreigner Entry Application Form," and prepare for job interviews as part of the job-hunting process. After studying potential companies, learners prepare the documents and submit them via email or deliver them to company representatives.

The fourth scenario is job interviews. Learners are interviewed and also serve as one of the job interviewers in an interview panel. In this way they can actively answer interview questions, listen to others answering questions, and ask interviewees questions. A set of authentic job interview questions can be adapted or used if desired. After two interviews, the representatives of companies announce the results of job interviews with rationale for each candidate in front of the entire class. Learners need to listen carefully about the job announcements, as they will have to reach decisions to accept or reject a job offer and explain why they accepted or rejected the offer. Following the job announcement, learners make an impromptu speech about their job-hunting and interview experience and share their insights about this immersion day.

Semester 3 Iso-Immersion
The Semester 3 iso-immersion is designed for learners at levels Advanced High/Superior (ILR 2+/3). Its theme is "US-China Business Fair." A US delegation (the learners) led by the secretary of commerce will attend the fair, which will be held at the Shanghai International Convention Center. The delegation is comprised of five groups (one to two representatives each), each representing a US company. At the fair each group presents a business plan with details such as objective, product, total investment, timeline, resources needed, office/plant location, staffing, and profit projection. Also attending are four to six delegations (one or two representatives each) from various Chinese cities that are interested in doing business with US companies.

First, learners in small groups brainstorm ideas for soliciting or attracting Chinese business people interested in working with their US counterparts. The different parts of the scenario serve to activate existing schemata and deepen target-language cultural understanding and competencies necessary for Superior (ILR 3) proficiency.

The scenario then continues in two parts. In the first part each group forms an "investment project team" that works together to create a business project it then presents. Teams do considerable research to devise their projects. Teams then take turns presenting their projects to Chinese city representatives. Q&A between US delegation members and city representatives follows. The second part involves establishing new business agreements between the two parties. After presenting the projects, both parties discuss the agreements. The activities culminate in a signing ceremony at which all learners make an impromptu speech.

The scenario includes large-group, small-group, and individual interactions among instructors and peers. Throughout, learners demonstrate cultural competencies (e.g., norms and etiquette), awareness of major historical or cultural events, idiomatic language, and cultural references needed for higher-level language proficiency.

This scenario requires substantial advance exposure to the range of area studies topics encompassed by the basic program. Learners find some of these topics (society, culture, and technology) easier to understand, likely because they have more relevance to their daily life. They often feel intimated by others, especially economics. During the reflection session at the end of the presentations, students expressed that they understood more than 90 percent of presentations, and that their grasp of the economic concepts presented was much improved. Teaching team members felt the same way. Students also shared that they had done extensive research in preparing for the presentations, and in so doing gained a deeper understanding of the topic they chose.

The Semester 3 immersion has proven to be a huge success. It improves learners' understanding of economic concepts and, more importantly, boosts their confidence and comfort level in discussing economics. When economic topics arise after the immersion, students demonstrate greater confidence and much improved comprehension of the topics addressed. The anxiety and perplexity they had previously demonstrated with economic topics were no longer noticeable, and their increased ease with—and command of—economic topics was palpable.

Two-Week Immersions at Concordia Language Villages and San Diego State University

DLIFLC Basic Programs currently have no immersions in mainland China or Taiwan due to the world situation. Instead, third-semester learners now participate in two-week immersions at Concordia Language Villages in Minnesota or San Diego State University. These intensive programs expose them to high-level Chinese listening, reading, and speaking. Both involve them in a wide range of interactive activities combining language and culture.

Concordia Language Villages

The Concordia Language Villages are a program of Concordia College in Moorhead, Minnesota, that offers a rich array of immersion programs for adults and children. Since 2006 they have offered customized training for US Army soldiers,[4] and in 2016 Concordia was designated a Language Training Center by the Defense Language and National Security Education Office. The Language Training Center provides residential iso-immersion sessions in a number of critical languages. For 2022–23, these included Modern Standard Arabic, Chinese Mandarin, French, Korean, Russian, Spanish, and Ukrainian.

The primary objective for the government language training programs is to "expedite language acquisition in a context that simulates realistic scenarios they might encounter when interacting with communities in which the target language is spoken" through "situated practice that encourages learners to apply language to unscripted, predictable and unpredictable interpersonal communication" (http://www.concordialanguagevillages.org/adult-programs/government-training/situated-learning, accessed in August 2023). The teaching philosophy is based on six guiding pedagogical principles, all well aligned with OACD. In abbreviated form, these are:

- giving learners courage,
- learner investment,
- linguistic and cultural authenticity,

- creating a need to communicate,
- experiencing the language, and
- learning within extended projects.

The teacher-learner ratio of 1:3 permits attention to individual differences.

The "Language Training Center General Course Description" (2023) specifies the following components:

- Small learning groups: in the mornings for three to four hours, learners review authentic texts and passages about area studies domains specified by DLIFLC.
- Authentic family-style meals: three hours per day in residential programs, where dishes are eaten family-style. Teachers are present to encourage conversation on a variety of topics or review material from the morning small-group sessions.
- Hands-on activities: two to four hours in the afternoons and evenings, completing job-related and cultural activities (one to two hours in virtual programs), where learners engage in "practical tasks that they might be required to do in their jobs, such as relaying or interpreting messages in the target language, preparing a brief, interpreting cultural artifacts for site exploitation" or working with a team on an assignment. "Other . . . activities require active interaction with cultural practices and products." This can be a simulation, such as involvement in a culturally specific event like a national holiday, or engagement in authentic music, arts, sports, and games.
- Independent projects: learners have multiple opportunities to research and present to the group on a topic of interest to them, with teacher support.
- Review of news and current events from the target-language region(s).
- Journal writing and study time, supported by teachers.

San Diego State University

The San Diego State University Language Acquisition Resource Center Language Training Center was established in 2011 with funding from Defense Language and National Security Education Office. It provides customized intensive language training and iso-immersions for military language specialists and others in a variety of languages. The primary objective of the iso-immersions at the Language Training Center at the San Diego State University Language Acquisition Resource Center is expressed in proficiency terms: by the end of the program, learners will be able to perform functions at a given level of proficiency in listening comprehension, reading comprehension, and speaking.

The teaching philosophy is learner-centered: learners are required to actively participate in the process of their learning, designing and delivering content and activities, an OACD core principle. For example, each day one or two learners lead a segment of the class, presenting and discussing a specific topic.

The "Language Training Center General Course Description" specifies the following components:

- In-class group listening and reading assignments. In the mornings, learners process authentic texts and passages provided by San Diego State University and researched by the learners themselves, supported by a teacher.

- Learner-led listening activities. One learner leads the class by:
  - reporting on a video clip,
  - identifying two to three relevant points about the clip,
  - critiquing and analyzing it (e.g., why certain points are significant), and
  - answering other learners' and teachers' questions.
- Learner-led reading activities. One learner leads the class by:
  - providing a copy of an article to learners,
  - reporting what it is about,
  - identifying two to three significant points,
  - critiquing and analyzing it (e.g., why those points are significant), and
  - answering other learners' and teachers' questions.
- Debates. Some topics are chosen by teachers, others by the learners themselves.
- Interaction with high-level target-language speakers. This is an important aspect of the program, involving learner interviews with college students, target-language community members, host families through routine visits, expert speakers through a seminar series, restaurant managers, shop owners, and others.
- Excursions. These may include the San Diego Zoo, a Buddhist temple, a Chinese school, and more. Learners are given tasks to complete at the excursion sites, such as translation and interpreting at the zoo, interviews with staff at the temple and school, and more.

Two-Week Immersion Outcomes

DLIFLC strives to attain the highest possible proficiency results from its two-week immersions, using until November 2023 both a pre- and post-immersion diagnostic assessment (Dababneh and Ruan, this volume) to determine gains. The goal has been to show proficiency growth in one or more skills, which is not unreasonable as indicated by the pre- and post-immersion diagnostic assessment results from a recent iteration in Table 4.1. At present, only the pre-immersion diagnostic assessment is being administered, due to staffing difficulties.

Given individual differences and typical times-to-next-level as described by the inverted pyramid construct (Corin 2020; Chapter 1, this volume), it is noteworthy that in many instances notable gains are in fact achieved, and post-immersion diagnostic assessment results generally show proficiency growth in at least one skill (listening, reading, or speaking) for most participants.

Pre-immersion diagnostic assessment results and teaching team input are sent to the immersion institution before learners arrive so the program can be tailored accordingly. Whenever possible, a DLIFLC teacher accompanies the learners. Following immersions, Concordia Language Villages and San Diego State University teachers provide input to the DLIFLC teaching team and discuss with them program strengths and weaknesses so adjustments can be made to the next iteration.

Table 4.1. Pre- and post-immersion diagnostic assessment results for the Chinese Mandarin iso-immersion held at the Concordia Language Villages, March 27–April 7, 2023 (n = 10). Results are cited according to the ILR scale.

Pre-immersion			Post-immersion		
Listening	**Reading**	**Speaking**	**Listening**	**Reading**	**Speaking**
1+ High	1+ High	1+ Low	1+ High	2+ High	1+ Mid
2 Mid	2 Mid	2 Mid	1+ High	2+ High	2 Mid
1+ Mid	1+ Mid	1+ Mid	1+ Mid	2+ Mid	1+ High
1+ Mid	2 Mid	2 Mid	2 High	2+ Mid	2 Mid
1 High	1+ High	1+ High	1 High	1+ High	1+ High
1+ High	1+ High	1+ Mid	2+ Mid	2+ Mid	1+ High
2 Mid	2 High	1+ Mid	1+ Mid	3 Low	1+ High
1+ High	2+ Mid	1+ Mid	2+ Mid	2+ Mid	1+ Mid
1 Mid	1+ Mid	1+ Mid	1 Mid	1+ Mid	1+ Mid
2 Low	2 High	1+ High	1+ High	2+ Mid	1+ High

Discussion

The two core OACD principles discussed earlier inform the one- to two-day and the two-week immersions. Predictably, opportunities for substantial on-the-fly curricular modification are more limited in the one- and two-day immersions than in the two-week ones. Nevertheless, both utilize learner and teacher feedback after each iteration to redesign and reorganize activities.

Learner Feedback

Effectiveness of immersions is best measured in terms of their intended purpose. In the case of Semester 1–3 iso-immersions at the DLIFLC immersion facility, their effect on learner motivation is reflected in learner feedback. Data gathered in 2022 from approximately 400 students in the Semester 1–3 immersions indicate they appreciate the immersion opportunity. Most reflect positively on the activities (though with some criticism of the relative allotment of time), enjoy the exchanges, and view them as a fun alternative to regular class. Many moreover state that the immersion helps them improve their speaking, listening, and grammatical competencies. They want to continue participating in immersions. Some felt more comfortable speaking Chinese in the immersion setting since it was required of all participants; in the classroom, extrovert, academically strong students tend to be more vocal and can monopolize activities. Some view certain immersion activities as challenging, but in a positive way. As one learner stated: "Immersions are an important part of the learning process and should be included more frequently." While a majority of the comments refers only incidentally to proficiency gain, learner feedback overall documents the effect on motivation and, by extrapolation, readiness for more autonomous, less scripted learning in the future.

In the case of two-week immersions at Concordia Language Villages, data gathered in 2022 at feedback sessions with two cohorts of 20 students each reveal that they routinely improved their proficiency scores after the Village experience on the "Online Diagnostic Assessment" tool that is available to the general public on the DLIFLC website (Dababneh and Yuan, this volume). Participants additionally report, as a whole, that the topics chosen were excellent and that most of the time the curriculum was well organized and applied.

Leaving aside some concerns about practical considerations (e.g., travel, food, free time), critiques related to learning are instructive. First, participants generally favored, rather than opposed, more rigorous immersivity (insistence on exclusive use of the target language):

- Learners should use Chinese only, employing circumlocution when needed and English only as a last resort.
- [Concordia] could go the extra mile with the immersive experience.
- Provide more activities to force students to come together and speak Chinese.

Just one introverted learner did not like being pushed to speak by the teachers. Second, some participants felt a need for DLIFLC to provide fuller formative assessment information to Concordia teachers:

- Teachers don't know what we don't know.

Taken together, diagnostic assessment data on proficiency gain (cited previously), self-reported data on Online Diagnostic Assessment proficiency gain, and learner feedback in the form of participant impressions all point to the effectiveness of the immersion experience, particularly those aspects that are aligned with OACD core principles.

In the case of the two-week immersions at San Diego State University, feedback sessions in 2022 paint a similar picture. Learners from one cohort of ten found the immersion effective overall. They especially liked interviewing native and near-native college students when doing assigned surveys because:

- It helped to have a real (not staged) conversation.
- It helped to learn the point of view of people who had arrived recently from China.
- It provided opportunities for unfiltered conversational language because both parties were the same age.

They also liked the contact with host families who open their homes to learners almost every evening for a meal and activities. At the end of the evening, learners return to their hotel to sleep. One learner did criticize the intensity of the program: "This immersion trip overall was good, but it was stressful and tiring." The military language instructors who accompanied the immersion reported:

Curriculum: Covering a wide variety of topics in a short time span is invigorating and beneficial to building language confidence. Guest lectures introduced previously studied topics and helped with deeper understanding.

Effect on Basic Program Proficiency Outcomes

For the one ten-learner cohort whose diagnostic assessment proficiency gain during their two-week immersions was cited previously, their end-of-program results are noteworthy: 77% ILR Level 2+ in listening; 80% Level 2+ in reading; and 72% Level 2 in speaking. The cohort graduated with a low attrition rate. It appears likely that the two-week immersion experience contributed to these results, considered outstanding for Chinese Mandarin and most DLIFLC basic programs. Unfortunately comparisons with cohorts that did not undergo this experience are not available.

Breadth of Applicability of OACD-Based Immersions

The field of world language learning recognizes the merits of immersions, especially in-country immersions or study abroad (e.g., Leaver and Campbell 2023; Davidson, Garas, and Lekic 2021; Basterretxea Santiso and Sanz 2023; Levine-West, Lam, and Schaeffer 2023; Shiri 2023; Morris 2023; Griffin 2023; Quan, Diao, and Trentman 2023). For a variety of practical reasons, it is not feasible for all learners in all programs to participate in open-architecture out-of-class immersions of the types described in this chapter, much less analogous open-architecture-type immersions in the target language country. It is likely that a larger proportion of government personnel have access to such immersion opportunities. Yet even for them the availability of such events and the amount of time spent in them is generally low. At DLIFLC, 20% of students currently enrolled in basic programs participate in two-week and four-week immersions, the latter typically in target-language-speaking countries, when circumstances permit. This relatively low percentage underscores the value of promoting an immersive environment in the classroom itself and OACD-based immersions that approximate in-country experiences.

Conclusions

Both immersion models described in this chapter were informed by two OACD core principles: curriculum structured around a theme-based syllabus (rather than a textbook) that integrates interchangeable unadapted authentic texts, tasks, and other activities; and continual and systematic (vs. occasional) tailoring to learner and cohort needs. Both have a motivational and confidence-building purpose as each gets learners out of the classroom and accustoms them to functioning in simulated real-world settings while meeting real or simulated needs. Available feedback, while incomplete, suggests that they meet both of these purposes well, of course with room for enhancement.

Both types of immersion have also served as stopgaps that address, if only to a limited extent, current limitations or challenges in the Chinese Mandarin basic program. The one- and two-day iso-immersions, used for many years, have helped fill a need for open-architecture activities during the interim while a new three-semester basic program curriculum is being designed. Two-week immersions at the Language Training Centers at Concordia Villages and San Diego State University mitigate the loss of in-country immersions in mainland China and Taiwan that once yielded considerable gains in proficiency and sociocultural competencies.

Finally, while only the two-week immersions may yield (and in most cases do yield) measurable proficiency gain, the one- and two-day iso-immersions are also perceived by learners as yielding enhanced target-language performance.

In order for DLIFLC basic programs to meet their long-term objective of Advanced High/Advanced High/Advanced (ILR 2+/2+/2) (listening, reading, and speaking, respectively) for 80% of the graduates, it is critical to have a curriculum expected to yield these results. Use of OACD-based immersions can contribute to achieving these results, as indicated by data at the Foreign Service Institute and DLIFLC (Chapter 1, this volume).

Study Questions

1. How could you integrate an OACD-based iso-immersion into your program? Think about logistics, facilities, time required, content/expertise needed, and learning resources.
2. If an iso-immersion, by the nature of its structure, is not possible in your teaching environment, what elements of an iso-immersion might you bring into your classroom?
3. Can you influence the immersion/study abroad programs in which your learners participate? If yes, how would you change them, using features of OACD, and what you expect to gain from the changes?

Notes

1. This chapter has been approved for public release by the Defense Language Institute Foreign Language Center's Public Affairs Office. For verification please email: mpao@dliflc.edu. Contents of this chapter are not necessarily the official views of the Defense Language Institute Foreign Language Center, nor are they endorsed by the Department of the Army, the Department of Defense, or the U.S. Government. All third-party products and materials featured in the chapter remain the intellectual property of their respective authors or originators. Use of outside materials is done under the fair use copyright principle, for educational purposes only. The content of this chapter is the sole responsibility of the author(s).
2. Iso-immersion are carried out "in isolation from the English language," (DLIFLC Immersion Language Office internet site, https://www.dliflc.edu/academics/immersion-language-office/, accessed June 26, 2023.
3. Program descriptions reflect their status of the time of writing; given the nature of DLIFLC and its requirement to respond to ever-changing needs of the military services it supports, the nature of some of the programs may differ in small or large details at the time of book publication. Readers interested in one or another program's current details should query the authors for an update.
4. All general information about the Concordia College Language Training Center is cited from several pages of the Concordia Language Villages internet site (http://www.concordialanguagevillages.org).

References

Basterretxea Santiso, Gorka, and Cristina Sanz. 2023. "Perspectives and Motives Involved in Study Abroad: COVID, Race and SES." *L2 Journal* 15, no. 2: 10–28. https://doi.org/10.5070/L215260145.

Corin, Andrew R. 2020. "The Challenge of the Inverted Pyramid in Attaining Distinguished-Level Proficiency." *Journal for Distinguished Language Studies* 7: 107–137.

Davidson, Dan E., Nadra Garas, and Maria Lekic. 2021. "Transformative Language Learning in the Overseas Immersion Environment: Exploring Affordances of Intercultural Development." In *Transformative*

Language Learning and Teaching, edited by Betty Lou Leaver, Dan E. Davidson, and Christine Campbell, 109–19. Cambridge: Cambridge University Press.

Griffin, Kim. 2023. "Study Abroad Programs in Transition from Pandemic to Endemic." *L2 Journal* 15, no. 2: 160–76. https://doi.org/10.5070/L215260153.

Leaver, Betty Lou, and Christine Campbell. 2023. "The Transformative Power of the Study Abroad Experience." *L2 Journal* 15, no. 2: 129–44. https://doi.org/10.5070/L215260151.

Levine-West, Glenn, Yeana Lam, and Gordon Schaeffer. 2023. "Study Abroad in a (Post-) Pandemic World: Our New Normal and Some Reasons for Optimism." *L2 Journal* 15, no. 2: 29–53. https://doi.org/10.5070/L215260146.

Morris, Kimberly. 2023. "When in Rome: Maximizing L2 Pragmatic Development in Study Abroad." *L2 Journal* 15, no. 2: 110–28. https://doi.org/10.5070/L215260150.

Quan, Tracy, Wenhao Diao, and Emma Trentman. 2023. "Returning to Normal?: Reimagining Study Abroad and Language Learning for a Sustainable and Equitable Future." *L2 Journal* 15, no. 2: 145–59. https://doi.org/10.5070/L215260152.

Shiri, Sonia. 2023. "Interactive Cultural Activities in Virtual Study Abroad during the Pandemic and Beyond." *L2 Journal* 15, no. 2: 54–70. https://doi.org/10.5070/L215260147.

van Lier, Leo. 2000. "From Input to Affordance: Social-Interactive Learning from an Ecological Perspective." In *Sociocultural Theory and Second Language Learning*, edited by James P. Lantolf. Oxford: Oxford University Press.

5

Introducing Open Architecture Curricular Design in an Egyptian Dialect Program[1]

KASSEMA JONES

ARABIC DIALECT PROGRAMS (LEVANTINE, Iraqi, and Egyptian) have become common at the Defense Language Institute Foreign Language Center (DLIFLC), with fluctuating enrollments over the past eight to ten years. In Semester 1 of these three-semester 63-week courses, students develop listening, translation, and transcription skills in dialect. At the end of each lesson, they analyze a short reading text in Modern Standard Arabic on the same theme as a previous listening passage. In Semesters 2 and 3, Modern Standard Arabic reading texts tied to dialect themes appear in a separate textbook. In all three semesters students speak in dialect. The instructional approach is, for the most part, standard fare of the last few decades: teaching for communicative competence, using a lock-step method of curricular presentation and design, including dependence upon a textbook throughout the course. Because faculty are expected to "cover" the textbook, on which summative learner assessments are based, they find little time for accommodating learners' personal and unique learning needs or for deviating from and supplementing the curriculum.

Learners in the Basic Program in Arabic have struggled to achieve the institutional proficiency objective of Advanced High (ILR 2+) in listening and reading. The minimal graduation requirements in 2017, the focus of this chapter, were Advanced (ILR 2) in listening and reading, and Intermediate High (ILR 1+) in speaking. Difficulty in reaching higher levels can be attributed, in part, to the static nature of textbooks, which do not change in response to events subsequent to their publication. This can affect learners' ability to deal with contemporary topics, but also their motivation, given the outdated materials in the textbook, even when authentic, and inflexibility to exploit unexpected learning opportunities (Gregory, this volume). One can further ascribe the difficulty to the nature of courses that center instruction upon a textbook: lockstep language training which can leave slower learners (often those with learning styles not supported by the textbook's activities) behind and hold faster learners back to the speed of a pre-conceived average learner (which, this author contends, does not in reality exist).

In 2017, some DLIFLC programs that had introduced *open architecture curricular design* (OACD) were showing improved proficiency results; for example, the Hebrew basic program (Oded & Oded, this volume) and all intermediate, advanced, and other post-basic courses (Leaver and Campbell 2015; Leaver and Campbell 2020; Corin 2021; Chapter 1, Dababneh and Yuan, and Wang, this volume). The author believed that Egyptian dialect learners might also benefit, even within the confines of a textbook-based program, from the application of certain OACD features and principles. The ones examined were:

- unadapted authentic texts, tasks, and activities from Day 1 of instruction;
- formative assessments; and
- ongoing learner involvement in the selection and delivery of course content and the design of activities and tasks.

Full application of OACD had been practiced by faculty in DLIFLC's Directorate of Continuing Education as early as 2006, with earlier applications dating back to 1984, when the Russian Department at the Foreign Service Institute implemented OACD. The term itself came into use in 2015 (Chapter 1, this volume).

This chapter will describe a 2017 case study involving five students and a two-person teaching team in which one teacher (the author of this article) introduced the OACD features and principle cited above into the Egyptian dialect program curriculum at DLIFLC. First, it will briefly describe the curriculum of the current Egyptian dialect program, noting its strengths and its weaknesses. It will then review how the teacher integrated the above-cited OACD principle and features into the curriculum.

The Curriculum of the Egyptian Dialect Program

The curriculum of the Egyptian dialect program was, and still is, textbook-based with limited individualization. It is sixty-three weeks in duration, teaches written and spoken skills simultaneously (a practice not without controversy, given the diglossic nature of Arabic[2]), with thirty class hours per week and assigned homework anticipated to require two to three hours each night. The schedule is divided into two-hour blocks of instruction, which is helpful when searching for time to incorporate OACD features and principles. Conventional summative tests and/or short quizzes are administered nearly every day.

Strengths of the Curriculum

Textbooks ensure that all learners are exposed to the same content, structure, and lexicon. Teachers at DLIFLC are provided with institutional teaching materials that ensure uniformity and save time and effort (at least within this system of instruction) of class preparation. The teacher need only design a good lesson plan using these materials. The ready-made curriculum is especially helpful to inexperienced teachers, who typically encounter difficulty finding a suitable topic or texts of suitable proficiency level during preparation hours.

The DLIFLC textbooks contain a plethora of reading texts in Modern Standard Arabic, followed by suitable tasks at proficiency levels 0+ through 3. For example, a task at Level 0+ requires identification of single words in context—names of countries, colors in a flag, and the like. A task at Level 1 requires the identification of basic information in a simple newspaper ad. The texts reflect the topical domains mandated by DLIFLC (Wang, this volume).

Egyptian Dialect is the *lingua franca* among learners and between learners and teachers for all communication—classroom activities and informal interactions. The learning space, whether at DLIFLC or online after hours, is intended to be an immersion experience.

As time allows, research projects on topics chosen by learners with observable outcomes such as written reports, oral presentations, and debates are part of the curriculum. These projects are carried out in pairs or groups in learner-centered classes under the teacher's facilitation and mentorship.

Weaknesses of the Curriculum

The curriculum displays at least three major weaknesses, all of which could be mitigated by introducing OACD features and principles. One relates to materials, the second to assessment, and the third to the involvement of learners in curricular development.

Materials

During the first sixteen weeks of instruction, most course materials are semi-authentic—that is, prepared for a pedagogical purpose. While many authentic materials—those prepared by native speakers for native speakers (van Lier 1996)—are easily accessible, such resources as on-line newspapers, documentaries, soap operas, songs, and films are not fully exploited until semesters 2 and 3.

Assessments

Assessments are summative—traditional decontextualized discrete-point achievement tests. This type of test, popular in the field of language learning in the 1970s and 1980s, includes texts that are not authentic, de-contextualized vocabulary lists, and discrete grammar items. Such achievement tests are administered after the end of each teaching unit throughout the program and are keyed to the curriculum. As a result, teachers feel constrained from deviating from the curriculum in ways beneficial to individual learners because of the need to cover material that will appear on the achievement tests.

Learner Involvement

Learners' sole role is to study the material in the textbook—grammar, vocabulary, and cultural notes. Decisions about curriculum, including adaptation and supplementation, are the exclusive domain of the teacher, as is "teaching."

Integrating the Use of Unadapted Authentic Materials from Day 1

The injection of authentic materials from the first day of instruction served as the primary intentional course adaptation in the direction of OACD. This adaptation appears to have made a substantial contribution to learners' proficiency development and represented no small administrative feat.

Many teachers are hesitant to use authentic materials early in instruction for several reasons:

1. Insufficient knowledge about proficiency levels: what texts to use at a given level of learners' proficiency
2. Insufficient training in the use of authentic materials from Day 1 in an immersion environment
3. Fear of losing learners early on in the program because of the misconception that novice learners cannot process authentic materials
4. Administrators who erroneously fear that deviation from a lock-step schedule will hamper language acquisition

The experience of the Egyptian Dialect Program described here showed that none of these fears were warranted, though novice teachers certainly need instruction in teaching strategies and proficiency levels, just as novice learners need instruction in learning strategies (Oxford 2017). In this case, the teacher was an experienced instructor and an oral proficiency tester. Most of the learners, however, were new to language study and benefited from instruction in language learning strategies such as guessing through context, taking advantage of cognates, risk taking, and "noticing" (defined by Schmidt and Frota 1986 as conscious awareness of [and attention to] input). "The noticing hypothesis states that what learners notice in input is what becomes intake for learning" (Schmidt 1995, 20).

In addition, the teacher scaffolded authentic materials, taking into consideration pragmatics and discourse types and, in spoken language, speed or tempo of speech. The teacher provided pre-listening and pre-reading activities to activate learner schemata related to the text/passage topic, asking learners what vocabulary they knew associated with the topic, what experiences they had had related to the topic, and the like. Grammatical features, semantics, phonological issues, and cultural and social background information were addressed as they emerged in textual context (Larsen-Freeman 2003; van Lier 1996; Thornbury 2005).[3] Early in the course, the teacher helped learners decode the situation and context of authentic materials. Later in the course, with the integration of more culturally and linguistically complex authentic materials, the teacher helped them navigate non-standard and colloquial language and process super-authentic language (spoken by two or more people with ambient noise, grammatical mistakes, fillers, and the like).

In processing the complexity of authentic reading and listening passages, learners had to understand both explicit and the implicit meanings, especially in the case of super-authentic texts. Understanding was facilitated by applying a top-down approach to get the main idea and supporting details, drawing on existing knowledge. At the same time, in a bottom-up approach, learners dissected the topic, deduced unknown words from context, and determined grammatical meaning and form from seeing or hearing it use.

Learners also benefited from a variety of instructional approaches. These included content-based, task-based, and project-based learning that integrated higher-order thinking skills.

Early Introduction of Authentic Materials

In the first week of the program, even before students finished learning all of the Arabic letters, the teacher showed them the first page of a famous Egyptian newspaper, *The Seventh Day*, and asked them to read the headlines aloud. The headlines of the first page included names of famous people; learners could guess names as they are cognates. The purpose of having the learners read aloud was to correct pronunciation and avoid the tendency of some, who do not subvocalize, to make up their own pronunciation and subsequently have difficulty understanding authentic pronunciation.

During the first week, the teacher also used authentic video clips. The topic of the first was a famous coffee shop in downtown Cairo called Café Groppi. The video clip was a documentary in Egyptian that tells the story of this coffee shop. It contains many words that learners had already encountered while working on the alphabet, e.g., *foreigner, Swiss,* dates and years, various kinds of drinks and sweets. The purpose for selecting such a topic early on was to determine whether learners might remember these words when heard in an authentic documentary. (The answer? Generally, yes.) Where words were completely new, meanings were teased out through scaffolding, hints, and applied learning strategies; where content was unfamiliar, background knowledge was provided.

From the middle of Semester 2, the teaching team chose more challenging authentic materials (in the sense of Child 1998) at ILR 2+—short news analyses, commentaries, and opinion pieces, that focused on the content areas they had studied. Learners were able to process the materials, guided by teachers using scaffolding.

After week 28, learners started watching movies and soap operas agreed upon in collaboration with the department chair.[4] These agreed-upon materials were placed on the schedule, with one episode of the television series taught over two days. Learners received a part of the series or a part of a movie to watch as homework the night before, along with open-ended comprehension questions encouraging elaborated responses. The following morning, learners turned in their homework. Either the teacher corrected the homework or had the learners, individually or in pairs, correct each other's. Then, they discussed their answers and their feelings and impressions about the episode. After this, the teacher replayed in class the parts that learners had not fully understood, providing background knowledge or missing schemata as needed.

A Content-Based Approach to Using Authentic Materials

Authentic materials reflected the topical domains mandated for DLIFLC basic programs and reflected in the textbook. In week 11, Unit 2, for example, where geography and weather are the topics, learners received one reading text from an Egyptian newspaper and one listening passage from an Egyptian television channel. The purpose here was dual: (1) to enhance what learners had already learned from the textbook and (2) to connect learners' classroom learning with the world at large.

The reading text was about rainy weather in the city of Safaga on the Red Sea and its impact on the roads, airport, and flight movements. Once the content was understood, learners were presented with alternatives to content questions such as short, personalized learner presentations (one-minute long) about weather in their hometowns, cultural comparison charts, simple discussion about weather, role plays—possible tasks are limited only by imagination.

The listening passage was a weather forecast for the next few days. The text and passage were followed by content questions. Because the learners were at ILR 0+/emerging ILR 1, they found it difficult to recognize words spoken at normal tempo in a native accent and to determine their meaning in an authentic context. For that reason, the teacher repeated in her own voice what was said in the passages and then asked the learners whether they had understood. Generally, the learners did understand once they heard the passage read by the teacher. Sometimes, the teacher repeated the sentences more than one time in order for the learners to understand fully. Then, they listened to the authentic passage again and could process most of it.

Some authentic materials incorporated into the Egyptian dialect program were keyed to textbook themes, while others related to current events, and learners soon began to watch and read on their own. They were especially pleased when, during after-class hours, they were able to understand words and phrases in cable programming because of their work with authentic materials in class. One learner was especially happy about an incident in his room in the barracks, watching his favorite Egyptian talk show. The talk-show host used a word in Egyptian dialect that the learner had been hearing in class since the course started, but had not understood. The following day in class, the learner happily reported his "aha" moment.

Task-Based Instruction

From the first hour of instruction, learners were assigned communicative tasks—those with a real-life purpose rather than just practicing language for its own sake (Richards and Nunan 1990). Communicative activities, composed of a series of tasks, can encourage learners to focus on content versus form as they work through the tasks.

The teacher set up tasks in pairs and or small groups where one learner had a bit more knowledge of the topic than other(s), using learners' zones of proximal development as a guide. Working together, learners helped each other understand the topic and answer questions, with the more proficient learner(s) explaining the complicated parts of the text/passage to those less proficient. In this way, the less adept learner could more facilely develop to the level of the more adept learner, moving the overall proficiency development of the class along faster.

As proficiency levels increased, authentic materials at Advanced High/Superior (ILR 2+/3) loaded with sociocultural references and background information were introduced. To compensate for the complexity, a pre-activity was used to stimulate learner schemata, followed by tasks where learners first worked alone and then with others. In negotiating passage meaning, learners worked together on solving a real-life problem, such as plausible recommendations for reducing pollution in Egypt. As needed, the teacher acted as an adviser, mentor, coach, explaining sociocultural references and providing background information, for example Egypt's approaches to certain societal issues. Group work provided learners with a safety net, increasing their comfort and lowering their affective filters.

For some tasks, the teacher divided learners into one dyad and one triad. In a jigsaw-like approach, each learner received a piece of authentic material, a text or passage with questions to work on alone. Following this individual work, each learner discussed the topic in the dyad or triad, comparing notes and negotiating meaning.

Then, groupings were reshuffled so that everyone had the opportunity to provide some missing information. As a culminating activity at Intermediate Low and Mid (ILR 1), the learners booked a trip to Egypt, playing tourist and travel agent roles, dealing with the details of the trip. When the learners were speaking, they made errors. The teacher used rephrasing or recasting to correct errors; gradually, more proficient learners started to correct their peers' errors.

Project-Based Instruction
The first short-term project (to be completed over the weekend and two additional evenings) was assigned in Week 17, the textbook theme being tourism. Learners could choose any topic they wished from among documents about the 1917 Balfour Declaration (promising Jews they could establish the nation of Israel), traffic in Cairo, the Soccer World Cup in Russia, and touristic ruins in Egypt. They could work individually, in pairs, or in a group. The tasks associated with this and future projects focused on higher-order thinking skills: analysis, synthesis, and evaluation (Bloom 1984).

Short-term projects were subsequently assigned once every two weeks. In Week 23, for example, each learner chose a topic to research in depth and present to the class. Chosen topics included the public transportation problem in Cairo, drug use, health, and housing problems. The teacher acted as a mentor/coach/advisor, helping learners with their research. Learners then made 5–7-minute presentations to their peers, using PowerPoint, original videos, and/or realia, with written notes to guide them.

Later, short-term projects became more elaborate. For example, two learners produced a video about touristic places in Monterey. Another found and categorized videos about touristic places in Egypt. One learner put into practice the OACD principle of ongoing learner involvement in the selection and delivery of course content, designing and teaching a lesson about a well-known children's story. The lesson's structure included review of unknown words, examination of the main idea, exploration into details, and a question about the moral of the story.

For projects in week 50, learners chose the topic of economy. They were permitted latitude in source selection (English, Arabic, or a combination) but were required to include both reading texts and listening passages. Oral reports, delivered formally to the class, teacher, other teachers, the department head, and the associate dean (who could—and did—ask questions) took a variety of forms: video, or presentations using PowerPoint or handwritten notes. The learners were asked to speak, wherever possible, without reading from slides or notes. One spoke about the complexities of austerity measures by the Egyptian government. Others talked about lifting government subsidies, floating the Egyptian pound, and proposed solutions to economic challenges. Through these oral reports, learners gained confidence in speaking, enhanced their fluency, and acquired experience in speaking Egyptian in front of native speakers. Administrators attending the oral reports found that learners could self-regulate, find pertinent authentic materials at Advanced/Advanced High (ILR 2 /2+), do research, and deliver course content in the process of becoming autonomous learners.

Integrating the Use of Formative Assessment

An important feature of OACD programs is the focus on formative rather than summative assessment (Dababneh & Yuan, this volume). Unlike summative testing, intended to provide information on learning outcomes, formative assessment seeks to inform learners and teachers about learner progress, identifying knowledge and skills needed to move to the next level of proficiency.

Formative assessment can be formalized, for example the diagnostic assessment tool described by Dababneh & Yuan (this volume) and others (Cohen 2020; Corin and Entis 2022); or informal, when teachers exploit daily activities for formative assessment to better identify learners' strengths, weaknesses, and readiness to learn particular aspects of language and culture. That readiness, i.e., the zone of proximal development, is the space between what a learner cannot do at all and what they can do with assistance. In essence, it refers to what the learner can do with a little help, such as hints, additional context, more examples, and minimal explanation.[5] Informal formative assessment includes observation of how learners carry out tasks and identification of the source of errors during in-class performance and in homework.

Given the lock-step structure of the Egyptian dialect program, with built-in summative testing at frequent intervals, formative assessment in the described case study was informal in nature. Feedback on projects and presentations, dyadic correction of homework, and work on building schemata and developing learning strategies all provided opportunities for formative assessment.

Integrating Ongoing Learner Involvement in the Selection and Delivery of Content and the Design or Directing of Activities

An important principle of OACD is ongoing involvement of learners in the selection and delivery of course content and the design of activities and tasks. As the Egyptian dialect program progressed, learners took on increasingly greater roles in teaching course materials. For example, peer teaching, either formally through presentations (e.g., project presentations) or via homework correction, was commonplace.

Learner Selection and Delivery of Course Content

In a well-established OACD program, learners would have negotiated the topics and the selection of most authentic materials with the teacher (in part locating the materials themselves) from the very beginning of the course. However, the tight control of content in the lock-step Egyptian dialect program precluded incorporating this OACD feature early on. Instead, it was introduced about a third of the way through the Program.

Flipped Classrooms

Flipped classes provided learners the opportunity to study materials from the textbook on their own in order to increase time in class for processing supplemental authentic materials. In the classroom, the teacher reviewed all learner questions emanating from textbook contents. As a result, the class spent as little as 30, rather than the typical (and assigned) 50 minutes on the textbook.

Discussion

Learners were not exempt from required summative tests. One major test, given at the beginning of week 18, permitted a comparison of learners who had had an OACD experience and those who had not. Two achieved grade A and three achieved grade B. The results of this class (C3) were 92.62%, while whose for C1, C2, and C4 (the other three classes in the same department) were 75%, 80.76%, and 81%, respectively.

At the end of the program, these learners, like all at DLIFLC, took the standardized exit test, the Defense Language Proficiency Test 5[6] for listening and reading, and Oral Proficiency Interview for speaking. On them, they achieved historical highs, with four of the five reaching Advanced High (ILR 2+) in one or more skills.

These results demonstrate the possibility of introducing authentic reading and listening materials and using the target language nearly exclusively from Day 1, the latter practice being fundamental to proficiency development (van Lier 1996). In the case of listening, teacher use of targeted scaffolding, learner application, and expansion of language learning strategies can span the gap between the known and the to-be-known that characterizes the experience of learning from authentic broadcasts and conversations. In the case of reading, research indicates that teaching and encouraging awareness, expansion, and application of reading strategies can improve reading comprehension (Alhaqbani and Riazi 2012).

Given the small size of the sample, the results presented here must be considered anecdotal. More definitive results would require a study following the experience of more learners over more iterations.

Conclusions

The unprecedented proficiency results achieved by the cohort of Egyptian dialect program learners described in this small case study suggest that the integration of the specified two features and one principle of OACD was an important contributing factor. These results were attained despite the textbook dominance and otherwise controlled, lockstep program.

Perhaps most importantly, opening up aspects of the program's curricular architecture in the direction of OACD, even in this very incomplete manner, proved motivational to learners as they negotiated aspects of the curriculum with the teacher and progressively became more autonomous. Learner feedback gathered throughout the course at routine three- to five-minute sessions at the end of every two-hour block indicated that they had a meaningful and enjoyable learning experience throughout the intensive, challenging, and often anxiety-provoking 63-week course.

Study Questions

1. This case study demonstrated one way to incorporate OACD features and principles in a lock-step, standardized, highly constrained program. Were these the most logical/reasonable choices, based on the description of the standardized program? Why or why not? Were the OACD features sufficiently exploited by the teacher? How might you have further exploited them?

2. Based on the program description, what other OACD features might have been included? How could this have been done?
3. Assess your own situation. How many features and principles of OACD does your program offer? How might you increase that number? What would you need to do that?

Notes

1. This chapter has been approved for public release by the Defense Language Institute Foreign Language Center's Public Affairs Office. For verification please e-mail: mpao@dliflc.edu. Contents of this chapter are not necessarily the official views of the Defense Language Institute Foreign Language Center, nor are they endorsed by the Department of the Army, the Department of Defense, or the U.S. Government. All third party products / materials featured in the chapter remain the intellectual property of their respective authors / originators. Use of outside materials is done under the fair use copyright principle, for educational purposes only. The content of this chapter is the sole responsibility of the author(s).
2. DLIFLC has wrestled for years with the question of how best to handle Arabic diglossia. Reading first? Speaking/listening first? Both together? It was long felt that teaching both together would overload learners, since they would be learning essentially two languages at the same time. However, experience showed that it was possible, as affirmed, for example, by Dr. Karin Ryding at an Arabic teaching methods conference hosted by DLIFLC in 2007.
3. Dr. Philip Johnson, a DLIFLC instructor at the time, referred to this approach as teaching "grammar in the wild" (personal communication, March 6, 2007).
4. The requirement for such agreement demonstrates the extent to which the Egyptian course was standardized and maintained under administrative control.
5. Vygotsky (1978, 86) defines the zone of proximal development as "the distance between the actual developmental level as determined by independent problem solving and the level of potential development as determined through problem solving under adult guidance or in collaboration with more capable peers."
6. The Defense Language Proficiency Test is the standardized exam administered to DLIFLC graduates and other Department of Defense language users. Information about the current version, the Defense Language Proficiency Test 5, can be found at https://www.dliflc.edu/resources/dlpt-guides.

References

Alhaqbani, Ahmad, and Mehdi Riazi. 2012. "Metacognitive Awareness of Reading Strategy Use in Arabic as a Second Language." *Reading in a Foreign Language* 24, no. 2: 231–255.
Bloom, B. 1984. *Taxonomy of Educational Objectives, Handbook 1: Cognitive Domain.* 2nd ed. Boston: Addison-Wesley.
Child, James R. 1998. "Language Skill Levels, Textual Modes, and the Rating Process." *Foreign Language Annals* 31, no. 3: 381–391.
Cohen, B. 2020. *Diagnostic Assessment at the Superior/Distinguished Threshold.* Hollister: MSI Press LLC.
Corin, Andrew R. 2021. "Foreign Language Learning Efficiency: Transformative Learning in an Outcomes-Based Environment." In *Transformative Language Learning and Teaching*, edited by Betty L. Leaver, Dan E. Davidson, and Christine Campbell, 51–60. Cambridge: Cambridge University Press.
Corin, Andrew, and Sergey Entis. 2022. "Protocol-Based Formative Assessment: Evolution and Revolution at the Defense Language Institute Foreign Language Center." *Journal of Distinguished Language Studies* 8: 95–115.
Larsen-Freeman, Diane. 2003. *Teaching Language: From Grammar to Grammaring.* Boston: Thompson-Heinle.
Leaver, Betty Lou, and Christine Campbell. 2015. "Experience with Higher Levels of Proficiency." In *To Advanced Proficiency and Beyond*, edited by Tony Brown and Jennifer Bown, 3–21. Washington: Georgetown University Press.
Leaver, Betty Lou, and Christine Campbell. 2020. "The Shifting Paradigm in Russian Language Programs from Communicative Language Teaching to Transformative Language Learning and Teaching. In *Art of teaching Russian*, edited by E. Dengub, I. Dubinina, and J. Merrill, 147–62. Washington: Georgetown University Press.

Oxford, Rebecca L. 2017. *Teaching and Researching Language Learning Strategies: Self-Regulation in Context*. London: Routledge.

Richards, J., and D. Nunan, eds. 1990. *Second Language Teacher Education*. Cambridge: Cambridge University Press.

Schmidt, Richard. 1995. "Consciousness and Foreign Language Learning: A Tutorial on the Role of Attention and Awareness in Learning." In *Attention and Awareness in Foreign Language Learning*, edited by Richard Schmidt, 1–64. Honolulu: National Foreign Language Resource Center.

Schmidt, R., and S. Frota. 1986. "Developing Basic Conversation Ability in a Second Language: A Case Study of an Adult Learner of Portuguese." In *Talking to Learn: Conversation in Second Language Acquisition*, edited by R. Day, 237–94. Rowley: Newbury House.

Thornbury, S. 2005. *Beyond the Sentence*. Oxford: McMillan.

van Lier, L. 1996. *Interaction in the Language Curriculum: Awareness, Autonomy and Authenticity*. New York: Longman.

Vygotsky, Lev. 1978. *Mind in Society: The Development of Higher Psychological Processes*. Edited by Michael Cole. Cambridge: Harvard University Press.

6

The Use of Project-Based OACD Modules in an Intermediate and Advanced Chinese Mandarin Program[1]

DANIEL WANG

THIS CHAPTER DESCRIBES HOW the use of project-based OACD modules, supplemented with a data analytics tool—the Learner Data Panel—facilitates learner involvement in the selection and delivery of content and the design and delivery of activities, a core OACD principle (Campbell 2021; Corin 2020a, 2020b), and learner-teacher negotiation. The Learner Data Panel provides the teacher with key information about individual and cohort error patterns, gaps in language-learning strategies, subject-matter knowledge, and application of knowledge to solve problems or complete tasks. The relationship between the project-based OACD module and the Learner Data Panel will be illustrated using an example from the intermediate/advanced Chinese Mandarin program.

OACD, Learner Individuality, and Tailoring Curriculum to Meet Learner Needs

No two learners are identical; no one curriculum fits all learners. OACD recognizes both individual learner differences and the "invisible classroom"—the learning-space dynamics that emerge within a group of learners (Dabbs and Leaver 2019; Ehrman and Dörnyei 1998). OACD therefore recognizes the benefits of co-creating curricula teacher with learners—to meet individual and cohort needs; it encourages learners, as stakeholders in their own success who are aware of their primary needs and goals, to actively contribute to the formation of the curriculum.

The goal is to have learning modules continually tailored through ongoing negotiation and collaboration between learners and teachers. Rather than adopting a static textbook with authentic materials that rapidly become dated, an OACD curriculum is a living document constructed from ongoing data—a portfolio of the learners' journey through the course—that evolves organically, naturally spiraling and recycling, where learners scaffold as well as are scaffolded. The design of the Chinese Mandarin course described here encouraged maximal interaction between learner and teacher in routinely negotiating aspects of the curriculum, so as to enable closer alignment of lesson rationale and design with individual learners' personal and learning preferences and compatibility with group norms.

OACD thus enables learners to be at the center of learning efforts. The teacher helps them develop autonomy and positively influences learner self-efficacy. In this context, learners' views of their own competency are informed by past performance, observation of others' performance, exhortations from others, especially those whom they trust such as the mentor/coach/advisor, and knowledge of their own state of emotional and physiological arousal, such as fear, anxiety, and stress (Bandura 1977).

A key factor in the development of learner autonomy is the recognition, influenced by Vygotsky's work in social constructivism, that meaning is constructed through social interaction, while learning occurs at the level of individual readiness for specific learning, referred to by Vygotsky as the zone of proximal development (Vygotsky 1978). Scaffolding (Wood, Bruner, and Ross 1976) and learning strategy instruction are thus critical to enhancing learners' probability of success by empowering them to transition from "other-regulation" to "self-regulation" (Kohonen 2006) on a path that leads toward increased autonomy. When lessons are teacher-delivered rather than negotiated, a gap inevitably grows between learner needs and lesson design, and learner self-efficacy and developmental autonomy are restricted. OACD enables the curriculum to remain flexible so as to incorporate learner input and updated information on learner needs as the course progresses.

Merrill's (2002) "First Principles of Instruction" emphasize material authenticity, the integration of new knowledge and demonstration of how it is utilized, and plentiful opportunities for learners to apply knowledge. OACD enables the curriculum to go further, evolving to match the adult learner's evolving exploration of an open space that expands in width and breadth. Learner-teacher negotiation determines the choices of texts and activities and ensures that learners are continually operating at the upper reaches of the zone of proximal development. Throughout, the teacher's continual support can guide learners through disorienting dilemmas—experiences catalytic to perspective transformation (Mezirow 2000), which are bound to occur when the culture of the learner authentically encounters the other culture (Leaver, Davidson, and Campbell 2021; Mezirow 2000).

Introduction of OACD in DLIFLC Chinese Mandarin Courses

The author taught in the intermediate/advanced Chinese Mandarin program in DLIFLC's School of Resident Education and School of Distance Learning between 2007 and 2021, where several variants of the Learner Data Panel were successfully used. The nineteen-week intermediate and advanced courses described here met thirty hours a week and focused on ten content areas: military, security, economy, politics, science, technology, culture, society, environment, and geography (DLIFLC 2004). Graduation objectives, measured by end-of-course Defense Language Proficiency Test for listening and reading and Oral Proficiency Interview for speaking, were Advanced High/Advanced High/Advanced (ILR 2+/2+/2) for intermediate courses, and Superior/Superior/Advanced (ILR 3/3/2) for advanced courses.

The nineteen-week course is composed of four weeks of distance learning followed by fifteen weeks of face-to-face study, including a four-week target language-country immersion event. Although the length of the courses was reduced by nearly 60%, i.e., from forty-seven to nineteen weeks, course outcome objectives remained unchanged, making it even more crucial that every lesson produce observable learner growth and that growth span all mandated content areas.

As these courses could be attended by up to eight learners with varying needs, they invariably involved multi-level teaching, but prior to 2006 the pre-built textbook-based curriculum did not accommodate the reality of learner diversity and many learners did not reach their proficiency goals. While the introduction of OACD led to significant enhancements in proficiency outcomes, the shortened course duration with unchanged course objectives required even greater learning efficiency.

Features of OACD essential to the revamped Chinese Mandarin program were:

- Use of modules, each lasting from three to eighteen hours, the former the case in an intensive course, with learners in contact with the teacher for six hours daily and assigned two hours of homework. OACD, which is the framework for the entire course described here, often incorporates modules into the course structure; this chapter describes one specific project-based module. Each project-based module is a complete set of materials comprised of *learning objects*. Learning objects may be foundational (teacher-chosen) or elective (chosen by individual learners). While the term *learning object* has many definitions, L'Allier's (1997) most closely reflects its use within these OACD modules: "the smallest independent structural experience that contains an objective, a learning activity and an assessment" (65). A classic example of a learning object includes a learning activity based on a reading text or listening passage and a formative assessment with an observable outcome. (See the abbreviated sample of a foundational learning object in the following section.)

    Each module focuses on the ten content areas. Each content area has sub-topics. Crucially, the teacher ensures systematic and tailored coverage of relevant *sub-topics/themes essential to progress*, termed **STEPs**. The STEPs tie the content areas selected by the teacher for the foundational learning objects and the learners for the elective learning objects and facilitate spiral learning (recycling of structural, lexical, and topical features of performance and proficiency at ever higher levels). For example, for the Economy content area dealing with the construction of a dam in China, which is described in detail in sections below, one related STEP is the post-construction concerns and costs associated with dam dredging and repairs due to sediment build-up and riverbank erosion, at different spots, over time. Figure 6.1 below illustrates the relationship between the learning objects, the STEPs, and the ten content areas.

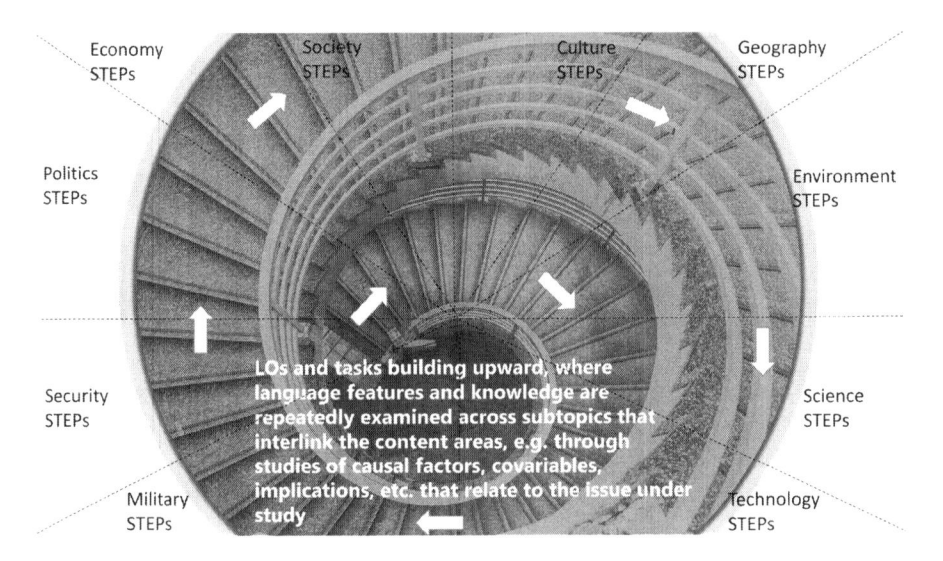

Economy STEPs
Society STEPs
Culture STEPs
Geography STEPs
Politics STEPs
Environment STEPs
Security STEPs
Science STEPs
Military STEPs
Technology STEPs

LOs and tasks building upward, where language features and knowledge are repeatedly examined across subtopics that interlink the content areas, e.g. through studies of causal factors, covariables, implications, etc. that relate to the issue under study

Figure 6.1. Language features and knowledge are examined in increasingly higher-level LOs across STEPs, or subtopics, that interlink the ten content areas

- Learning strategy instruction, and
- Culminating task-based scenarios with real-world application (Wang 2016).

In each module, learners analyze real-world problems, seeking teacher advice and coaching as needed in resolving disorienting dilemmas where their native world views conflict with Chinese world views. Upon completion of each module, teachers and learners identify the next real-world problem, of increased sophistication and greater profundity, with opportunities for reinforcement of mastered language. During this process, teachers, like sports coaches working with athletes to draft individualized improvement programs, support learners materially and psychologically, so that each learner develops and practices what is specifically and personally needed, avoiding time wasted on one-size-fits-all exercises.

In such a learning environment, learners need objective and actionable information pertaining to their individual needs so that the learner-teacher negotiation proceeds from data and autonomous learner initiative is most usefully directed. One tool for objectifying data is the Learner Data Panel. With this panel, teachers track learner errors and learner-teacher joint efforts at error resolution; they provide learners access to this data for use in negotiating the learning experience. In addition to error patterns, the panel gathers information about needs pertaining to language learning strategies, subject-matter knowledge, and application of knowledge to solve problems or complete tasks. With this panel, learners can visualize their own progress across multiple content areas and multiple proficiency levels (Wang 2018). The panel is especially important in the quest to attain near-native levels of language proficiency, where fossilized errors represent an obstacle (Ehrman 2002). Details of the

THE USE OF PROJECT-BASED OACD MODULES   83

Learner Data Panel will be discussed later in this chapter, following an illustration of OACD in action that exemplifies the contexts in which the Learner Data Panel has been employed.

A Module in the Chinese Mandarin Program: Actualizing OACD

The following Chinese Mandarin project-based OACD module combines asynchronous and synchronous learning and proved well-suited for both face-to-face and distance learning programs. It can be adjusted to various lengths, including a shorter variant for short courses. The module offers learners a chance to explore freely China's Three Gorges Project, an ambitious waterworks project with long-term benefits as well as consequences, an attractive topic for a multi-day module since it can be analyzed from the perspectives of multiple content areas. OACD learners negotiate with the teacher and each other in successive, adjustable STEPs. In this project (or scenario), learners engage in high-level discussion about the Three Gorges Project, sorting themselves into two groups, one believing that the Three Gorges Project's costs outweigh the benefits, the other that the Project's benefits outweigh the costs. The culminating task for each group is to create handouts and/or presentation slides to organize their argumentation and then engage in a debate on the costs versus benefits of the Three Gorges Project.

The Three Gorges Project module is different each time it is used because learner-teacher negotiation results in a unique set of learning objects. Learning objects serve as the cobblestones on the learner's personalized learning path through the STEPs. With each iteration of an OACD course, learners and teacher create new learning objects and/or supplement with previously designed ones. The entire curricular architecture is modular, with interchangeable and updatable components utilizing individualized authentic materials.

Teachers create the foundational learning objects that provide essential knowledge and scaffolding; they also ensure that the elective learning objects developed through learner-teacher collaboration are achievable. Learners individually choose one or two content areas, driven by their own interests or learning needs, within which they will develop a pool of shared elective learning objects through iterative learner-teacher negotiation and collaboration.

The process helps ensure the requisite repetition for retention (see also Bondarenko, this volume) with (1) activities of increasing sophistication and greater profundity spiraling upward, and (2) each STEP building on previously explored STEPs, with follow-on STEPs providing opportunities for learners to draw deeper insights from the contents, processes, and products of previously explored STEPs. Through this process, learners grow increasingly autonomous, with mentoring from the teacher.

The phases of the process that includes (1) development and use of both foundational and elective learning objects, (2) culminating task, and (3) post-task reflection, are shown in Figure 6.2:

    Phase 1. Establish learning needs for the next module, with a focus on the next STEP.
    At the end of the previous module, the teacher had discussed with each learner the focus for the upcoming module, shared data on current learning needs (discussed

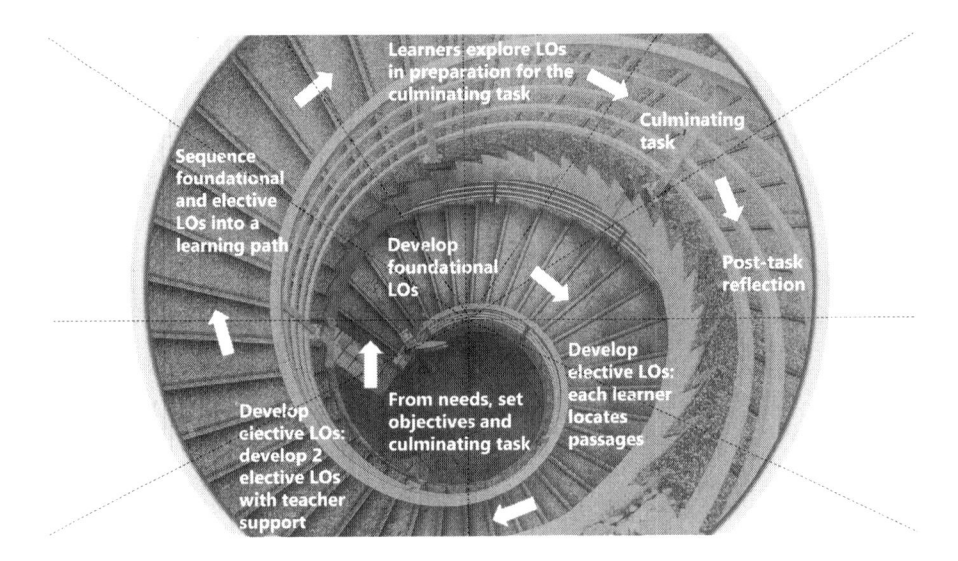

Figure 6.2. Process phases, with learner-teacher negotiation throughout

in the next section) and obtained learner input. If the Learner Data Panel system is in use, the two-way communication tends to be precise and succinct, so that the learner and teacher often reach a quick consensus.

Phase 2. Set objectives for the STEP.

With each learner's current needs and the topic in mind, the teacher and learners set objectives, specifying audience, behavior, condition, and degree. For example, to improve learners' accuracy in analyzing linguistic features to determine whether authorial opinion in a reading text or listening passage exists, the following objectives may be set:

- Given a pool of learning objects at Advanced High (ILR 2+) and Superior (ILR 3), intermediate course learners can identify the presence and bias of authorial opinion with 80% or higher accuracy for 80% of the passages examined.
- Learners can use discourse features such as syntactic and lexical connecting devices, rhetorical strategies, style/register markers, etc., in a cost-benefit discussion of the Three Gorges project, voicing their opinions with greater than 80% accuracy in the number and suitability of the features used.

Phase 3. Set a culminating task to focus learner efforts.

Through learner-teacher discussion, identify a communicative task that can be used to measure attainment of the STEP's objectives and allow room for individual exploration. In this case, the culminating task is a multi-stage debate based on a cost-benefit analysis of the Three Gorges Project. Each learner chooses one or two of the content areas to examine.

Phase 4. Develop the foundational learning objects.

The teacher locates authentic reading texts or listening passages and, from them, develops two learning objects, each focused on two or more content areas, each complete with objective(s), learning activities and an assessment to gauge the objectives' attainment. The abbreviated sample of a foundational learning object below is based on a listening passage extolling the reliability and capabilities of the Three Gorges Dam. The passage includes descriptions of the dam size, features, and anticipated strengths in terms of flood control, power generation, and boosting transportation. As a foundational teacher-developed learning object, it ensures learners grasp essential language features and background knowledge crucial for understanding the opinion pieces explored in the elective learning objects to follow, which are learner-developed with the teacher's support. The learning object activities include comprehension checks using a combination of level-appropriate short-answer content and open-ended questions, and a "correct the false statements" exercise. The transcript of the listening passage below is only an excerpt; the statements in the exercise address the entirety of the passage.

听两遍，然后按照段子的内容判断各句的正误，并纠正错误的部分。Listen to the passage twice, then mark each statement as True or False and correct the parts that make the statement false.

部分文本：	**Partial transcript:**
...举世闻名、史无前例的的三峡工程堪称现今全人类建设史中的规模最大的、难度也最高的水利工程。经过十多年的艰辛努力，三峡大坝终将于本月竣工。其发电功效、防洪效果与运输功能均可谓无可比拟。...	... The historically renowned and unprecedented Three Gorges Engineering Project can be considered the greatest and most difficult waterworks engineering project in human architectural history. Through more than ten years of laborious efforts, the Three Gorges Dam will finally be completed this month. Its electricity generation capabilities, flood prevention effectiveness, and transportation functions could all be considered incomparable....

a. 兴建三峡工程的首要目的是防旱。The foremost purpose behind building the Three Gorges Project was to prevent droughts.
b. 三峡地区自古以来经常遭受洪涝之害。Throughout history, the Three Gorges region frequently endured flood disasters.
c. 三峡大坝虽然能够承受极其严重的洪灾，但其能耗要求较高。The Three Gorges Dam could withstand extremely severe floods, but its energy consumption demands are rather high.
d. 设计师在设计时有考虑到大坝可能遭受敌人武器的攻击。During the design phase, the architects had considered the possibility of the dam coming under attacks from enemy's weaponries.

The foundational learning objects aim to ensure that the foundational knowledge and basic linguistic needs for this STEP are covered so that learners can fully benefit from each other's elective learning objects. As the teacher works with the learners on developing the elective learning objects, the foundational learning objects may need to be revised or changed entirely to provide the necessary content knowledge or strategic scaffolding to ensure the elective learning objects are accessible to the learners.

Phase 5. Develop the elective learning objects: learner identifies potential reading texts/listening passages.

As homework, the teacher asks each learner to look for three short, challenging authentic reading texts/listening passages on the Three Gorges Project, with the emphases being on what each learner wishes to learn and the need for coverage of a variety of content areas. The learner summarizes each text/passage, in the case of reading passages, highlighting challenging parts and, in the case of listening passages, transcribing the challenging parts using a combination of Pinyin and Chinese characters. The teacher reminds learners to look for texts/passages that are challenging but within grasp; if a text/passage is deemed too difficult, the teacher helps either by making the contents accessible through scaffolding for the learner or by preparing it for other learner(s) in the class who are at higher proficiency levels.

Phase 6. Develop the elective learning objects: learner chooses final two texts/passages and designs and develops activities using the teacher's sample.

a. Day 1 hour 1. Learners turn in three texts/passages to the teacher. The teacher then has one-on-one conferences with each learner to complete two tasks while the other learners are reading each other's texts/passages. The first is to advise them how to identify the best two texts/passages for in-depth sharing and study (features that match learners' needs/errors, relevance to the key topic and culminating task, difficulty level, length, etc.). The second is to negotiate with the learner activities that address the learner-identified challenges in the texts/passages, where the teacher as mentor produces one sample activity for a targeted challenge, fostering learner autonomy by suggesting practical activities learners can use to develop new skills or knowledge.
b. Day 1 hour 2. Using the teacher-provided sample activity targeting text/passage challenges, each learner designs and develops activities for one of his/her two chosen texts/passages and, on a separate document, submits his/her model answers for these activities. This helps the learner understand how to explore these types of texts/passages via activities geared toward experiential or investigative inquiries—skills needed for the evening's follow-on research and for the cost-benefit discussions the next day.
c. Day 1 hour 3. As learners begin to develop activities for the second text/passage, the teacher reviews each learner's activities for the first text/passage and writes feedback to ensure key aspects of the texts/passages are captured in the activities and that the model answers are suitable in terms of accuracy and depth.
d. Day 1 hour 4. Learners make necessary adjustments to the first text/passage, possibly changing the objectives and/or modifying the design of the activities based on the teacher's feedback. The teacher then reviews the second text/passage and activities.
e. Day 1 hour 5. Now, learners make the necessary adjustments to the second text/passage and its associated activities, as the teacher sequences all text/passage (two from each learner, two from the teacher) into a hyperlinked timeline of the Three Gorges Project from completion through the present (see Figure 6.3).

Hyperlinked Timeline

Instructions: You'll find 11 hyperlinks to reading/listening passages in the row marked "pool of materials." They're in chronological order, from the time when the Three Gorges construction project was completed up to the present. For each passage, determine whether the passage espouses the strengths and virtues of this construction project, warns of its potential weaknesses or consequences, or does neither, by providing the specifics in the appropriate row. For example, if the passage does not pertain to either the strengths or weaknesses of the project, in the last row enter what it mainly discusses instead.

	Start of the timeline	Elective LO (1)	Elective LO (2)	Elective LO (3)	Elective LO (4)	Elective LO (5)	Elective LO (6)	Elective LO (7)	Elective LO (8)	Elective LO (9)	Present
Pool of materials	Foundational LO (1)										Foundational LO (2)
Passage mainly focuses on the project's strengths, which are ___											
Passage mainly focuses on the project's weaknesses or potential consequences, which are ___											
Passage does not pertain to either the strengths or weaknesses of the project, instead it mainly discusses ___											

Figure 6.3. Hyperlinked timeline for learner exploration of the Three Gorges Project

(It was decided to start from completion for practical reasons, specifically, media coverage over time reveals greater details, and the benefits and consequences of the project emerge over time, following the Project's completion.) Learners can easily click-and-enter each text/passage to optimize the ease of exploration and centralize their findings to pave the way for the culminating task. The hyperlinked timeline provides three possible communicative purposes for each text/passage (Figure 6.3):

Phase 7. Learners explore the jointly composed module.
a. Day 1 hour 6. The teacher incorporates all last-minute changes (the hyperlinked timeline does not need to be changed as only the documents need to be updated), provides a short lesson on discourse features of typical argumentation in the Chinese Mandarin language, and distributes the hyperlinked timeline for the learner-teacher jointly composed module. Each learner examines the hyperlinked timeline with the culminating task in mind by (1) listening to/reading other learners' texts/passages and completing the activities and (2) applying the discourse features lesson (day 1 hour 6) and drawing on his/her own Chinese language work on the topic of the Three Gorges Project (day 1 hours 2–5) to label each text/passage's communicative purpose using the last three rows of the table.
b. Day 2 hours 1–3. Learners continue working individually, and collaboratively in small groups when the activity design calls for it, on the foundational and elective learning objects, which are accessed via the hyperlinked timeline. This timeline provides learners a visual way to study the Three Gorges Project's costs and benefits over time. To ensure learners can work in parallel in the same learning environment (either in-person in the same classroom or remotely via distance learning) without frequent interruptions from other learners' discussions with the teacher, the teacher provides live advice/mentorship/coaching via collaborative platforms such as Google Docs, Class Notebook's collaborate feature, Teams' Wiki feature, or Adobe Connect's notes pods. This also ensures each learner gets live help in a private and respectful fashion.
c. Day 2 hour 4–5. Taking turns, each learner takes on the role of subject-matter expert to help others understand the model answers to their texts and answers other learners' queries, while the teacher assists and supports in preparation for the next day's discussions on costs vs. benefits.
d. Day 2 hour 6. The teacher provides feedback (privately if learner-specific; openly if pertaining to most learners). Learners and teacher then negotiate to determine other unexplained aspects of the Three Gorges Project. The homework consists of two or three additional texts/passages, to be found and analyzed by learners, to support their argument as to whether the costs outweigh the benefits. For example: What effects has the Project had on the growth of the surrounding regions and on the national strength (economic-social-political)? What historic sites were flooded in the process and what population was displaced (social-cultural)? What climate impact is suspected in the years since its completion (scientific-environmental)? What kind of construction was used for the dam, from a defense perspective (technology-military-security)? Then, the

THE USE OF PROJECT-BASED OACD MODULES

Criteria \ Points	1-2	3-4	5-6	7-8	Total
Overall Organization	Completely disorganized; audience/opposing party cannot follow or understand.	Poorly organized; audience/opposing party follows with difficulty.	Generally organized; audience/opposing party follows.	Well organized; audience/opposing party follows with evident ease.	
Contents	Main idea has no support, or no evident main idea presented.	Main idea is poorly supported, or main idea is at times unclear or has consistency issues.	Main idea is generally supported and clear.	Main idea is well supported and completely clear.	
Knowledge Demonstrated	Subject matter knowledge is absent or generally erroneous.	Some subject matter knowledge is present, but with some errors.	Subject matter knowledge is present with very few errors.	Subject matter knowledge is present in abundance with no errors.	
Language Accuracy	The speech is incomprehensible due to lexical and structural errors; misuse of terms abounds.	The speech is mostly comprehensible, but paraphrasing is often needed due to lexical and structural errors; word choice is sometimes not appropriate or accurate.	The speech is comprehensible with few lexical or structural errors; word choice is generally appropriate and accurate.	The speech is easily comprehensible, with no lexical or structural errors; word choice is highly precise and contextually appropriate.	
Elocution	The speech is incomprehensible due to unclear pronunciation, poor projection, poor pace, poor inflexion, poor intonation, and culturally/contextually unsuitable poise.	The speech is difficult to comprehend due to occasional issues relating to pronunciation, projection, pace, inflexion, intonation, and poise.	The speech is generally comprehensible, albeit with a few issues relating to pronunciation, projection, pace, inflexion, intonation, and poise.	The speech is easy to comprehend; speaker's pronunciation, projection, pace, inflexion, intonation, and poise clearly enhance the speech.	
				Total Points	

Figure 6.4. Sample rubric for the culminating task

teacher provides learners the assessment rubric (see Figure 6.4) for the culminating task—the multi-stage debate.

e. Day 3 hours 1–2. Each learner develops and prepares to support her/his opinion, and selects one or two content areas to focus on. As needed, the teacher holds one-on-one conferences with each learner to answer questions.

Phase 8. Do culminating activity.

a. Day 3 hours 3–4. Learners share their views and sort themselves into two groups: one believing that the Three Gorges Project's costs outweigh the benefits, the other that the Project's benefits outweigh the costs. Then, each group meets separately to create handouts and/or presentation slides, drawing on the discourse features identified in day 1 hour 6 and reviewed up through day 2 hour 3.

b. Day 3 hours 5–6. Learners engage in a debate, with each learner functioning as a subject matter expert for his/her content areas of the Three Gorges Project. The teacher scores the debate, using the rubric chosen for the event, adding a standard of accuracy that addresses each learner's previously determined dominant error patterns. At the end of the debate, the teacher provides general feedback and afterward, learner-specific feedback.

The Learner Data Panel: Facilitating Data-Driven Learner-Teacher Negotiation

In a project-based OACD module like the one examined above, it is critical to base learner-teacher negotiation on objective data sufficiently detailed to effectively support planning aspects of the curriculum. Targeted aid can promote de-fossilization of errors, correct deficiencies, and educate learners about the proper use of learning strategies. The Learner Data Panel is a data analytics tool designed to provide real-time data to meet that goal.

As referred to earlier, the Learner Data Panel[2] is a navigational display with which the learner and teacher chart the evolving learning path. As such, it can be tailored to a range of course objectives and designs. It provides an at-a-glance display of individual or cohort performance in four key categories: error patterns, needs pertaining to language learning strategies, subject matter knowledge, and applications of knowledge to solve problems or complete tasks.

The steps for using the Learner Data Panel are as follows:

1. Teacher evaluates individual and cohort performance during an extended project or activity (a multi-stage debate, a presentation activity requiring research, an essay requiring data collection and graphics, or similar) according to the four key categories listed above.
2. Teacher logs key data onto a spreadsheet, generating a chart for either an individual or the cohort (see Figure 6.5). The chart is continually updated so each learner and/or cohort can see improvements/needs by category. Each learner has access to his/her own charts.
3. Teacher meets with the learner or cohort to negotiate where to focus attention in upcoming lessons.
4. At the end of the extended project or activity, the learner-teacher team reflects on overall performance and improvement.

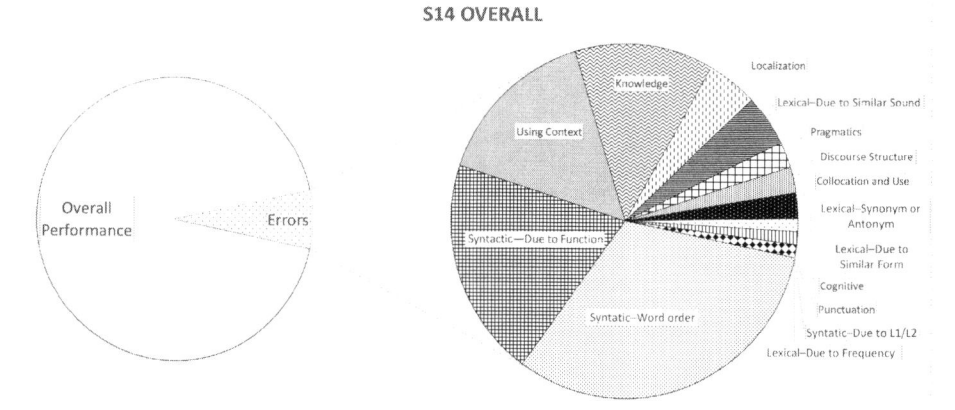

Figure 6.5. Panel for learner no. 14 (S14)

The panel provides specifics that inform the use of the learning objects, which are constructed to reflect ever-changing learner needs and interests. The panel above pertains to one learner, named S14, who participated in a version of the Three Gorges Project STEP. As S14 progressed through the unit, the teacher analyzed in-class and out-of-class language production data and identified error patterns, language learning strategies needs, and gaps in subject-matter knowledge. S14's challenges included word order errors resulting from first language interference; a tendency to read and listen sequentially rather than utilizing function words to organize meaning; inability to use context to determine meaning; and knowledge deficiencies relating to the unit topics.

Learner-teacher negotiation on OACD aspects of the curriculum inspired the creation of the Learner Data Panel. This data analytics tool for formative assessment produces actionable data enabling data-driven learner-teacher discussions that support the learner's role as a stakeholder in learning success.

Conclusions

This chapter describes how the use of project-based OACD modules, supplemented with a data analytics tool—the Learner Data Panel, facilitates both learner involvement in the selection of content and design and delivery of activities, an OACD core principle, and learner-teacher negotiation. With this type of module, learners individually choose one or two content areas, driven by their own interests or learning needs, within which they will develop a pool of shared elective learning objects through iterative learner-teacher negotiation and collaboration. The module design differs from a one-size-fits-all static one as it provides the flexibility crucial to promoting a seamless fit between learners and their individual learning paths. That fit is further enhanced through the use of the Learner Data Panel. Learner Data Panel information can help teachers better tailor instruction to address individual and cohort error patterns, needs pertaining to language learning strategies, subject-matter knowledge, and applications of knowledge to solve problems or complete tasks. With tailoring that is continual and systematic, learners can become more autonomous, more confident and, ultimately, more proficient.

Study Questions

1. Given your students, likely a more disparate group than DLIFLC students, what eight to ten topics would you consider might best meet their needs and interests as a cohort? How might you sequence them? What STEPs (sub-topics/themes essential to progress) would you develop as segue and to maximize recycling and spiraling?
2. The module examined was developed for an intensive program. How would you adapt it to a typical university or high school course?
3. Learners in the described program had tested proficiency at Advanced and Superior (ILR 2 and 3). How would you adjust the program for learners whose proficiency is either lower or higher than those levels?

Notes

1. This chapter has been approved for public release by the Defense Language Institute Foreign Language Center's Public Affairs Office. For verification please email: mpao@dliflc.edu. Contents of this chapter are not necessarily the official views of the Defense Language Institute Foreign Language Center, nor are they endorsed by the Department of the Army, the Department of Defense, or the U.S. Government. All third-party products / materials featured in the chapter remain the intellectual property of their respective authors / originators. Use of outside materials is done under the fair use copyright principle, for educational purposes only. The content of this chapter is the sole responsibility of the author(s).
2. Readers interested in further information about accessing and populating the Learner Data Panel can refer to the author at daniel.wang.1D@gmail.com for further information.

References

Bandura, Albert. 1977. "Self-Efficacy: Toward a Unifying Theory of Behavioral Change." *Psychological Review* 84, no. 2 (March): 191–215.

Campbell, Christine. 2021. "Open Architecture Curricular Design: A Fundamental Principle of Transformative Language Learning and Teaching." In *Transformative Language Learning and Teaching*, edited by Betty Lou Leaver, Dan Davidson, and Christine Campbell, 43–50. Cambridge: Cambridge University Press.

Corin, Andrew R. 2020a. "Open Architecture Curriculum and Transformative Language Learning Revisited. Part 1. The Relationship between Open Architecture Curricular Design and Transformative Language Learning." *ACTR Letter* 46, no. 3–4: 1–2, 4–5.

Corin, Andrew R. 2020b. "Open Architecture Curriculum and Transformative Language Learning Revisited. Part 2. Toward a Constrained Definition of OACD." *ACTR Letter* 47, no. 1: 1–2, 4.

Dabbs, Laura, and Betty Lou Leaver. 2019. *The Invisible Foreign Language Classroom: Bringing Hidden Dynamics to Light for Individual and Group Harmony and Success*. Hollister: MSI Press.

DLIFLC. 2004. "DLIFLC Regulation Number 350-1." Accessed July 15, 2020. https://mlitraining.weebly.com/uploads/9/4/5/6/9456290/350-1jul2004_dli_forms.pdf/.

Ehrman, Madeline E. 2002. "The Learner at the Superior-Distinguished Threshold." In *Developing Professional-Level Foreign Language Proficiency*, edited by Betty Lou Leaver and Boris S. Shekhtman, 245–59. Cambridge: Cambridge University Press.

Ehrman, Madeline E., and Zoltan Dörnyei. 1998. *Interpersonal Dynamics in Second Language Acquisition: The Visible and Invisible Classroom*. Thousand Oaks: Sage.

Kohonen, Viljo. 2006. "On the Notions of the Language Learner, Student and User in FL Education: Building the Road as We Travel." Accessed July 15, 2020. https://citeseerx.ist.psu.edu/viewdoc/download?doi=10.1.1.539.6397&rep=rep1&type=pdf.

L'Allier, James J. 1997. "A Frame of Reference: NETG's Map to Its Products, Their Structures and Core Beliefs." In *Utah State University Ninth Annual Summer Instructional Technology Institute Conference Proceedings August 27–30, 1997*, 60–78. https://files.eric.ed.gov/fulltext/ED416849.pdf.

Leaver, Betty Lou, Dan Davidson, and Christine Campbell. 2021. *Transformative Language Learning and Teaching*. Cambridge: Cambridge University Press.

Merrill, Marriner D. 2002. "First Principles of Instruction." *Educational Technology Research & Development* 50, no. 3: 43–59.

Mezirow, Jack. 2000. "Learning to Think Like an Adult. Core Concepts in Transformation Theory." In *Learning as Transformation: Critical Perspectives on a Theory in Progress*, edited by J. Mezirow, and Associates, 3–33. San Francisco: Jossey-Bass.

Vygotsky, Lev. 1978. *Mind in Society: The Development of Higher Psychological Processes*. Cambridge: Harvard University Press.

Wang, Daniel. 2016. "Reading Strategies at Higher Proficiency Levels." Paper presented at California Language Teachers Association 2016 Conference, March 19, 2016.

Wang, Daniel. 2018. "Achieving 3+ through Individualized Formative Feedback in a Multi-Level Classroom." Paper presented at LEARN Conference, 26 September 2018.

Wood, David, Jerome S. Bruner, and Gail Ross. 1976. "The Role of Tutoring in Problem Solving." *Journal of Child Psychiatry and Psychology* 17, no. 2: 89–100.

Part 3
OACD in US Military Service Academies
Programs at the US Military Academy (West Point)

7

Emulating Proficiency-Increasing Features of the Semester Abroad Experience through Open Architecture Curricular Design

E. John Gregory

THIS CHAPTER DEMONSTRATES HOW open architecture curricular design (OACD) in an advanced Chinese media course sequence can replicate some of the most effective attributes of a well-designed semester abroad experience—self-sequenced modularity,[1] opportunities to revise activities and tasks, and learner autonomy. Also key to OACD's game-changing potential is its ability to promote the development of learners' metapragmatic awareness[2] though the examination of unadapted current authentic materials. This awareness, arguably one of the most effective components of the semester abroad sociolinguistic experience, is largely missing from the traditional advanced-level language classroom. OACD provides a particularly effective way to bring elements of this metapragmatic environment into the language classroom, especially when OACD's flexibility is guided by a strategy-based framework such as critical discourse analysis relevant to the particular language or region. The experience at the US Military Academy at West Point (West Point) suggests that such an approach can arrest or delay post-SA proficiency attrition (proficiency loss) and lead to greater proficiency gains in the advanced language classroom.

Three Proficiency-Enhancing Features of the Out-of-Class Portion of the Semester Abroad Experience

Most scholars agree that the semester abroad environment is, in general, a better environment for rapidly increasing language proficiency than a home university environment (Llanes 2011). West Point's Chinese semester abroad experience is consistent with this view, with students on average gaining one-half to a full step improvement in at least one of three domains (listening, reading, and speaking) as measured by both pre- and post-semester abroad Defense Language Proficiency Test and ACTFL Oral Proficiency Interview.

Formal structured class forms a critical component of a semester abroad program (Brecht and Robinson 1995). Sunderman and Kroll (2009), for example, asserts that without a formal component deliberately building the necessary internal resources, the learner will generally not be able to take full advantage of the immersive social environment. West Point's Chinese semester abroad program, currently conducted primarily in Taiwan, has a formal classroom component in which learners spend at least 200 hours in the classroom during the semester abroad experience. For learners who begin the semester abroad program in the Intermediate Low/Mid (ILR 1) to Intermediate High (ILR 1+) range in the three domains of listening, reading, and speaking, these classes focus on mechanical increase in Chinese-language knowledge—internal resource building at the basic level—in a more-or-less traditional fashion. For learners at the Advanced Low to Superior (ILR 2 to 3) range prior to beginning the semester abroad program, their overseas programs are customized with private tutors and subject-area classes taken together with native students. If formal classroom instruction were solely responsible for semester abroad proficiency gains, one would expect to see similar gains from intensive nonimmersion programs at the home institution, but this is generally not the case.

What is it about the semester abroad immersive environment that in a relatively short time period contributes to proficiency gains, and how does this environment highlight the value of OACD to home college course design? Three specific features can be highlighted: self-sequenced modularity; opportunities to revise activities and tasks; and learner autonomy.

Self-sequenced modularity occurs naturally in the semester abroad environment as learners engage in unique, everyday language acts, either organized or impromptu, such as the unexpected chat at a restaurant with a native speaker curious about the learner's culture. Llanes (2011, 190) posits as key to proficiency growth in the semester abroad environment: "multiple opportunities that students have to practice any of the four skills (listening, speaking, reading, and writing)." In other words, the unique, out-of-class opportunities available in the semester abroad environment foster proficiency growth. According to Isabelli-García (2006) and Juan-Garau and Pérez-Vidal (2007), the informal, immersive social component of semester abroad is as at least equally important as the formal component. This nonclassroom component of semester abroad is also often credited with building sociolinguistic competence (Regan and Lemée 2009). While all Chinese semester abroad learners at West Point spend significant time in the formal classroom component, most curious students will also spend significant time experientially learning within the informal environmental context. This is where many of them will gain critical mega-pragmatic knowledge of the Chinese language environment (Kinginger and Farrell 2004). The knowledge they gain in class is reactivated and reinforced continually as they interact in their dorm rooms with native students and participate in the social life of the communities surrounding their semester abroad universities while (ideally) building a mental picture of how social discourses are constructed.

This informal component, the canvas of society in the semester abroad environment, provides the diligent learner with the epitome of a nonfixed, non-one-size-fits-all curricular learning model. It is naturally *modular*, with the "transportation module," the "convenience shop module," the "random-interaction-with-a-stranger module," the "curious-engagement-with-a-veteran module," the "intense-talk-in-the-coffee-shop-about-politics module," among others, to reinforce the vocabulary and sentence structures learned in class in a completely *self-sequenced* manner. These modules are absorbing and inherently cross-referencing language acts in real time, which enables learners to accumulate and distill metapragmatic knowledge.

Concerning the second feature—opportunities to revise activities and tasks, once the learner is abroad in the immersive environment, opportunities for change in this open-air curriculum arise without additional resources. "Let me take the bus today instead of the subway" provides a whole new set of material for the "transportation module." The opportunities occur naturally, providing learners ways to engage autonomously in ever deeper experiential learning. In other words, the informal semester abroad environment is, in many ways, for the curious student, what West Point seeks to deliberately reproduce through the intentional use of OACD in designing the home classroom environments.

Regarding the third feature—learner autonomy—West Point makes focused, deliberate efforts to empower its students to take responsibility for their learning throughout their time at the institution. A key part of the education of the majority of West Point students is the semester abroad experience. Most travel abroad during their junior year. The semester abroad experience can significantly enhance learner autonomy as students grapple with the challenges of communicating and communing with native speakers.

In the Chinese program, many who travel abroad during the second semester of their junior year will complete their required Chinese course credits for the major while on semester abroad, meaning that many students will not continue to take Chinese after they return from their semester abroad. Over the past three years, students have generally lost one-half to a full level of proficiency in the two semesters after returning from semester abroad. Even if the students continued to take some Chinese courses post-semester abroad, seldom did their proficiency remain at the same level or improve post-semester abroad.

However, following the OACD redesign of LC 475–476, a two-semester advanced course sequence focused primarily on Chinese media, for those students that take this course sequence after semester abroad preliminary analysis suggests that this decrease in proficiency has been arrested, mitigated or, in some cases, reversed. Moreover deliberately incorporating a significant writing component using the OACD features discussed subsequently appears to have contributed to gains in writing proficiency across the two-semester sequence as measured by the ACTFL Writing Proficiency Test (WPT).

Heightening Learners' Metapragmatic Awareness through the Examination of Unadapted Current Authentic Materials

In addition to addressing the problem of post-semester abroad attrition, the OACD redesign of LC 475–476 described in this chapter has allowed West Point to construct a Chinese media course sequence that not only replicates important aspects of the semester abroad immersive experience but also allows learners to develop metapragmatic awareness of the influence of the Chinese Communist Party on discourse. In fact, this aspect of the metapragmatic environment is often lacking when Chinese-language semester abroad is conducted outside of China itself, for instance in Taiwan where the Chinese Communist Party lacks the ability to exert such strong control over Chinese-language discourse formation. For the Chinese language critical awareness of the Chinese Communist Party's role in discourse formation is not mere additional critical understanding of society but rather necessary linguistic training in meaning-informing metapragmatics. As Elizabeth Perry and others have written, the Chinese Communist Party relies on "cultural governance" to maintain and solidify its power in an ever more diverse and complex Chinese society and world (Shue and Thornton 2018). Semester abroad students studying in China often naturalize Chinese Communist Party discourse as "just the way you speak Chinese," whereas semester abroad students studying in Taiwan, a politically independent Chinese-speaking country, are, for the most part, not exposed to Chinese Communist Party-inflected discourse. The linguistic component of this Chinese Communist Party program involves a significant and ongoing resignifying of the public terms of discourse across media platforms and formats. Within Chinese Communist Party-moderated society, this linguistic project starts in elementary school, where children are taught the basic terms of discourse that preclude effective criticism of the party itself (Gregory 2018). For Chinese language learners, understanding and recognizing the party's voice throughout the linguistic environment, including within the majority of ostensibly nongovernmental communications, is critical.

Metapragmatic awareness in the Chinese context allows learners to develop both a greater mechanical understanding of the Chinese-language media they are consuming and a deeper perception of the way in which those media are constitutive of greater reality-forming discourses in the Chinese speaking world, including outside of China's borders, through what Edney (2016) has called the "globalization of Chinese propaganda (19)." Metapragmatic awareness allows the learner to approach the language environment critically and insightfully, through a process analogous to that experienced during the informal semester abroad experience (in China), as discussed by Kinginger and Farrell (2004). Development of this metapragmatic knowledge has become more difficult since China's government has made it more difficult for foreigners to study freely in China.

While the central and dominant role of the Chinese Communist Party in Chinese linguistic transformation and discourse formation has long been documented by scholars outside the language learning field, it has been almost wholly ignored within Chinese language teaching programs (Brady 2006). Part of the reason for this is likely political, not disciplinary. Many Chinese teachers who were educated within the Chinese Communist Party-controlled educational system simply naturalize Chinese Communist Party influence in discourse formation and pass that on to their American students, resulting in language learners who often unwittingly adopt ideologically infused terms. For instance, it is not uncommon to hear American Chinese learners refer to North Korea in terms that implicitly delegitimize the Republic of Korea (South Korea) because they "learned" the "right word" for North Korea "in

Chinese." Since, until recently, a significant portion of Chinese language education in the US is funded by the Chinese Communist Party through the Party's Hanban organization and Confucius Institutes, American Chinese textbook publishers have little incentive to highlight this important context for Chinese language learning lest their textbooks be banned for use in Chinese-financed programs or considered too "political" by Chinese Communist Party-educated teachers. Even the reflexive dismissal of "political topics" by Chinese Communist Party-educated speakers is often a reflection of an inherent component of the Chinese Communist Party-dominated metadiscursive environment in which it is inappropriate to speak of political matters except in strict, formulaic ways that affirm Chinese Communist Party authority. For West Point, whose mission is cultivating critical leaders to lead the nation, ignoring a uniquely powerful meaning-forming agent within the Chinese discursive environment is not an option.

Coupling OACD with a Strategy-Based Framework for Enhancing Metapragmatic Awareness through Analysis of Unadapted Authentic Materials

Since OACD, by definition, loosens course structure, the commitment to a strategy-based framework can play an important role in enhancing course unity. What specific strategy is used will be highly dependent on the language and the goals of the course. West Point's advanced Chinese media sequence currently uses critical discourse analysis as its unifying strategy-based framework to facilitate scrutiny of unadapted authentic materials.[3] Critical discourse analysis's focus on how unequal gender and race "power relations" shape social and political discourse has led some scholars to criticize or dismiss critical discourse analysis's methodologies as politically informed. For Chinese, however, where the Chinese Communist Party occupies such a dominant role in the formation of discourse, it is precisely this methodological focus on the influence of power in discourse formation that is important in the advanced Chinese language learning context (van Dijk 2015). In a different language or with a different regional focus, a different strategy might be preferred. For instance, a French media course could use the French sociolinguistic construct of *laïcité* as a unifying analytical theme across texts. For Chinese, the critical discourse analysis strategy exploits OACD, with its emphasis on the use of unadapted authentic materials, by requiring learners to engage and develop higher-order and critically reflective thinking skills, key enablers for the attainment of Superior (ILR 3) and Distinguished (ILR 4) proficiency.

Van Dijk (2015) explains that "the central notion" in most critical discourse analysis work "is that of power, and more specifically social power of groups or institutions" (469). With a critical discourse analysis lens, learners are encouraged to engage with Chinese media sources to discern discourse power relations which tend to lead them to the Party's voice. Why might peaceful democracy protestors be portrayed as "radical rioters" in a particular media product? How might that relate to where and when it was published? What does "radical" even mean when it appears in Chinese Communist Party-moderated discourse? These are the kinds of questions that a critical discourse analysis lens encourages within the Chinese context.

The Implementation of OACD in the Chinese Media Course Sequence

OACD is reflected in five aspects of the course design that re-create the naturalness, nonsequenced modularity, and learner autonomy of the semester abroad environment while at the same time allowing students to gain metapragmatic knowledge through the application of critical discourse analysis to unadapted authentic materials:

1. The course uses a cloud-based platform that supports a rapid swapping out of materials as well as continual learner-learner and learner-teacher interaction.
2. All units, after the methodological introduction in Unit One, are topical, allowing the specific content material to be easily swapped out depending on what is trending and salient on real-life Chinese media contemporaneous with the class.
3. All units can be moved around—resequenced—to best accommodate currency and recency of important and interesting events in the Chinese media discursive sphere, allowing learners to observe and even engage in real time dialectic development.
4. Learners are required to engage with the Chinese media environment themselves to find media related to the topic of the lesson.
5. Learners are required to engage critically with the material with their classmates (in person orally and online in writing), as well as with the teacher and a contracted writing tutor based in Taiwan.

OACD is best served by an effective learning platform in which assignments can be easily viewed, uploaded, and downloaded by learners, teachers, and others involved in the course. Such a platform should support the execution of units in any sequence. Ideally, it would provide learners spaces to engage in teacher-moderated written discussions. The platform must be able to support multiple forms of media.

The units in LC 475 are as follows:

- Unit 1: Chinese Media Discourse Analysis: Background and Methodology
- Unit 2: The Party's Self-Narrative of the Role of the Press
- Unit 3: "Rule of Law" and Society
- Unit 4: Economy, Entertainment, and Sports Writing as Spaces of Discourse Construction and Critique

For each unit there are three main parts. The first begins with learners reading unadapted authentic materials, specifically a Chinese media selection on a topic chosen by the teacher (the teacher provides this selection). Prior to coming to class, learners are expected to upload five questions or statements regarding the provided text to the online platform. The questions or statements are used as the nucleus of the class discussion, ensuring that the learners have prepared the material prior to arriving in class since classroom discussion and engagement is a critical aspect of the course. Usually, the discussion of the text material extends over two days. Each unit also includes a teacher-selected video from Chinese media on the unit topic. The video is used for in-class listening exercises.

Another important aspect of the course is small-group organization. Once per unit, each small-group student member must select an article on his or her own related to the topic of the group. The student is required to summarize the article and to make comments on the other students' self-selected articles, further increasing the opportunity for engagement and autonomous exploration of the Chinese media environment. Each student is required to lead a class discussion on the self-selected article. Without the OACD format, this type of timely selection of unadapted authentic materials would be difficult.

In addition to requiring learners to provide critical discourse analysis-informed written reflections on the assigned reading, each unit requires learners write a 500-character paragraph, using critical discourse analysis principles learned in the first unit about the Chinese discursive environment related to that topic. In this paragraph, they must consider all the sources they have engaged with in class. They post the draft of this paragraph to the online platform. Since all the course materials and student submissions are managed on the online platform, it is easy to have an offsite-contracted teacher correct the mechanical aspects of the paragraphs, the time-intensive red-lining of their document with notes about grammar and punctuation. This allows the main course teacher to focus more on the content and analysis aspects and thereby address such matters as learners' actual understanding of the article and its interpretation, as well as critical approach and language register. Throughout the revision process of the 500-character paragraph, learners are provided additional opportunities to engage with the teacher on the material.

An Example of How OACD Allowed US-Based Learners to Participate in Unfolding Linguistic Events within the Target Language Culture

To illustrate how effective the ability to move around units (modules), a feature of OACD, is, consider the multimillion-person marches for democracy that were taking place in Hong Kong during the Fall 2019 academic semester. From protest speeches, emblazoned in songs and posters, to official response, this was a tremendous Chinese linguistic event. How were Chinese media representations of the protests influenced by the Chinese Communist Party? How were Chinese media outside of Chinese Communist Party control covering the protests? How were Chinese bloggers behind the "Great Firewall"[4] understanding, processing, and linguistically engaging with the Chinese Communist Party-moderated information that was flowing out of Hong Kong into "mainland" China? What were the terms of discourse and how were they defined, explicitly and implicitly? One should assume that advanced learners of Chinese would be interested in such a current and important topic. The abstract questions of hypothetical futures, rule of law, freedom of expression, and contested opinions parallel the precise functional content of Superior-level proficiency. OACD allowed this topic to be flexibly and seamlessly sequenced into an ongoing course through learner-teacher collaboration. The addition of the topic was not a disruption but an opportunity, not fully known but anticipated when the semester began. In other words, OACD provides a framework that encourages the teacher to incorporate this type of material because the administrative and disruption costs are low.

At the time of the Hong Kong protests, the class was just completing Unit One on critical discourse analysis. Rather than wait for later in the semester, *Unit 3: "Rule of Law and Society"* was moved up and changed to Unit 2. But unlike a traditional course, the change was not limited to mere resequencing of the same material, which would entail a lack of deliberate progression or building in the course. The course also switched out Hong Kong-related articles for the original property-confiscation articles. Even though the Hong Kong protests differ significantly from the property confiscation cases that were the original material for the original Unit 3, in the OACD environment this shift allowed the class to take advantage of the unique opportunity that the protests presented without disruption or laborious reworking. The idea of "rule of law" (*fazhi* 法治) has become a contested term highly amenable to critical discourse analysis, with the Chinese Communist Party media and education apparatus trying to resignify the term as a synonym for "law and order" obedience to Party directives. Using the current Hong Kong movement as the underlying basis for media articles, class discussions and online writing allowed learners to "immerse" themselves and participate in a contested discourse unfolding in real time.

Conclusions

Currently there exist two sets of proficiency assessments (listening, reading, writing) for two complete iterations of the OACD-based media course sequence. As noted previously, typically West Point students gain a half to full level in proficiency in one or more of the assessed domains of reading (Defense Language Proficiency Test), listening (Defense Language Proficiency Test), and speaking (Oral Proficiency Interview) during their semester abroad in Taiwan or China, which generally takes place in either the first or second semester of their junior year. Since West Point administers the Defense Language Proficiency Test to all students in their last semester prior to graduation, it has some idea of what happens to proficiency after their return from semester abroad. What it has found is that students usually experience significant Chinese proficiency attrition between the time they take the Defense Language Proficiency Test right at the end of the semester abroad and their final graduating Defense Language Proficiency Test, with the atrophy proportional to the number of months that have passed since the student returned from semester abroad. This is not inconsistent with what other scholars have found (Westley and Antadze 2010). Interestingly, for those students who took the OACD-based media course sequence, while some still experienced degradation in one or more domain, many maintained their post semester abroad proficiency, and several experienced significant gains. West Point saw especially strong gains in writing, with several students reaching the Intermediate High (ILR 1+) or even Advanced Low (ILR 2) level of writing on the ACTFL Writing Proficiency Test.

Beginning with the Class of 2018, West Point initiated testing in the second course in the sequence, LC 476 (which has the same general structure as LC 475 but is focused on media topics related to international, diplomatic, and military matters). Of the twelve students who took the course, all but three improved in proficiency level in at least one of three skill areas (reading, listening, speaking) as compared with their scores when they returned from semester abroad. This contrasts with the situation, discussed in the literature, where students' proficiency significantly deteriorates after semester abroad. For the writing skill each student had been administered a baseline ACTFL Writing Proficiency Test at the beginning of LC 475: ten of twelve students reached Intermediate Mid (ILR 1) or above, with one student who started as Advanced High (ILR 2+) reaching Superior (ILR 3). For students who took the course in 2019 (2019–20), of fourteen who were semester abroad-returnees, the results were more mixed, with two improving in at least one domain with no apparent attrition in the others, while four maintained their proficiency levels and eight had some attrition in one or more skill. All nineteen students who took the course were able to reach Intermediate Mid (ILR 1) or above on the ACTFL Writing Proficiency Test, including seven students who were able to score Advanced Low (ILR 2) or above. While the sample size renders this data anecdotal, at the very least these results suggest that gaining critical awareness of the megapragmatic environment in Chinese need not come at the expense of maintaining communicative proficiency. The data suggests that OACD course redesign can improve proficiency.

In conclusion three features of OACD—self-sequenced modularity, opportunities to revise activities and tasks, and learner autonomy, in combination with its ability to promote the development of learners' metapragmatic awareness through the examination of unadapted current authentic materials, have been shown to be indispensable for re-creating within the home college course environment some of the most effective conditions of an immersive semester abroad environment while also enabling a broader, living, real-time, critical engagement with metapragmatic knowledge of the language. From this brief experience, courses that incorporate features of OACD demonstrate promise in addressing the problem of language attrition following a semester abroad experience. Perhaps more importantly OACD features are essential to designing a Chinese course that engages with and makes students aware of the current broader sociolinguistic environment. Anecdotal evidence from two iterations of the LC 475–476 media course sequence at this point suggests that the OACD format, coupled with a flexible online platform and a strategy for facilitating learners' scrutiny of unadapted authentic materials (which may be different based on considerations particular to a given language or metapragmatic linguistic environment), can be used both to promote language proficiency and to provide a necessary environment for gaining critical insight into the discursive context.

Study Questions

1. If you are at an institution where study abroad programs are not aligned with classroom instruction, how might you bring the benefits of OACD to either or both of these programs? What steps might you need to take and whose assistance might you need to enlist?
2. The program described in this chapter utilized critical discourse analysis as a strategy for facilitating analysis of unadapted authentic materials. What alternative or additional strategies might be employed to support or enhance coherence of activities in an OACD environment?
3. What three takeaways from this chapter might benefit your own classroom or program?

Notes

1. "Self-sequenced modularity" refers to the practice of learners, or learners and teachers in collaboration, creating (or selecting) and then using modules such as "Taking Public Transportation," in which learners develop and apply target language competencies in a variety of contexts either within the target language culture or in home country classrooms.

2. Kinginger and Farrell define metapragmatic awareness as "knowledge of the social meaning of variable second language forms and awareness of the ways in which these forms mark different aspects of social contexts" (2004, 20).
3. Critical discourse analysis refers to a strategy of analyzing texts that seeks to reveal how power is manifested and reproduced in the formation of discourse. Critical discourse analysis achieves this through a reader's deliberate awareness that discourse is a constituent element of society and culture, discourse is an ideological tool, power relations are discursive, and discourse is linked to history.
4. The "Great Firewall" is a catchall phrase for the Chinese Communist Party's control of the internet in China. It involves restricting international content as well as policing and fabricating domestic content on a wide scale.

References

Brady, Anne-Marie. 2006. "Guiding Hand: The Role of the CCP Central Propaganda Department in the Current Era." *Westminster Papers in Communication and Culture* 3, no. 1.

Brecht, Richard D., and Jennifer L. Robinson. 1995. "On the Value of Formal Instruction in Study Abroad: Student Reactions in Context." In *Second Language Acquisition in a Study Abroad Context*, edited by B. F. Freed, 317–34. Amsterdam: John Benjamins.

Edney, K. 2016. *Globalization of Chinese Propaganda: International Power and Domestic Political Cohesion*. London: Palgrave Macmillan.

Gregory, E. John. 2018. "Control Issues Are Feeding China's Discourse Power Project." *The National Interest*, August 15, 2018. https://nationalinterest.org/feature/control-issues-are-feeding-chinas-discourse-power-project-28862.

Isabelli-García, C. 2006. "Study Abroad Social Networks, Motivation and Attitudes: Implications for Second Language Acquisition." In *Language Learners in Study Abroad Contexts*, edited by M. DuFon and E. Churchill, 231–58. Clevedon: Multilingual Matters.

Juan-Garau, Maria, and Carmen Pérez-Vidal. 2007. "The Effect of Context and Contact on Oral Performance in Students Who Go on a Stay Abroad." *Vigo International Journal of Applied Linguistics* 4: 117–34.

Kinginger, Celeste, and Kathleen Farrell. 2004. "Assessing Development of Meta-Pragmatic Awareness in Study Abroad." *Frontiers: The Interdisciplinary Journal of Study Abroad* 10: 19–42.

Llanes, Àngels. 2011. "The Many Faces of Study Abroad: An Update on the Research on L2 Gains Emerged during a Study Abroad Experience." *International Journal of Multilingualism* 8, no. 3: 189–215. https://doi.org/10.1080/14790718.2010.550297.

Regan, Vera, Martin Howard, and Isabelle Lemée. 2009. *The Acquisition of Sociolinguistic Competence in a Study Abroad Context*. Clevedon: Multilingual Matters.

Shue, Vivienne, and Patricia M. Thornton. 2018. *To Govern China: Evolving Practices of Power*. New York: Cambridge University Press.

Sunderman, Gretchen, and Judith F. Kroll. 2009. "When Study Abroad Experience Fails to Deliver: The Internal Resources Threshold Effect." *Applied Psycholinguistics* 30: 79–99.

Van Dijk, Teun A. 2015. "Critical Discourse Analysis." In *The Handbook of Discourse Analysis*, edited by Deborah Tannen, Heidi E. Hamilton, and Deborah Schiffrin, 466–85. Malden: Wiley Blackwell.

Westley, Frances, and Nino Antadze. 2010. "Making a Difference: Strategies for Scaling Social Innovation for Greater Impact." *The Innovation Journal: The Public Sector Innovation Journal* 15, no. 2: 2–20.

8

Optimizing Flexibility in a Distance Learning Immersion Course at West Point
Three Examples of Open Architecture Curricular Design

SHERRY A. MAGGIN, ZACHARY F. MILLER, JOSHUA ENSLEN, JOHN PENDERGAST, AND OLGA DOBRUNOFF

THIS CHAPTER DESCRIBES HOW OACD optimizes flexibility to create transformative experiences for study abroad learners through critical reflection in a distance learning immersion course at the US Military Academy's (West Point) Department of Foreign Languages.

West Point's OACD-Based Distance Learning Immersion Course for Study Abroad Students

West Point places over 150 cadets into semester-long immersion programs in sixteen different countries annually. An important element of the program curriculum is the experiential learning course, Advanced Language and Culture Studies through Distance Learning (LN451). Grounded in *open architecture curricular design* (OACD), this modular course offers flexibility in content and sequence with variation across the eight different language programs within the Department of Foreign Languages. LN451 encourages cadets to examine cultural norms, preparing them to become better global citizens, critical thinkers, and military leaders. Through a series of essays based upon experiential learning and introspection, learners exercise significant autonomy by choosing specific learning events in the immersion environment as they complete fifteen weekly modules. These learning events are designed to challenge learner perspectives by exploring the language and culture of the host country and, after reflection and comparison, provide an opportunity for transformative shifts in perspective.

OACD's Flexibility as an Enabler for Individualization, Critical Reflection, and Transformative Growth

OACD is fundamentally flexible, learner-centered, and personalizable. Its use in language instruction permits teachers to tailor objectives, expectations, and methods to provide each learner with a unique learning experience (Altman 1979; Campbell 2021). For decades, as an alternative to fixed curricula and rigid syllabi, colleges and universities have begun exploring individualized language learning programs to align better with learner interests and learning goals. The exploration has led to adoption of curricular designs such as OACD, which has been implemented to differing degrees in select government institutions within the language teaching community such as the Foreign Service Institute and the Defense Language Institute Foreign Language Center, where its application is constantly evolving (Leaver 1989; Stovicek 2018).

According to Campbell (2018), "Open Architecture (OA), as it refers to language learning, is a curriculum design principle that encourages teachers to add and swap activities and tasks on a continual basis according to learner needs, specifically their styles, strategies, level of fossilization, interests, and zone of proximal development" (27). This observation highlights the malleability of course design within OACD since teachers can modify course content and L2 learning approaches to best meet the needs of individual learners. By emphasizing flexibility, learner experiences, and learner autonomy, OACD becomes a platform for "teacher-learner collaboration" (Campbell 2021), while leveraging the immersive environment to stimulate independent thought and creativity. The ability to swap out, exchange, and reorganize various components of a curriculum as a hallmark of OACD supports this level of flexibility: "[t]he open architecture curricular design is controlled by syllabi that do not include textbooks; that is to say, lesson components can be added or upgraded easily, which promotes flexibility and creativity" (Chen 2018, 45). In some settings, OACD may intertwine task-based instruction with more traditional learning modules (Derderian 2017) or even utilize a learning contract in lieu of a syllabus. OACD is particularly useful in the curricular design of nontraditional courses like distance learning, study abroad, and other types of experiential learning.

Experiential learning is the process of acquiring knowledge through concrete experiences along with reflective observation (Kolb and Kolb 2005). This reflective practice, facilitated by the principles of OACD, may contribute to the personal transformation of the learner. With respect to language learning, for example, Murphy (2005) states that critical reflection and the learners' active engagement in developing their plan of study are "crucial in the development of autonomous language learners" (22). Critical introspection, as a component of the learning process, is often exercised through written compositions that "require learners to externalize their reflective experience" and "provide a means for both reflecting and recording previous thoughts that can be shared with others and returned to and reflected on when most relevant" (Taylor 2016, 9). Critical reflection, as an outcome from OACD, can be used to promote language and cultural development and can contribute to a transformative learning experience.

A number of studies have examined the relationship between OACD and transformative learning experiences. Through an analysis of students enrolled in an online graduate course, Boyer, Maher, and Kirkman (2006) discovered that certain elements of OACD (e.g., self-directed learning and teacher as mentor/coach/advisor) were key factors that positively influenced the transformative learning process. Mezirow (2000, 2016) established that experiential learning is also critical for transformative development. Tarrant (2010) examined this theory in the context of overseas immersion opportunities and concluded that learners were likely to challenge their own worldviews, values, and norms through study abroad programs that were experientially structured.

Based upon previous research, immersion opportunities may offer a fruitful environment for examining the interplay of OACD with transformative learning, given that the context is rife with unfamiliar cultural and linguistic experiences and potential for disorienting dilemmas. As OACD allows for increased flexibility and learner autonomy, it creates a space that maximizes the potential for reflective observation. OACD-oriented study abroad courses, where learners drive the overall content and select experiences on which to critically reflect, provide a proper framework for encouraging experiential activities and assessing transformative learning outcomes. The following examples from cadets participating in West Point's study abroad programs illustrate how the course LN451 adheres to the principles of OACD.

Examples from Advanced Language and Culture Studies through Distance Learning
Course Objectives and Description

The Department of Foreign Languages at West Point offers instruction in eight foreign languages: Arabic, Chinese, French, German, Persian Farsi, Portuguese, Russian, and Spanish. To supplement language training and cultural development, West Point affords cadets the opportunity to participate in semester-long study abroad programs spread across civilian and military academic institutions in sixteen different countries. As a part of the curriculum, the Department of Foreign Languages provides cadets the option of enrolling in the distance learning course, LN451. This specialty course encourages cadets to self-reflect on myriad transformative experiences encountered during their immersion. Course assessments include weekly composition assignments (graded by instructors) and language proficiency testing (Oral Proficiency Interview).

As stated in the syllabus, the two principal objectives of LN451 are (1) to increase cadets' language proficiency and (2) to develop cadets' cultural and regional competencies in an immersive environment. Pedagogically LN451 cultivates these goals by linking personal experiences with self-reflective activities. Over the course of a semester, instructors assign cadets up to fifteen different topics upon which to reflect through essays written in the target language. These topics (e.g., politics, religion, and cultural geography) are designed to consider the specific location and individual interests of each student. Further this approach permits cadets to select, plan, and execute the tasks autonomously.

To facilitate course administration, each language section has adopted a preferred method of electronic communication and dissemination of course products. The use of collaborative technology complements the flexibility in the course design, creating efficiencies in the submission process and further promoting learner autonomy. For example the Russian program maintains a shared folder for each cadet on Google Drive. The cadets can access their folders at any time to create and modify weekly assignments. Instructors then review these assignments and provide feedback within the same folders. The Portuguese program has adopted email correspondence and Microsoft Teams as the primary methods of communication. The Spanish program utilizes Microsoft Teams for administration of the course and the online e-book platform, Book Creator, as a repository for essay collections in e-book format, allowing students to curate their written assignments with photos and other media. Regardless of the platform the electronic interface promotes learner autonomy and interactivity between cadets and their teachers from an OACD perspective, allowing for easy submission, assessment, and archiving of assignments.

Data for this chapter, which are presented in the next section, were derived from weekly compositions assigned to cadets enrolled in LN451. Analysis of the essays follows qualitative coding procedures as outlined by Baralt (2012). For the Russian, Portuguese, and Spanish examples, which highlight different aspects of OACD flexibility, coding was informed by the literature review. All quotes have been translated from the target language into English. To preserve anonymity, student names used are pseudonyms.

Modular Flexibility in the Russian Course

LN451 has been offered to cadets studying Russian in four different Russophone countries: Latvia, Ukraine, Moldova, and Kazakhstan. The unique linguistic and cultural environments of these nations vary significantly, which necessitates a high level of flexibility in how LN451 is designed and implemented for each cadet. Instructionally LN451 utilizes task-based assignments that can be easily organized into modular components and completed nonlinearly throughout a semester. General topics upon which to reflect include a visit to a local museum or monument, observations on societal notions of time and space, and conversations of political relevance with a host nation acquaintance. Although assignments are scheduled in a similar timeframe across the various locations, cadets may choose to complete their essays at different junctures within their program. The examples addressed subsequently demonstrate the modular flexibility of OACD.

In the course syllabus module fourteen requires cadets to visit and evaluate a live theater performance. The syllabus includes some recommendations for venues to explore. However the decision of what to see is left entirely up to the learner, which affects the timing of both the event and the essay submission. For example Cadet Ulmer decided to see the opera *Carmen* during his second week, Cadet Kay viewed *Swan Lake* during her eighth week, and Cadet Moon saw a play during his twelfth week. Cadet Luck made a very interesting decision: in his tenth week, while on vacation in Moscow and away from his study location, he decided to attend a performance of the ballet *Spartacus* at the Bolshoi Theater.[1] These examples underscore the autonomous nature of LN451 that allows cadets to select performances based upon their own interests and individual timeframes.

One learning objective of module fourteen is to reinforce vocabulary related to theater and leisure time. While many of the associated Russian terms are English cognates, spelling can be difficult, and mastering the transformations to produce each of the six case forms requires repetition. The module's final assignment is designed to elicit several verb types, such as those related to motion, decision-making processes, appreciation, and enjoyment. Beyond this the thematic content of each essay (i.e., "I went to theater X and saw Y") should maintain a similar structure and ultimately prompt an interpretive assessment (e.g., "I liked it because..."). Despite the high degree of flexibility and autonomy of the module, the following examples indicate that the four cadets met the specified learning objectives.

All cadets demonstrated satisfactory usage of the theater lexicon. On the interpretive level the cadets made several interesting observations. From Cadet Luck at the Bolshoi: "I'm not a ballet expert but could tell that I was in the presence of the highest level of art in the world." From Cadet Ulmer in Kiev: "Carmen and the soldiers wore beautiful costumes, but I was sad that her face was not very pretty. The fourth part was better and more interesting, but I don't understand why Jose killed Carmen." These comments suggest that the cadets made personal connections to the performances, likely a byproduct of their ability to select a theatrical event based upon their own interests. On a mechanical level, the teacher was able to provide the cadets with quick and detailed recommendations for improving their lexicon and grammar. As a result these errors usually vanished from later essays produced throughout the semester. The Russian example demonstrates how OACD's flexibility and modularity can contribute to executing this distance-learning course across multiple countries.

The task-based learning activity from module fourteen was inherently experiential. The learners needed to select a performance, purchase tickets, locate and find the theater, and attend the performance. It also aligned with Derderian's (2017) conditions for *task-based open architecture language teaching*: the immersion environments provided conditions ideal for second language acquisition, the module was part of the syllabus, the assignment was a real-world activity, and selection of the venue was entirely learner-centered.

Personalized Flexibility in the Portuguese Course

The reflective essay assignments for Portuguese students of LN451 cover a broad range of cultural topics, from museum visits and church gatherings to reflections on local expressions and idioms. The purpose of these prompts is to allow cadets to register common experiences across all study abroad locations (Brazil and Portugal) and to facilitate self-reflection after the occasion. These prompts are not entirely rigid, as the teacher can offer personalized flexibility for content customization based on personal background, life experiences, or unique circumstances. The following example demonstrates this characteristic of OACD using an exchange between a cadet and his teacher aimed at modifying a week-twelve writing task.

Prior to studying in Portugal, Cadet Cole exhibited high levels of proficiency in Portuguese while enrolled in basic and intermediate-level courses. To capitalize on these successes, he chose to further develop his linguistic capabilities during a semester-long immersion at a foreign service academy. According to Cadet Cole, attending the Portuguese Military Academy would provide exposure to a foreign military and potentially enrich his development as a West Point cadet and future Army officer. He expressed a positive attitude and was excited to explore the language and culture of the host nation.

While abroad Cadet Cole diligently completed his weekly LN451 assignments and scored high marks in all his work. In these essays he demonstrated the ability to thrive in a foreign environment while overcoming numerous challenges centered on the Portuguese language and general academics. In the twelfth week of the semester, Cadet Cole was invited to participate in a week-long field training exercise with the Portuguese Army. Since this was a new development in the academy exchange, the LN451 syllabus provided no opportunity to reflect on this unique experience. Instead the prompt for week 12 required cadets to "attend a religious service" and compare the attendees' behaviors and attitudes at the service with those of attendees' experiences at such a service in their hometowns in the United States. Testing the flexibility of the curriculum, Cadet Cole made the following request via email:

> Looking ahead to week twelve, I was wondering if I could write about a different topic. I am not religious and do not know how to compare a religious service in Portugal to one in the U.S. I was wondering if I could instead write about my experience during the academy's field training exercise. I have a lot to say about the differences in the training and tactics. (Cadet Cole, email to teacher)

The teacher concluded that an assignment comparing religious services was not the best fit for Cadet Cole. The field exercise, however, appeared more relatable to his professional goal of becoming an Army officer. As such the teacher agreed to the modification, which better suited the cadet's circumstances "on the ground" and still satisfied the intent of the assignment to compare cultural practices.

In his essay Cadet Cole detailed the differences and similarities between the American and Portuguese military cultures. Some key reflections from the experience, which appeared to challenge his own initial perceptions of the foreign military academy, are as follows:

> One of the biggest differences between West Point and Portuguese Military Academy is that the Portuguese Military Academy conducts military training during the year, not only during the summer. As such, the Portuguese Military Academy cadets can practice [military skills] before going to the field. I thought that this practice would make the field training more efficient, but when we arrived at camp, we did not do much. . . . I thought we would train, but we sat [on our rucksacks] instead . . . when we finally finished the mission, I was happy. We gave each other fist-bumps after six hours of marching. (Essay 12)

As Cadet Cole explained, the highly anticipated field exercise did not entirely fulfill his expectations but still provided a chance for finding common ground between American and Portuguese cadets. He expressed disappointment in how the exercise was ultimately executed but still enjoyed the shared experience of training with his Portuguese counterparts.

> For five days we rested during the day, marched during the night, and completed our missions during the morning. The whole time, our rucksacks were heavy, and the food was horrible. But the cadets and I had a good time because we like being soldiers. I think that American soldiers and Portuguese soldiers are very similar [in this regard]. (Essay 12)

This overall example highlights the personalized flexibility of LN451, a key component of OACD. Here Cadet Cole successfully negotiated with his teacher to modify an existing assignment from the course syllabus. The teacher approved of the change after considering Cadet Cole's own background, interests, and professional goals within the scope of the course. The modification proved fruitful and enabled the cadet to self-reflect on a more meaningful and personal experience during his immersion in Portugal.

Sequential Flexibility in the Spanish Course

LN451 supports a variety of learning approaches. For a number of years the Spanish program included only project-based learning that partnered study abroad students with at-home learners to explore topics related to politics and identity within the host country. Since 2018 the Spanish section has focused on promoting critical reflection and introspection among the study abroad students during their immersion experiences in Mexico, Spain, and Chile. Until recently, only one Spanish study abroad location utilized LN451, and students were assigned a schedule of sequenced topics to complete that encouraged iterative reflection. Cadets often wrote about similar experiences, given that they were spending the majority of their time together and generally followed the prescribed weekly assignment schedule. Although rare, requests for time extensions were approved to support topic completion. While the course granted a measure of flexibility, cadets preferred to complete their essays on time and according to schedule.

In the fall of 2019 the Spanish program experimented with increasing learner autonomy by allowing learners to determine which topic they would complete each week. The Spanish course teacher, inspired by the significant flexibility and high level of learner independence that OACD encourages, decided to pilot a version of LN451 that removed the linear sequencing of topics for cadets studying in Spain. In the new model learners were still required to complete nine critical reflection essays to record aspects of experiential learning and transformative developments. Instead of assigning a specific topic to each week, however, the mentor presented learners with a list of thirteen topic prompts at the beginning of the semester. Consequently cadets were then free to complete any nine topics out of thirteen they preferred and could even propose new topics to the teacher, based upon their unique and transformative experiences.

Cadets selected certain topics in common throughout the nine weeks, yet no two cadets chose the same sequence. Additionally not a single learner completed the essays in the numerical order found in the syllabus. Overall two or more learners chose the same topic five of nine weeks. Some similarities in topic selection were obvious. In week 1, for example, multiple cadets chose to reflect on topic one, which asked them to articulate goals for their upcoming semester abroad experience. Other parallels were driven by the cadets' participation in the same experiences. In week 5, for instance, many cadets chose to write on topic seven, "describe a recent trip," after making a journey together. Cadets generally developed their own unique topic sequencing, with no more than four learners sharing a topic in a single week. Additionally at least two learners proposed their own prompts, writing about topics of personal interest as part of their reflective experiences.

While trends emerged in weekly topic choice based on similarities in activities within the group, learners truly crafted their own unique collection of essays, taking the lead on documenting their experiential learning through individual critical reflection. To further increase learner autonomy, the Spanish program experimented with transforming these weekly, discrete essays into a collection of mini chapters using an e-book platform. The platform not only allowed learners to express themselves in text but also required them to curate and enrich these essays with photos, backgrounds, and other media available on the platform.

At the end of the course, through informal feedback, learners expressed appreciation for the more personalized topic sequencing. They also lauded the use of the e-book platform to creatively showcase their transformative experiences through a variety of media. These two additions to LN451 facilitated innovation and learner autonomy and fit squarely within the OACD principles of sequential flexibility and self-directed learning.

Conclusions

As the findings from these three examples demonstrate, the distance learning immersion course LN451 utilizes the flexibility that characterizes OACD to create transformative experiences for study abroad learners through critical reflection. The Russian program's example showcased the modular flexibility of LN451 through one assignment centered on a theater performance where cadets selected plays at different points in the semester that best reflected their own interests and timelines. As a result the cadets were able to achieve stronger connections to the Russophone culture through an individually tailored learning experience (Altman 1979). The Portuguese program's example highlighted how cadets can modify and tailor assignments centered on their prior experiences, future goals, or unique circumstances that occurred during the immersion. Based upon Cadet Cole's interest and professional objectives, participating in and reflecting on a military training exercise, rather than a religious service, made more sense. The decision to modify academic requirements at the individual level showcases how LN451 leverages OACD's flexibility and personalization. The Spanish program's example demonstrated how LN451 promoted learner autonomy through sequential flexibility. Cadets were allowed to arrange their own course assignments based upon a variety of factors, such as personal interest, opportunity, and task relevance (Taylor 2016). Nonlinear task organization, a key component of OACD, ensured that learners were able to reflect on experiences that occurred naturally and in real time rather than through a rigid and contrived format (Chen 2018). In sum the flexible, modular design of the LN451 course, along with its focus on experiential activities and self-reflective assessments, provided excellent opportunities for in-depth cultural and language learning to occur.

These examples from the Russian, Portuguese, and Spanish programs highlight the positive effects of OACD in driving autonomous, learner-centric, and transformative experiences grounded in critical reflection. Critical reflection is key for the development of future Army leaders who are required to function within international and unfamiliar contexts. Study abroad programs in civilian universities may also benefit from utilizing aspects of OACD in their own curricula to promote independent thought, cultural competency, and language development in learners. Future research into OACD in study abroad would benefit from the inclusion of interview data in a longitudinal framework (Rowan-Kenyon and Niehaus 2011) to afford greater nuance in the analysis.

Study Questions

1. If you already have an immersion (study abroad) component to your language course or program, identify the extent to which it is transformative, using the characteristics described in this chapter. Are you seeing transformation in your learners? How might you enhance that transformation further? If you are not seeing transformation, how might you adjust your study abroad design, applying some of the experiences of Maggin et al.?
2. Learners today usually do not arrive in language courses with fully developed reflective skills. How are your learners' skills? How might you enhance their capacity for critical reflection while developing their language and intercultural proficiency?
3. If you are in the initial stages of developing a study abroad program, identify ways in which you can incorporate Maggin et al.'s experience advantageously.

Note

1. This trip took place prior to 2022.

References

Altman, Howard B. 1979. "Foreign Language Teaching: Focus on the Learner." In *Foreign Language Teaching: Meeting Individual Needs*, edited by Howard Altman and C. Vaughan James, 1–16. Oxford: Pergamon Press.
Baralt, Melissa. 2012. "Coding Qualitative Data." In *Research Methods in Second Language Acquisition: A Practical Guide*, edited by Alison Mackey and Susan M. Gass, 222–44. West Sussex: Wiley-Blackwell.
Boyer, Naomi R., Patricia A. Maher, and Suzanne Kirkman. 2006. "Transformative Learning in Online Settings: The Use of Self-Direction, Metacognition, and Collaborative Learning." *Journal of Transformative Education* 4, no. 4: 335–61.
Campbell, Christine. 2018. "Introduction to Proceedings of the 'Actualizing Open Architecture in the Classroom' Summit." *Dialog on Language Instruction* 28, no. 1: 27–8.
Campbell, Christine. 2021. "Open Architecture Curricular Design: A Fundamental Principle of Transformative Language Learning and Teaching." In *Transformative Language Learning and Teaching*, edited by Betty Lou Leaver, Dan E. Davidson, and Christine Campbell, 43–50. Cambridge: Cambridge University Press.
Chen, Yali. 2018. "Using Authentic Materials in Teaching Language." *Dialog on Language Instruction* 28, no. 1: 45–51.
Derderian, Ani. 2017. "Designing for Teaching and Learning in an Open World: Task Supported Open Architecture Language Instruction." *International Journal of Adult Vocational Education and Technology* 8, no. 3: 55–67.
Kolb, Alice Y., and David A. Kolb. 2005. "Learning Styles and Learning Spaces: Enhancing Experiential Learning in Higher Education." *Academy of Management Learning & Education* 4, no. 2: 193–212.
Leaver, Betty Lou. 1989. "Dismantling the Classroom Walls for Increased Foreign Language Proficiency." *Foreign Language Annals* 22, no. 1: 67–74.
Mezirow, Jack. 2000. "Learning to Think like an Adult: Core Concepts of Transformation Theory." In *Learning as Transformation: Critical Perspectives on a Theory in Progress*, edited by Jack Mezirow and Associates, 3–34. San Francisco: Jossey-Bass.

Mezirow, Jack. 2016. "Transformative Learning Theory." In *Transformative Learning in Practice: Insights from Community, Workplace, and Higher Education*, edited by Jack Mezirow and Edward W. Taylor, 18–31. San Francisco: Jossey-Bass.

Murphy, Linda. 2005. "Critical Reflection and Autonomy: A Study of Distance Learners of French, German and Spanish." In *Distance Education and Languages: Evolution and Change*, edited by Börje Holmberg, Monica Shelley, and Cynthia White, 20–39. Clevedon: Multilingual Matters.

Rowan-Kenyon, Heather T., and Elizabeth K. Niehaus. 2011. "One Year Later: The Influence of Short-Term Study Abroad Experiences on Students." *Journal of Student Affairs Research and Practice* 48, no. 2: 213–28.

Stovicek, Thomas. 2018. "An Open Architecture Approach to Individualized Instruction." *Dialog on Language Instruction* 28, no. 2: 9–22.

Tarrant, Michael A. 2010. "A Conceptual Framework for Exploring the Role of Studies Abroad in Nurturing Global Citizenship." *Journal of Studies in International Education* 14, no. 5: 433–51.

Taylor, Edward. W. 2016. "Fostering Transformative Learning." In *Transformative Learning in Practice: Insights from Community, Workplace, and Higher Education*, edited by Jack Mezirow and Edward W. Taylor, 3–17. San Francisco: Jossey-Bass.

Part 4
OACD in Academe

9

Using OACD and Macrostrategies Frameworks to Enable the Practical Application of Sociocultural Theory in a College Russian Course

JEFF R. WATSON

SOCIOCULTURAL THEORY IN RELATION to language learning (SCT-L2) represents a holistic description of second language acquisition that encompasses the cognitive functions, that is, Vygotsky's "higher mental functions" (Vygotsky 1997), sociocultural variables, and individual differences of L2 learners. According to SCT-L2 intentional classroom language learning should be fostered in an environment in which there is a "unity of perception, speech, and action" (Vygotsky 1978), keeping in mind that language learning behavior, indeed, all "behavior results from the integration of socially and culturally constructed forms of mediation into human activity" (Lantolf 2000). SCT-L2 is informed by three core concepts that underly SCT theory: (1) *mediated learning*, (2) *internalization*, and (3) *zone of proximal development*[1] (Lantolf and Pavlenko 1995; Lantolf 2006). Of importance to second language acquisition is the belief that language learning is a socially mediated activity. Mediated learning leads to *internalization* through the engagement of higher mental functions, also known as higher-order thinking skills (Bloom et al. 1956). Intentional language acquisition can be defined, then, as a mediated process in which human mediators (teachers, peers, and others) assist learners in using and assimilating symbolic mediators (in the sense of SCT: learning environment, learning tasks, curricula, textbooks, authentic materials) in order for the learners to internalize the L2 (Kozulin 2003; Byrnes 2002). The human mediators must operate in the zone of proximal development, in which a more knowledgeable interlocutor assists a less knowledgeable one.

In the classroom environment where SCT-L2 is actualized, learners have opportunities to mediate their learning through self-regulation and interaction with mediating tools. L2 learning in such an environment is considered to be of a "transcendent character" (Kozulin 2003, 22), meaning that it provides broader developmental benefits such as learner autonomy, self-regulation, and increased learner motivation (van Lier 1996, 2000; Dörnyei 2005).

As the preceding paragraphs indicate, the level of abstraction in the SCT-L2 literature has tended to hinder the actualization of the type of classroom environment that it seeks to promote (Lantolf and Poehner 2014), and little research has been conducted on ways to holistically translate SCT-L2 with its various principles into practice. The study described in this chapter examines one instance of the practical application of SCT-L2 through the use of both OACD and macrostrategies frameworks in supplementary modules in a second-year college Russian course at Bryn Mawr College.

OACD as an Enabler for SCT-L2

OACD principles, specifically the ongoing learner involvement in the selection and delivery of content and the design or directing of activities—align practically with SCT-L2, through the manner in which OACD shapes learner interaction (with other learners or with other mediating tools in the learning environment), motivation, and autonomy. The OACD framework is inherently learner-focused, enabling the promotion of learner autonomy and self-regulation (Campbell 2018) as well as task-, content-, project-, and scenario-based learning (Derderian 2017; Corin 2020). The learning opportunities in this environment are affordances (van Lier 2000)—teacher-guided learning activities that allow learners to choose from a variety of specifically created interactive and collaborative learning tasks or scenarios that best meet their learning needs. This further promotes the self-regulation that will allow learners to best take control of their own learning in various task- or scenario-based contexts.

Macrostrategies and OACD in the Exploitation of SCT-L2

According to Kumaravadivelu (2003), a macrostrategy is "a broad guideline, based on which teachers can generate their own situation-specific, need-based, microstrategies or classroom techniques" (38). In the study described in this chapter, the practical application of SCT-L2 was made possible through the use of macrostrategies in supplementary OACD-based modules in a second-year college Russian course. Five macrostrategies informed course structure:

1. Foster and enhance learner self-awareness
2. Account for individual differences to promote strategic self-regulation
3. Provide learning affordances
4. Facilitate collaborative problem-solving
5. Foster multidimensional language awareness

Foster and Enhance Learner Self-awareness

Donato and McCormick (1994) state that learners become "competent members of a language learning community" through their individual "ability to develop, reflect upon, and refine their own learning strategies" (453). Gillette (1994) further states that learners' goals and motivations determine "their strategic approaches to language learning" (196). Teachers in an OACD environment are mentors, coaches, and advisors (Campbell 2021) who help learners to identify their goals and personal learning strategies and style, which in turn influences the type of behavior they exhibit during the language learning process.

Account for Individual Differences to Promote Strategic Self-Regulation
Once learners identify their goals, motivations, strategies, and style preferences, they can be advised by teachers in the OACD environment about how to understand those differences in order to take charge of the learning process and set meaningful goals. This self-regulation is optimized through transformation of the classroom—no longer a place learners go primarily to receive and manipulate input but instead an environment where they are encouraged to "stretch themselves" (i.e., to adapt to learning activities that do not match their specific preferences), reflect on past performance, self-assess and set new goals, develop a broad repertoire of learning strategies to reach their goals, and understand that achievement and further development can be attained by continuously renewing this cycle of activity (Donato and McCormick 1994, Oxford 2016).

Provide Learning Affordances
Learning affordances are situations that provide (or *afford*) learning opportunities selected and acted upon individually by the learner according to what the learner finds relevant. Van Lier (2000) states that an affordance "affords further action (but does not cause or trigger it)" (252). In light of SCT-L2, this shifts the focus in curricular design away from the necessity of specific or contextualized linguistic input toward the activity that a learner engages in. Affordances situate learners in a linguistic, cultural, historical, and social environment that allows learners to identify the property of that environment most relevant to them and then to act upon it. OACD, with its principles of ongoing learner involvement in the design and delivery of content and the design and delivery of activities, provides learners with ample affordances through a variety of task-, content-, project-, or scenario-based classroom activities (Corin 2020).

Facilitate Collaborative Problem-Solving
The basis for Vygotsky's zone of proximal development is the belief that interaction between a more competent or knowledgeable interlocutor, an *expert*, and a less competent one, a *novice*, facilitates the transfer of knowledge from the social plane to the cognitive plane (i.e., internalization) (Antón 1999). Although this novice-expert paradigm is helpful, other studies have shown that novice-novice and/or expert-expert collaborations can be equally helpful (Donato and McCormick 1994; Ohta 1995). The OACD classroom helps learners deal with cognitive and affective challenges when learning the L2 by promoting *collaborative problem-solving* that can facilitate the internalization of the behavior attended to in the task. Such collaboration can take place in both native and target languages depending on the proficiency of the learner. This approach provides learners the assistance needed until they "become self-regulated" and their "performance becomes automatized" (Antón 1999, 304). It may also aid in dealing positively

with the "disorienting dilemmas and ... cognitive distortions" (Campbell 2021) of language learning and inhibit "premature stabilization of interlanguage forms" (i.e., fossilization) (Byrnes 2002). The role of language as a social problem-solving tool in the first language is then extended to foster development in the target language.

Teach Multidimensional Language Awareness
Multidimensional language awareness incorporates not merely the form and function of a piece of language but also awareness of its sociocultural, historical, ideological, and other genre-specific aspects—in other words, the cultural embeddedness of language. Language is not simply "a system of forms, to which meanings are then attached" but is more accurately, as Halliday (1994) asserts, "a system of meanings, accompanied by forms through which the meanings can be realized" (xiv). With this assertion in mind, Byrnes (2001, 2002, 2005) suggests a systemic-functional approach to language curriculum design that aligns well with OACD principles in which cultural awareness and intercultural competence are important goals. In this approach, language course content is authentic, preferably unadapted, and taught in functional areas (i.e., areas of language use in social context) according to the complexity of the function's genre (i.e., the way in which social context informs language use). Byrnes (2005) claims that a genre includes not only literary forms (e.g., poems, narratives, short stories, novels, and plays) but also any oral, written, pragmatic, and functional forms, public or private (e.g., appointment making, service encounters, and news broadcasts). Such an extended definition and use of genre would include a focus on grammar when appropriate but would also allow for a more holistic integration and synthesis of culture, history, environment, and ideology into the language curriculum. This aligns well with the OACD classroom, which strives to be immersive and focuses on building intercultural competence.

Using OACD and Macrostrategies Frameworks to Develop Supplementary Modules in a Second-Year College Russian Course: A Study

The study described here hypothesized that combining the OACD and macrostrategies frameworks to develop supplementary modules within a textbook-based course can enable the practical application of SCT-L2.

Participants and Timeline
The study involved an intensive, second-year, college Russian course meeting seven hours a week for one semester. Five hours per week were dedicated to vocabulary and grammar reinforcement and practice while two hours were dedicated to conversation and culture. Five learners (four sophomores, one freshman) were enrolled in the course, which used *Russian Stage Two: Welcome Back* (Martin 2001).

Integration Process and Course Phases
The integration of the OACD principle of *ongoing learner involvement in the selection and delivery of content and design and directing of activities* into the course occurred mainly during the

USING OACD AND MACROSTRATEGIES FRAMEWORKS 123

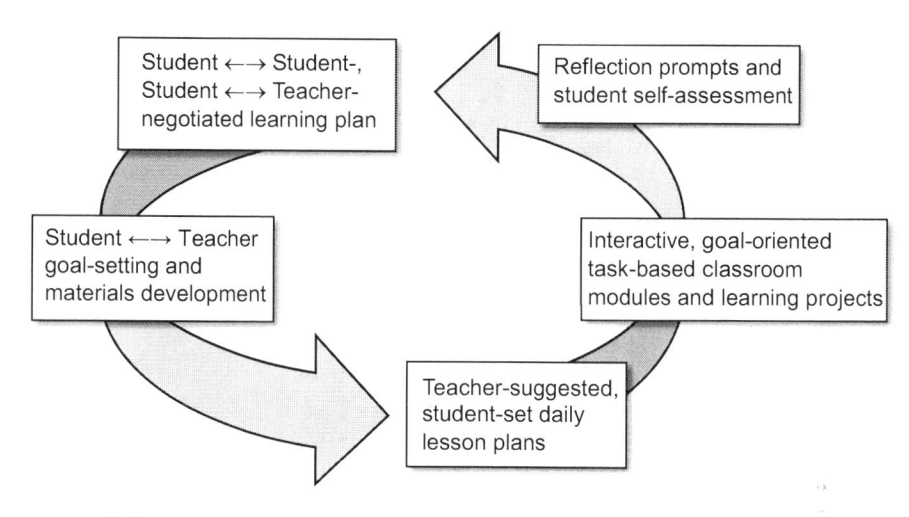

Figure 9.1. OACD integration in the learning environment

hours otherwise devoted to vocabulary and grammar teaching and reinforcement, with only limited integration during the conversation sections. The learners were exposed to the five in-class phases (see Figure 9.1) of the integration process, approximately three to four hours per week, with the variance due mainly to the amount of material to be learned and to the unit quiz and exam schedule. In addition, learners were asked to write reflection essays out of class approximately one additional hour per week.

The process in Figure 9.1 fostered the development of a fluid learning plan, that is, a learner-teacher negotiated plan that could be readily changed on a monthly, weekly, or even daily basis should the learners and teacher feel it necessary to accommodate learners' zone of proximal development, among other reasons. This process (minus the initial learner training) was repeated whenever a new unit was started throughout the semester:

1. *Preplanning phase—Learner strategy and self-awareness training:* Learning strategies and awareness of one's learning style are cognitive and metacognitive "tools" that mediate a learner's interaction with other people and with other semiotic tools (tasks, materials, texts) within a language learning environment. This training was included as a preliminary step prior to beginning coursework with the goal of improving learning choices made during the course. In this phase learners were administered surveys to elicit self-assessment of their learning strategies and styles (see Appendix A for the Perceptual Learning Styles Survey). Each survey contained twenty-two to twenty-five statements with a seven-point Likert scale followed by a self-evaluation section in which the learners could evaluate their responses to better understand what conclusions they might draw from their responses. Class discussion was held after each survey to allow questions to be asked and thoughts to be shared.
2. *Goal-setting phase—The learning plan:* Explicit goal setting in the OACD classroom provides another tool to help mediate learners' interaction in and with their

environment. Since second-year Russian during this time used the *Russian Stage Two: Welcome Back* (Martin 2001) textbook, which presents a daily schedule of review topics, the envisioned modular OACD environment was built on this foundation. At the beginning of each unit, learners completed a learning plan activity to familiarize themselves with the upcoming material as well as give them a chance to reflect on that material and to choose what topics to focus on based on their previous experience (or lack thereof). Each learning plan activity consisted of two sections: (1) a topic list, with learners asked to reflect on which topics they were familiar with to some degree, and (2) a vocabulary and/or grammar list, with learners asked to reflect on which terms and/or grammar features they were (more or less) familiar with. Class discussion was held to flesh out learners' perceptions, understanding of the upcoming material, and readiness to assimilate it, so as to better respond to the learning plan prompts (see Appendix B). Learner responses were then assessed by the teacher to determine which topics needed more attention than others throughout the unit.

3. *Task selection phase—Learner negotiation:* Once a list of prioritized topics from the unit was negotiated, the teacher used the textbook (and other supplementary authentic) materials to create tasks in which the learners learned about the chosen topics. Since SCT-L2 and OACD inherently imply a task-, content-, project-, or scenario-based teaching environment, all learning events were arranged around the completion of one or more tasks or projects. For each negotiated topic, two or three tasks were developed to allow learners a choice based on their varying learning preferences. At the beginning of each class in which a new topic was initiated, the learners were given a task selection handout on which the topic was introduced and on which a brief written description of the tasks they could choose from was presented (see the sample task selection handout in Appendix C). One task might involve more writing (creative focus) while another might involve listening to a recorded audio text and completing an activity (auditory focus). The learners then reflected on their personal learning preferences, chose a task based on this reflection, and negotiated among themselves to find a partner (or two) for work on the task. At first learners were asked not to work alone. The learners were also asked not to all work on the same task, which often required further negotiation. Since the OACD environment promotes learner autonomy, learners were allowed to choose which aspect of the environment (i.e., which task) to interact with. This feature in the process was added specifically to promote activity aligned with macrostrategies three, four, and five as an integrated approach to providing affordances for learner-focused, task-based, problem-solving interaction.

4. *Task completion phase—Learner interaction and collaborative problem-solving:* Each pair (or threesome) selected one task packet and one set of activity instructions requiring them to work together and interact using a specific type of interaction that van Lier (2002) calls *triadic interaction*, two or more learners working together in conjunction with a semiotic tool of some kind (a computer, text, CD player, etc.). Each task typically involved three sections: (1) a topic presentation section, (2) an interactive activity section, and (3) a classroom discussion section. The

learners worked in pairs (or threesomes) to complete their chosen tasks (with teacher involvement, modeling, and corrective feedback as needed). Using the guidelines provided, they prepared and gave a short presentation to the class about what they had learned from the task. A full-class discussion followed to reinforce and practice learned material jointly. This was carried out in both Russian and English as needed. Each unit consisted of several of the task-selection and task-completion activities based on the number of topics chosen to be covered from the learning plan for that unit.

5. *Task reflection phase—Learner retrospection and introspection:* Following most of the units, learners were assigned one or two reflection prompts to elicit more self-assessment of their learning experiences. Each reflection essay prompt was specifically structured to elicit information about learners' motivations, use of learning strategies, perceptions of the learning process, and so on (see Appendix D). This aspect of the course was designed to promote learner reflection as an interaction-mediating cognitive tool and to elicit emic data—that is, data on how the participants understand the meaning of the interaction they participated in.

Learner Interviews—Learner Awareness and Motivation Check

At the end of the semester, the research practitioner interviewed each participant to elicit reflections, feelings, and perceptions concerning motivation before and after the course, motivation to study further, as well as any thoughts on the effectiveness of the course environment. These interviews were digitally recorded and later analyzed.

Results

Throughout the study insights were gained into the practical application of SCT-L2 through the use of OACD and macrostrategies frameworks to develop supplementary modules within a textbook-based course. Specifically examined was the OACD principle of *ongoing learner involvement in the selection and delivery of content and design and directing of activities ("ongoing learner involvement" hereafter)*. Direct teacher observation of learner performance and written reflections were the main source of insights, in addition to analysis of the videotaped interviews. These insights were either immediately incorporated into the design for improvement purposes or noted for consideration later. Overall OACD seemed uniquely capable of promoting many of the learning behaviors supported in the SCT-L2 literature. The modular design successfully led most learners to a higher awareness of the learning process and encouraged them to make sense of it, take control of it, and self-regulate within it.

During an end-of-course interview, learners were asked to assess their likes or dislikes regarding their own *ongoing involvement* in the task selection activities, the learning plan activities, and the reflection entries using a scale of one to five (five being a high level of like and one being a high level of dislike). Overall learner perception was positive (three or above) with only one learner expressing some indifference as to the reflection opportunities offered in class. See Table 9.1.

Table 9.1. Learner likes or dislikes

	Learner Likes or Dislikes (on a scale of 1-5)	
S1:	Task selection activities	3.5
	Learning plan activities	3.5
	Reflection entries	2
S2:	Task selection activities	5
	Learning plan activities	4
	Reflection entries	5
S3:	Task selection activities	2.5
	Learning plan activities	3
	Reflection entries	3.5
S4:	Task selection activities	4.5
	Learning plan activities	3
	Reflection entries	3
S5:	Task selection activities	4
	Learning plan activities	4.5
	Reflection entries	4.5

The impact of the integration of the OACD principle of *ongoing learner involvement*, based on analysis of learner feedback in their reflection essays, the end-of-course survey, and interviews, is summarized and discussed as follows in terms of the five macrostrategies identified previously:

1. *Promoting learner autonomy:*
   The learner surveys used in the learner training phase as well as the learning plans and task selection activities were designed to facilitate learner autonomy. After familiarization with these processes, as learners progressed through the course, they exhibited more autonomy in collaborating and negotiating the goal-setting and decision-making processes. In their reflection essays, learners reported increased self-awareness of their preferences throughout the course with only one learner reporting that she perceived these elements as primarily only useful "to understand what the teachers were thinking." In some cases learner completion of the reflection prompt activities did not always correspond to expectations. In hindsight, these prompts, though structured, could have been more effective in promoting the message of increasing learner self-awareness and eliciting more detailed reflections on the more relevant aspects of the OACD learning environment (see Appendix D).

2. *Accounting for individual differences:*
   The course elements designed to take account of individual differences seemed to work well. Learners reported looking forward to these tasks and enjoyed being a part of the decision-making process at the beginning of each unit.

3. *Providing learning affordances:*
   Many of the course activities were structured to provide learners with choices on how to process required language material in ways that were most relevant to them and that would motivate further study outside of class and in the future. In terms of the former, as mentioned previously, learners enjoyed the decision-making and reflective aspects of the OACD environment. In regard to the latter, the use of authentic Russian-language music, poetry, and websites during the course tasks also proved highly motivating. Learners requested lyrics and copies of the Russian music used in class and reported completing follow-up activities outside of class using the internet to research Russian music and film. Certain activities used during class tasks, such as using a search engine to verify the correct context for a word or phrase, were picked up by learners, who reported using them in their personal language learning initiatives going forward.
4. *Facilitating collaborative problem solving:*
   Collaborative scaffolding and problem solving as a goal of the interactive tasks in the study was observed often and worked well as a learning tool. After several instances of requiring learners to collaborate to complete the task exercises, it became clear that with certain activities some learners would respond better to a task environment in which they could work individually first and then collaboratively in their pair or group to compare answers and discuss differences. This change, combining individual work with collaborative work in the same pair or group, was very well received by the learners and was used as the norm in the remaining task completion phases of the course. This observation seems to support Chaiklin (2003) in that task-based activities work well to activate learning in learners' zone of proximal development by observing what they can accomplish individually followed by what they can accomplish through interaction and/or collaboration with others and then adjusting curriculum and task to account for it.
5. *Promoting multidimensional language awareness:*
   Although one cannot hope to develop multidimensional language awareness, as described previously, in one course alone, steps were taken to raise awareness of the language's multifaceted cultural embeddedness by incorporating authentic materials from a wide variety of historical, cultural, and genre-specific sources. While the genres of music and poetry were used frequently during the course, other literary and speech genres came into play as well, including newspaper excerpts, political opinions, and historical film analysis. Russian music, popular and otherwise, was used frequently in class not only as the main focus for listening and oral practice but sometimes as soft background music during task completion to promote a sense of "immersion." Furthermore learners were encouraged to find and bring in their own Russian music for this purpose. The learners responded well to these course elements, and OACD allowed for this flexibility and creativity.

Discussion

Here findings suggest that using OACD and macrostrategies frameworks to develop supplementary modules within a textbook-based course can enable the practical application of SCT-L2. In future iterations it will be imperative to increase efficiency in material preparation. While the OACD-based framework worked well for the purposes of this study, the initial effort of preparing the learning plans, the negotiated task activity handouts, and the multiple task worksheets based on the course materials was intensive and time-consuming because it required the quick creation of two or three alternative sets of activities based on the learning preferences and strategy sets exhibited by the learners. When given a textbook as organized and comprehensive as *Russian Stage Two: Welcome Back* (Martin 2001), some teachers may be unwilling or unable to devote the time needed to develop a large amount of supplementary materials for each unit. To mitigate the time challenge while promoting the OACD principle of *ongoing learner involvement*, teachers can ask the learners to co-create the materials or at least draw them into the process of defining them. Corin (2020, 2021) speaks to the time issue, arguing that a complete integration of OACD principles into a course, versus a partial one, achieves flexibility in a manner that limits demands on teachers and course developers.

Furthermore, while the supplementary tasks used in this study were thoughtfully created to elicit specific behaviors from the learners and encourage learning in the zone of proximal development, "(t)ask design . . . ultimately cannot determine the nature of the activity engaged in by learners" (Ohta 2000, 76). In the study, unexpected activity was observed on occasion—for example, journal prompts that elicited unexpected feedback based on an individual learner's unanticipated (mis)perceptions, or task selection activities that resulted in unexpected learner interaction within ensuing pair/group work. Since learner perceptions and their subsequent reactions based on those perceptions are vital concepts in the language classroom, the lessons learned about the tasks can inform future studies.

The simultaneous application of both the OACD and macrostrategies frameworks discussed previously present practical challenges for the K-16 practitioner. One approach the language educator interested in experimenting might take is to integrate OACD principles in one course, then macrostrategies in another, ultimately deciding whether to combine the two in a third iteration.

Conclusions

The study described in this chapter presents a small sample of participant data from a more in-depth study that includes a quantitative analysis of treatment and nontreatment group proficiency tests. The current findings, based on extensive learner feedback through reflection essays, surveys, and interviews, provide useful insights for designing future studies focused on the practical application of SCT-L2. The findings suggest that using both the OACD and macrostrategies frameworks to develop supplementary modules within a textbook-based course can enable the practical application of SCT-L2 and, ultimately, benefit learning.

Study Questions

1. If you are currently using a textbook, identify the juncture points at which you can add macrostrategies to create greater learner affordances. Do they fit in

easily—or do you have to make some adaptations, either to the textbook or to your classroom practices? What would these adjustments look like?
2. Explore more deeply. What kinds of motivations do your learners exhibit? How skilled are they in self-regulation and learner autonomy? How can you use macrostrategies to help them become highly motivated, expert learners?
3. Be creative. Even if you must use a textbook for a variety of reasons, how can you take advantage of the principles of OACD and the advantages of macrostrategies to provide a more individualized, flexible learning experience for your learners?

Note

1. The zone of proximal development "is the distance between a learner's actual developmental level as determined by independent problem-solving and the level of potential development as determined by what they can learn through problem-solving under adult guidance or in collaboration with more capable peers" (Vygotsky 1978, 86).

Appendix A: Sample Learner Profile Survey: Perceptual Learning Styles
Intermediate Russian-Learning Styles Survey

Directions: Read the following statements and give your honest response by circling the appropriate number, then go on to the next section to see how to compile and interpret your score. Be sure to respond quickly, without pausing to think too much; your first thought will be the best.

> 1 = completely disagree
> 2 = strongly disagree
> 3 = disagree
> 4 = undecided
> 5 = agree
> 6 = strongly agree
> 7 = completely agree

1) I learn things best when the teacher explains them to me.	1	2	3	4	5	6	7
2) I remember new words best when they are written on the blackboard.	1	2	3	4	5	6	7
3) I learn better when my hands are occupied.	1	2	3	4	5	6	7
4) I learn a lot from participating in role plays.	1	2	3	4	5	6	7
5) I understand best when the teacher tells me what to do.	1	2	3	4	5	6	7
6) I prefer to read about something first before it is explained to me in class.	1	2	3	4	5	6	7
7) I study best by making drawings and diagrams of what I am learning.	1	2	3	4	5	6	7
8) I remember things longer when I have read about them in a book rather than heard about them in class.	1	2	3	4	5	6	7
9) My favorite kind of learning is doing experiments.	1	2	3	4	5	6	7
10) I learn lists of vocabulary in a book quite easily.	1	2	3	4	5	6	7
11) Copying words and sentences from the blackboard into my notebook is a very useful exercise for me.	1	2	3	4	5	6	7
12) I like to read aloud sentences and dialogues from the textbook.	1	2	3	4	5	6	7
13) In order to make progress with a new topic of study, I will read anything I can lay my hands on.	1	2	3	4	5	6	7
14) I am not a particularly good speller in any language.	1	2	3	4	5	6	7
15) Repeating words and phrases after the teacher is a very useful activity for me.	1	2	3	4	5	6	7
16) I prefer to practice dialogs and conversations by acting them out.	1	2	3	4	5	6	7

USING OACD AND MACROSTRATEGIES FRAMEWORKS

17) My friends tell me I am a good listener.	1 2 3 4 5 6 7
18) I learn more by reading textbooks than by listening to lectures.	1 2 3 4 5 6 7
19) I like to use a lot of gestures when practicing speaking a new language.	1 2 3 4 5 6 7
20) I like to learn things by listening to audiotapes, for example, when I am driving.	1 2 3 4 5 6 7
21) I intend to get my hands on as many types of radio broadcasts and other types of speech in a foreign language as I can.	1 2 3 4 5 6 7
22) When I do a grammar exercise from a textbook, I like to copy out the whole sentence for extra practice.	1 2 3 4 5 6 7
23) I enjoy making things for a class project.	1 2 3 4 5 6 7
24) I really enjoy playing charades.	1 2 3 4 5 6 7
25) I learn a lot from doing hands-on projects.	1 2 3 4 5 6 7

Part II: Scoring and Interpretation

Write your score for each item in the spaces below, then add up the total for each category. Divide the total by the number of items in the category as indicated and write the result in the spaces at the bottom of the page.

VISUAL
Item 2 = _____
  6 = _____
  8 = _____
  13 = _____
  18 = _____
TOTAL _____
÷ 5 = _____

AUDITORY
Item 1 = _____
  5 = _____
  14 = _____
  17 = _____
  20 = _____
  21 = _____
TOTAL _____
÷ 6 = _____

MECHANICAL
Item 3 = _____
  7 = _____
  11 = _____
  12 = _____
  15 = _____
  22 = _____
  25 = _____
TOTAL _____
÷ 7 = _____

KINESTHETIC
Item 9 = _____
  16 = _____
  19 = _____
  23 = _____
  24 = _____
TOTAL _____
÷ 5 = _____

Average Scores
VISUAL _____ AUDITORY _____ MECHANICAL _____ KINESTHETIC _____

These scores might be interpreted as follows:

5.3 – 7.0 = Major learning style preference
3.6 – 5.2 = Minor learning style preference
1.0 – 3.5 = Not a significant preference

Appendix B: Sample Learning Plan
Learning Plan: Unit 6

Часть А
В этой главе, мы будем рассматривать следующие темы:

  how to be a guest in a Russian setting / how to receive guests graciously
  how to express your reactions and evaluations
  how to use the preposition ПО + dative
  how to express <u>doubt</u>, <u>certainty</u>, or <u>hope</u> about the likelihood of something
  how to state your intentions
  how to talk about famous people
  how to use кто-то/что-то and *кто-нибудь/что-нибудь*

REFLECT: First, think about your experience (or lack thereof) with these topics (they are not all new). Then, please put 1 – 7 next to the topics in their order of familiarity to you (1=most interesting, 7=least interesting). In other words, which of these topics are you more familiar with and which ones are you less familiar with? Rank them from 1 to 7.

Часть Б
В этой главе, мы будем также изучать следующие выражения/слова:

- брать интервью
- быть в гостях (у кого-то) / ходить в гости (кому-то)
- играть роль
- кстати
- Не за что (not to be confused with ни за что)

- Проходите. Будьте как дома.
- Прошу (вас)!
- Умоляю вас!
- Какими судьбами!
- Надо + verb
- О том, что…
- Работать над чем…

- Profession names such as:
  - актёр (актриса)
  - секретарша
  - учитель
  - милиционер
  - композитор
  - официант(ка)

USING OACD AND MACROSTRATEGIES FRAMEWORKS

- Adjectives used for describing famous people:
  - *великий*
  - *замечательный*
  - *известный*
  - *классный*
  - *профессиональный*
  - *бывший*

- Short form adjectives: ***знаком(а)(ы), уверен(а)(ы)***
- Verbs like:
  - *ждать-подождать*
  - *задавать-задать*
  - *продавать-продать*
  - *участвовать*
  - *репетировать*
  - *советовать(ся)*
  - *сомневаться*
  - *случиться*
  - *надеяться*
  - *посылать-послать*

REFLECT: First, put a plus sign (+) next to any of the above phrases and/or words, verbs, etc. that you are familiar with and a minus sign (−) next to those words, phrases, etc. that you aren't familiar with. Then, put a check mark next to those words, phrases, etc. that you think would be most useful to you (put 2 check marks if you think something would be <u>really</u> useful).

Appendix C: Sample Task Selection Handout
Day 2: быть в гостях / ходить в гости

GOAL: To become familiar with the phrases *быть в гостях у кого-то* (to be a guest at someone's place) and *ходить в гости* (to go to someone's place as a guest)

DIRECTIONS: Read each of the following task synopses and decide which task you want to work on. Think about the following things when making your decision:

- Which of these exercises seems best for my learning style?
- Which of these tasks will benefit me most?
- Which of these tasks is the most interesting to me?

Based on your choice, find a partner or two to work on the task with. (You will need to form two groups—one group of two and one of three.)

Task One: In this task you will be given three short dialogs in which the target phrases are used. You will read these dialogs and answer the follow-up questions that follow. The dialogs will deal with being a guest at someone's home and the language used in such situations.

Task Two: In this task you will type the target phrases into a search engine and find several Russian-language websites where this language is used. You will record several examples from the websites, translate them, and analyze the differences between them as well as the other language used in the same context. *Not as easy as it seems!*

Appendix D: Sample Reflection Prompt and Learner Responses
Weekly Journal 2

Question 1 Reflection Essay Prompt
In as detailed a manner as you can, tell me what you learned this week. Think back to the grammar sessions and conversation sessions. What insights did you gain? Did you get a new understanding of anything that you previously knew (or thought you knew)? What are you still unclear about?

Learner Answers:

S1: I gained a clearer understanding of надо versus нужно. And also when to use должна. They all are similar and for a long time I had mixed up which one takes a logical subject and which one doesn't. I also gained a better understanding of кто-то, etc. The -ся words versus their counterparts are much better understood. I feel like I know better which case they take and in what context to use them. I have never completely gotten the никуда не, etc. format. I feel like I do now. But it will take more usage to make it become a part of my everyday vocab. I could work a little more with ли and how it's used in reported speech.

* * *

S2: I think the topic I learned the most about this week was how to use the two "to meet/invite/etc." verbs. When to use the "-ся" and not and what form the subjects should take on in either case. I was very unclear about all of those rules, but after our worksheet work with those concepts the rules are clearer.

* * *

S3: I'm still really unclear about reported speech. And I'm not really sure about kotorii clauses. But I think I have a much better grasp on to meet/to get acquainted with.

* * *

S4: The main thing I learned was about "to meet," which I think I'd learned differently in high school and mostly forgotten anyway. Since Teacher 1's explanation was different from Teacher 2's understanding, I'd kind of like to hear hers and see if that would gel my understanding of it a bit more. I don't think I remember anything specific from the riddles/poems session, but I did like it best of all the stuff we've done in the last few weeks.

Question 2 Reflection Essay Prompt:
Thinking back about the different lessons that you've been in this year in Russian class, what kind of lesson leaves you the most motivated? In general, what motivates you?

Have any of the lessons this semester given you a strong desire to pursue the topic of that lesson further on your own? Have any of the lessons this week given you a desire to pursue the topics covered further? If so, which ones?

Learner Answers:

S1: I find that I really want to practice ideas or do the exercises in the book or workbook when we do the individual/group diagraming work—where we're given examples and have to figure out the rules. Even if I/we get the rules all wrong the interaction still makes me want to explore it further. I also like the progression of doing those sheets, and then maybe doing something out of the textbook using the same ideas and then seeing the content in the work book. An example from this week would be the exercise I mentioned previously.

* * *

S2: I think the Russian lesson that has left me with this desire to learn or do more with it came last year when we learned the song that the teacher taught us on his guitar. I sang that song over and over because it had such a beautiful melody and I enjoyed getting the pronunciation just right. The lesson we did this week on Russian poems, sayings and riddles was also motivating. The desire to pursue information additionally was not strong enough for me to research any further this weekend, but I feel like it is something that could capture my interest if I came across it again outside of class. I like memorizing the poem last year for Teacher X. It was hard, but it was rewarding to be able to recite several stanzas by memory.

* * *

S3: I really liked the conversation class with the little rhymes, I thought they were very cute, and they're sort of culture as well as translation practice as well as speaking practice. That makes me motivated to like Russian, for instance I read a review of one of my favorite movies in Russian just to see what I could pick out of it.

* * *

S4: I do like the choosing tasks and doing translations or defining how a phrase is used in different sentences. (Actually, I think I just like translations.) I guess the lesson on "to meet" made me realize I need to learn it better on my own, but that was mostly because I'm still not entirely clear on when to use what.

References

Antón, Marta. 1999. "The Discourse of a Learner-Centered Classroom: Sociocultural Perspectives on Teacher-Learner Interaction in the Second-Language Classroom." *Modern Language Journal* 83, no. 3: 303–18.

Bloom, Benjamin S., Max D. Englehart, Edward J. Furst, Walker H. Hill, and David R. Krathwohl. 1956. *The Taxonomy of Educational Objectives, Handbook I: The Cognitive Domain.* New York: David McKay Co., Inc.

Byrnes, Heidi. 2001. "Curriculum Construction at the Post-Secondary Level." Presentation at Summit Conference on the Future of Language Learning. Washington, DC.

Byrnes, Heidi. 2002. "Toward Academic-Level Foreign Language Abilities: Reconsidering Foundational Assumptions, Expanding Pedagogical Options." In *Developing Professional-Level Language Proficiency*, edited by Betty Lou Leaver and Boris Shekhtman, 34–58. Cambridge: Cambridge University Press.

Byrnes, Heidi. 2005. "Perspectives on Curriculum Construction at the Postsecondary Level: Contexts, Approaches, Principles." *Russian Language Journal* 55, no. 1: 143–67.

Campbell, Christine. 2018. "Introduction to Proceedings of the Actualizing Open Architectures in the Classroom Summit." *Dialog on Language Instruction* 28, no. 1: 27–28.

Campbell, Christine. 2021. "Open Architecture Curricular Design: A Fundamental Principle of Transformative Language Learning and Teaching." In *Transformative Language Learning and Teaching*, edited by Betty Lou Leaver, Dan E. Davidson, and Christine Campbell, 43–50. Cambridge: Cambridge University Press.

Chaiklin, Seth. 2003. "The Zone of Proximal Development in Vygotsky's Analysis of Learning and Instruction." In *Vygotsky's Educational Theory in Cultural Context*, edited by Alex Kozulin, Boris Gindis, Vladimir Ageyev, and Suzanne Miller, 39–64. Cambridge: Cambridge University Press.

Corin, Andrew R. 2020. "Open Architecture Curriculum and Transformative Language Learning Revisited. Part 2. Toward a Constrained Definition of OACD." *ACTR Letter* 47, no. 1: 1–2, 4.

Corin, Andrew R. 2021. "Foreign Language Learning Efficiency: Transformative Learning in an Outcomes-Based Environment." In *Transformative Language Learning and Teaching*, edited by Betty Lou Leaver, Dan E. Davidson, and Christine Campbell, 51–60. Cambridge: Cambridge University Press.

Derderian, Ani. 2017. "Designing for Teaching and Learning in an Open World: Task-Supported Open Architecture Language Instruction." *International Journal of Adult Vocational Education and Technology* 8, no. 3: 55–67.

Donato, Richard, and Dawn McCormick. 1994. "A Sociocultural Perspective on Language Learning Strategies: The Role of Mediation." *Modern Language Journal* 78, no. 4: 453–64.

Dörnyei, Zoltán. 2005. *The Psychology of the Language Learner: Individual Differences in Second Language Acquisition*. Mahwah: Lawrence Erlbaum Publishers.

Gillette, Barbara. 1994. "The Role of Learner Goals in L2 Success." In *Vygotskian Approaches to Second Language Research*, edited by James Lantolf, and Gabriela Appel, 195–213. Norwood: Ablex.

Halliday, Michael Alexander Kirkwood. 1994. *An Introduction to Functional Grammar (2nd ed.)*. London: Edward Arnold.

Kozulin, Alex. 2003. "Psychological Tools and Mediated Learning." In *Vygotsky's Educational Theory in Cultural Context*, edited by Alex Kozulin, Boris Gindis, Vladimir Ageyev, and Suzanne Miller, 15–38. Cambridge: Cambridge University Press.

Kumaravadivelu, B. 2003. *Beyond Methods: Macrostrategies for Language Teaching*. New Haven: Yale University Press.

Lantolf, James, ed. 2000. *Sociocultural Theory and Second Language Learning*. Oxford: Oxford University Press.

Lantolf, James. 2006. "Sociocultural Theory and Second Language Learning: State of the Art." *Studies in Second Language Acquisition* 28: 67–109.

Lantolf, James, and Aneta Pavlenko. 1995. "Sociocultural Theory and Second Language Acquisition." *Annual Review of Applied Linguistics* 5: 108–124.

Lantolf, James, and Matthew Poehner. 2014. *Sociocultural Theory and the Pedagogical Imperative in L2 Education*. New York: Routledge.

Leaver, Betty Lou, and Boris Shekhtman, eds. 2002. *Developing Professional-Level Language Proficiency*. Cambridge: Cambridge University Press.

Martin, Cynthia. 2001. *Russian Stage Two: Welcome Back*. Dubuque: Kendall Hunt.

Ohta, Amy. 1995. "Applying Sociocultural Theory to an Analysis of Learner Discourse: Learner-Learner Collaborative Interaction in the Zone of Proximal Development." *Issues in Applied Linguistics* 6: 93–121.

Ohta, Amy. 2000. "Rethinking Interaction in SLA: Developmentally Appropriate Assistance in the Zone of Proximal Development and the Acquisition of L2 Grammar." In *Sociocultural Theory and Second Language Learning*, edited by James Lantolf, 51–78. Oxford: Oxford University Press.

Oxford, R. L. 2016. *Teaching and Researching Language Learning Strategies: Self-Regulation in Context*. New York: Routledge.

van Lier, Leo. 1996. *Interaction in the Language Curriculum: Awareness, Autonomy, & Authenticity*. London: Longman.

van Lier, Leo. 2000. "From Input to Affordance: Social-Interactive Learning from an Ecological Perspective." In *Sociocultural Theory and Second Language Learning*, edited by James Lantolf, 245–60. Oxford: Oxford University Press.

van Lier, Leo. 2002. "An Ecological-Semiotic Perspective on Language and Linguistics." In *Language Acquisition and Language Socialization: Ecological Perspectives*, edited by Claire Kramsch, 140–64. London: Continuum.

Vygotsky, Lev. 1978. *Mind in Society*. Cambridge: Harvard University Press.

Vygotsky, Lev. 1997. *The Collected Works of L. S. Vygotsky: The History of the Development of Higher Mental Functions*. Vol. 4. New York: Springer Science & Business Media.

10

Inter-Institutional Collaboration in Curriculum Development
The Design of Flexible Modules in the Less Commonly Taught Languages Partnership

KOEN VAN GORP, EMILY HEIDRICH UEBEL, AND LUCA GIUPPONI

IN RESPONSE TO DECLINING numbers of students enrolled in world language courses and increasing budgetary constraints, many institutions of higher education have begun to establish inter-institutional collaborative partnerships as a means to increase access and improve performance in language learning, especially for less commonly taught languages. Successful collaborations require a shared vision and commitment from partners at all levels, including a willingness to explore and apply newer approaches to education, such as course sharing and online instruction, and to forefront proficiency-oriented models of learning and teaching. This push toward inter-institutional collaboration has created space for a paradigm shift in programs for the less commonly taught languages by (1) creating a collaborative mindset within and across institutions, programs for the less commonly taught languages, instructors, and even students; and (2) focusing a collaborative effort on creating high-quality and flexible proficiency-oriented practices and curricula.

Since 2016 Michigan State University, supported by the Andrew W. Mellon Foundation, has facilitated the Less Commonly Taught Languages and Indigenous Languages Partnership Project (henceforth Less Commonly Taught Languages Partnership) within the Big Ten Academic Alliance. This project aims to create communities of practice both among less commonly taught languages instructors for particular languages (by establishing working groups for specific less commonly taught languages) and across all instructors of less commonly taught languages of the Big Ten Academic Alliance (through professional development). The working groups collaborate to develop open architecture curricula to support proficiency-oriented pedagogies such as task-based language teaching and project-based language learning[1] and to promote the goal of more learners reaching at least Intermediate High (ILR 1+). To achieve this goal, language pedagogy specialists at Michigan State University team with instructors of less commonly taught languages to help them move beyond their institutional contexts and work with colleagues to develop open educational resources (OERs). In this project the OERs are modules that function as blueprints for curricular organization of courses. This chapter describes how inter-institutional collaboration in curriculum development can produce quality materials for less commonly taught languages like the OACD-enabled OER modules.

Key Challenges in Less Commonly Taught Languages Instruction Today

Changes in Enrollment

Enrollment in languages other than English continues to drop in US colleges and universities. The Modern Language Association Census shows a drop of 9.2% in enrollments between the fall 2013 and fall 2016 census, this being the second-largest decline in the history of the census, which started in 1954 (Looney and Lusin 2018). This steady decline is happening almost uniformly across the fifteen most commonly taught languages; only two (Japanese and Korean) showed a slight increase in enrollment during that time. Less commonly taught languages, which account for 1.8 percent of the overall enrollment figures, showed a small increase in enrollments of 0.2 percent between 2013 and 2016. The Modern Language Association defines less commonly taught languages as all languages not included in the top fifteen most commonly taught languages. As the Modern Language Association report's definition of less commonly taught languages can change from year to year, depending on which languages are the "fifteen most commonly taught" for any given year, a more stable definition of less commonly taught languages is "all languages other than English and commonly taught European languages of German, French and Spanish," a definition which is used by the National Council of Less Commonly Taught Languages.[2]

The Modern Language Association report points out that "[l]ess commonly taught languages] offerings can be fragile and transitory, since the programs tend to be small and may depend on a single instructor" (Looney and Lusin 2018, 3). Looking at the figures, one cannot help but conclude that enrollments in the less commonly taught languages are indeed volatile and vulnerable: ninety-seven of these languages are taught at a single institution, and 164 languages at three institutions or less. A total of forty-three languages were dropped since 2013, and forty-four new languages were added (Charitos 2018). More and more institutions of higher education struggle to keep their language programs overall, with universities losing a "stunning" 651 language programs from 2013 to 2016 (Johnson 2019) due to a variety of factors relating to availability and competencies of instructors of the less commonly taught languages, student interest, and budgetary constraints. For example in the academic year 2019–20, Michigan State University was forced to cut some of its less commonly taught languages courses after a Title VI grant was cut and was only able to reinstate some of these languages with other grant money.

Professional Development Needs

With the ebb and flow (lately more ebb than flow) of course offerings, it is crucial that the learners who need instruction in less commonly taught languages for their studies and future careers have a path to pursue their studies and receive high quality instruction. However given the uncertainty and constant changes in programming, less commonly taught languages programs may resort to short-term hiring of native speakers with limited to no pedagogical background in order to keep offering the language. For those instructors who do have some training, as shown by Johnston and Janus's 2003 survey of teachers of less commonly taught languages in higher education, "many instructors indicated that their primary source of 'training' consisted of the years they had spent in the classroom" (8).

Instructors of less commonly taught languages are often the sole instructors of that language in their institution, with comparatively few resources or opportunities for professional development (Johnston and Janus 2003). As a result, they have to rely on textbooks that, if not already outdated, can be of questionable pedagogical value (more form-focused than reflecting current pedagogical methods) and so do not meet learner needs or bring them to a more advanced level of proficiency (Johnston and Janus 2003).

Even before the Covid-19 pandemic, institutions of higher education were transitioning more and more instruction online, evidenced by the fact that at least one in every three students was enrolled in at least one online course in any given semester (Seaman, Allen, and Seaman 2018). With the number of online or hybrid courses that have continued after the pandemic, instructors of less commonly taught languages face the additional challenge of being asked to develop courses for a hybrid/blended or fully online environment.

More than ever instructors of less commonly taught languages need to be flexible and adapt their teaching to learner needs if they want to keep them motivated to learn the language up to an advanced level of proficiency. This challenge becomes more acute every year, and universities and colleges are looking for new solutions and innovative ways to address instruction in the less commonly taught languages.

Answering the Challenge: Proficiency-Oriented, OACD-Enabled OER Modules Collaboratively Designed by Instructors of Less Commonly Taught Languages from Multiple Institutions

The Less Commonly Taught Languages Partnership wanted to address some of the challenges instructors of less commonly taught languages across the Big Ten Academic Alliance faced. It brought together instructor teams from different languages to develop, collaboratively, OERs aimed at building learner language proficiency to Intermediate High (ILR 1+) and Advanced (ILR 2). Given the uneven professional and pedagogical background of instructors of less commonly taught languages in the project, the Michigan State University team determined that a good starting point for the work would be a community of practice for professional development in which individual practitioners developed skill sets and knowledge while the community developed a collective mindset with a common vision and mission. Communities of practice are "groups of people who share a concern or a passion for something they do and learn how to do it better as they interact regularly" (Wenger-Trayner and Wenger-Trayner 2015). With this in mind, regular professional development opportunities were established to connect instructors from a wide range of less commonly taught languages across the Big Ten Academic Alliance. Professional development efforts focused on topics like OERs, reverse design, the use of authentic materials, task-based language teaching and project-based language learning, alternative assessments, flipped and online pedagogies, and so on. Through two-day workshops and one-and-a-half day symposia, instructors of less commonly taught languages could work together and engage in conversations with pedagogy specialists as well as other instructors of less commonly taught languages, and communities of practice were established that helped support a sustained collaborative effort in creating flexible teaching materials aimed at improving learner language proficiency.

Working to establish the communities of practice and the requisite collaborative efforts was not a simple process. The participants in our working groups felt "getting to hear what other people have to say and getting feedback and comments about [their] work"[3] was beneficial, but they sometimes questioned whether their interactions regarding instructional materials focused too much on negative feedback as opposed to encouragement and whether they were merely cooperating or truly collaborating. Collaborative efforts, like material design, involve an iterative process that needs thought and curation.

The next section will examine how inter-institutional collaboration in curriculum development led to the incorporation of a core OACD principle—the use of a flexible, textbook-free curriculum—in the design and development of OER modules.

Incorporating a Core OACD Principle—The Use of a Flexible, Textbook-Free Curriculum in the Design of Collaboratively Designed OERs Modules

OACD embraces the use of authentic materials and eschews the use of textbooks beyond the acquisition of basic linguistic features of a language. A rather radical departure from tradition for some commonly taught languages, it is not so for learning environments for less commonly taught languages, where materials and textbooks have generally been limited or nonexistent for more advanced language study in many less commonly taught languages. As indicated previously most teachers participating in the project had typically relied on form-focused materials in the past. As a result working to create materials that embodied the tenets of proficiency-oriented language learning was a change from their past practices. For this project the flexible, modular approach facilitated the wider use of the materials. The materials developed as part of the Less Commonly Taught Languages Partnership are freely available on https://lctlpartnership.celta.msu.edu/.

The modules, based on broad themes, made up the theme-based syllabus, with individual units covering topics within each theme. For example a Hindi module on weddings contained units such as matrimonial alliances, traditional wedding announcements, and wedding processionals. A Swahili module helped prepare students for topics they would encounter while studying abroad (see chapters in this volume by Gregory and Soyan for additional examples on how features of OACD can be used to help students prepare for study abroad experiences). Several instructors in the pilot process chose individual units to pilot, fitting them in response to learner interest and as time allowed. Teachers who are looking to implement OACD principles in their classroom can easily use these materials to create a dynamic learning environment characterized by high-leverage teaching practices to align with students' needs, either by using parts of entire module or just one or two units within the module. However these materials were not meant to be static. Unlike materials developed as a part of a traditional publishing process, which have copyright and use restrictions,[4] thus limiting their widespread use or modification, or materials developed by individual teachers that never get shared, the materials developed in the project were designed to be released as OERs once piloting and revision were complete. Following the tenets of OER, which allows users to retain, reuse, revise, remix, and redistribute the content, the Michigan State University team encouraged the working groups to design their materials in such a way that would make it as easy as possible for other teachers to practice these "5 Rs." Particularly relevant to OACD features are the "revise" and "remix" tenets of OERs. Instructors are encouraged not just to choose to insert a unit into their syllabus (although they could do so if needed) but rather to adapt and supplement the content of the unit freely on the occasion of each use, in other words, adapt each unit to their own and students' needs. For more information on how open licenses can be used to allow for the sharing of similar material, see Creative Commons (www.creativecommons.org).

One important consideration for developing open materials is the choice of technology used to create and distribute the materials. As David Wiley, the founder of the OER movement, explains, "poor technical choices [can] make open content less open" (Wiley n.d.). It was essential for teachers to select technologies that would maximize the likelihood the material would be distributed widely. For example publishing learning materials in a format that can only be revised or remixed using tools that are expensive to purchase or license, or that run on an obscure or discontinued platform, practically negates the open nature of these materials. Likewise, publishing materials using platforms that require significant expertise (e.g., Adobe InDesign) or that make it more difficult to edit a published product (e.g., PDF) also reduces openness, and, as a consequence, increases barriers to adoption.

Given these considerations, Michigan State University encouraged the Hindi and Swahili teams to develop and distribute their materials using the Google Drive platform. The platform encourages openness through the following features:

- Real-time multiuser layered collaboration (editing, revising, commenting, and direct communication are embedded in the tool)
- Low to no learning curve
- End-user ability to duplicate, download, and revise/remix within the application
- Free and easily accessible
- Long-term stability and sustainability
- One-click offline backups

The disadvantage to creating materials within Google Docs was the lack of "polish" of the materials. One of the Swahili teachers created modules in Pressbooks, which, while not as open as Google Docs, has the advantage of the ability to integrate interactive activities and has an easily navigable and more pleasing aesthetic appearance. The Michigan State University team worked with teachers and graduate students to create advice for other teachers about how to adapt the more open, but perhaps less aesthetically appealing, materials on Google Docs to their needs, such as putting materials on learning management software platforms.

The next section will explore some of the focal points of the community of practice that are particularly relevant to OACD: reverse design, task-based language teaching and project-based language learning, and alternative assessments. Our discussion will focus on the experiences of the Swahili and Hindi working groups.

Incorporating Reverse Design and Select OACD Features—Task-Based Language Teaching, Project-Based Language Learning, and Alternative Assessments in the Design of Collaboratively Designed OER Modules

Reverse Design
Part of the role of the Michigan State University group was to help guide the working group discussion regarding material design. Giving guidance on pedagogical best practices without impeding the creative process or questioning teacher pedagogical knowledge based on many years of teaching can be a challenge. The Swahili and Hindi working groups went through similar processes to identify topics and levels. First the groups described their learner populations and what kinds of objectives those populations were trying to achieve. For example learners might be enrolled in the language to connect with their heritage or for professional purposes, such as engaging with nongovernment organizations or for fieldwork in their academic discipline. The Michigan State University team asked the working groups to consider topics or themes that might be unique to the cultures where the language is commonly spoken and what obstacles might hinder their ability to get their learners to the Intermediate High or Advanced levels. This analysis of their particular language, its corresponding culture(s), and student demographic primed the working groups to begin the process of reverse design—the design of instructional materials beginning with the end goals in mind. One might argue that reverse design should be implicit in all curricular design, especially open curricula, but the authors found that explicitly leading instructors through the process of identifying barriers and proficiency goals helped instructors think of a broader range of possible materials and how to better meet the needs of their students. Like Oded and Oded (this volume), providing professional development opportunities for instructors was a crucial element of this project. The process of reverse design helps prime teachers to consider learner needs, styles, and interests as they design materials and frameworks that are as open as possible so as to empower learners to engage deeply and in individual ways with the materials. This process is an important tool that teachers can use as they continually and systematically (vs. occasionally and in a limited way) tailor to learner and cohort needs, one of four fundamental principles of OACD.

In order to identify the goals toward which learners would be working, the working groups reviewed the ACTFL proficiency level descriptions (ACTFL 2012) and decided on appropriate levels to target in their materials. Once they identified the proficiency level, they also identified Can-Do statements[5] (see https://www.actfl.org/publications/guidelines-and-manuals/ncssfl-actfl-can-do-statements) they felt should have a particular focus. Individual topics for modules in the theme/topic-based syllabus were left up to the instructors after a number of possibilities were identified jointly by the group. Some of the topics of modules were designed to address particular gaps in learner knowledge (such as preparing them for study abroad or to understand the traditional elements of a cultural wedding), while others arose from a need for the ability to use authentic materials, such as data from fieldwork, that could be adapted to classroom uses. All topics addressed learner needs and were conceptualized with the use of authentic materials in mind. As these modules are created before using them with students, learners did not have input on the creation of the materials but rather could provide input on which themes might get chosen by the instructor to implement; the modular design also allowed for the possibility of switching out particular materials on an as-needed basis during actual use. By adopting reverse design, we noticed that the instructors started to think more about what students needed to do with the language in real life rather than focusing on the grammatical and lexical content of a module. Further discussion of the flexibility and openness of these materials will follow in later sections.

Task-Based Language Teaching

The Michigan State University team also highly encouraged the working groups to operationalize proficiency-oriented instruction in terms of task-based language teaching and project-based language learning and to design assessments in line with the identified Can-Do statements and the real-life tasks they wanted their students to master.

Task-based language teaching has progressively gained support since the early 1990s, and evidence for the impact of tasks on language proficiency development is growing (Bryfonski and McKay 2019; Long 2015). One might argue that task-based language teaching and proficiency-oriented instruction have become synonyms, since proficiency-oriented instruction requires students to demonstrate that they have acquired knowledge and skills, and this is often achieved by having students complete tasks (whether real-life tasks or pedagogical tasks). For example the *ACTFL Proficiency Guidelines* describe the tasks that speakers can handle at each proficiency level (ACTFL 2012). Many scholars have defined "task" differently, but all definitions view a task as primarily a meaning-based activity. Van den Branden (2006) defines a task as "an activity in which a person engages in order to obtain an objective, and which necessitates the use of language" (4). In a strong view of task-based language teaching (Long 2015), the objective to be obtained is a real-life goal that situates the task in a communicative context, often with a communicative problem to solve. Put differently there is some kind of clearly defined outcome that has some sort of relationship to real-world activities (Van Gorp and Bogaert 2006). These principles can be hard for teachers to incorporate in the development of lesson materials (Erlam 2016) or in their actual teaching practices (Vandommele, Van den Branden and Van Gorp 2018).

It took time for some teachers to adjust their more traditional ways of thinking about curricular materials. For example one of the teachers commented: "I was very much the traditional communicative [kind of instructor], but very much focused on how learners learn rather than what kind of actual skill or language solving problem activities they need to do ... what real-life situations that they will encounter." The primary challenges were how to create tasks that, although created for pedagogical purposes, were as close to real-life situations as possible and how to get learners to pay attention, in pre-and post-task activities, to forms they needed to learn. See Krasner (this volume) for additional examples of task-based activities incorporated into a world language classroom.

Project-Based Language Learning
Introducing a project-based approach on top of a task-based approach turned out to be the way forward. Project-based language learning has also been around for a long time and has more recently gained in popularity, as evidenced by the multiple resources provided by the National Foreign Language Resource Center at the University of Hawai'i at Manoa (see https://nflrc.hawaii.edu/projects/view/2014A/). Project-based language learning engages learners "in investigation of authentic problems" (Blumenfeld et al. 1991, 369) and should, according to the Buck Institute for Education that formulated Gold Standard Project Based Learning, include student-oriented goals, a challenging problem or question to solve, sustained student inquiry, authenticity, student voice and choice, reflection, critique and revision, and a public product (see https://www.pblworks.org/what-is-pbl/gold-standard-project-design).

The basic idea of project-based language learning was picked up by the working groups in the Less Commonly Taught Languages Partnership by identifying a project in which learners work toward an overarching specific outcome (for example, writing a brochure comparing higher education in India and the United States or planning a cross-cultural wedding). Such a project allowed them to link a series of tasks that have a unique contribution to the project outcome. This series of tasks allows for contextualized language work and retention of a focus on meaning over a longer stretch of planned teaching (Skehan 2014). Thinking about a project and a clear public product that the learners were working on thus helped shape assessments of the teaching materials the teachers were working on.

Alternative Assessments
It was an adjustment for some of our instructors to steer away from traditional assessments toward an assessment of such a final product, which could effectively show what the learners had actually learned, that is, what learners were able to do with language at the end of the module. Depending on the length of the module and the number of units, a number of products were identified as possible assessment tasks. For example in a unit on climate and weather in East Africa, the following end-of-unit project was formulated to serve as an effective summative and formative assessment tool in addition to learning-related objectives, thus aligning with the OACD feature of minimal use of summative assessments that lie outside the learning process and emphasis on formative ones:

Conduct a research project on natural disasters that have affected: (1) a country in East Africa; and (2) your country. Report on one from each category; what it was, where and when it occurred, its effects, and how it was dealt with. Present your findings to your teacher for assessment.

Five assessment criteria, scored on a four-point scale ranging from "does not meet expectations" to "exceeds expectations" were identified relating to the project and the work done in class:

1. The learner can interpret a weather report in written and spoken forms. *(interpretive listening/reading)*
2. The learner can ask for and provide information about the climate and weather of a place. *(interpersonal speaking)*
3. The learner can interpret and summarize contents of a multimedia presentation on weather, climate, and climate change in writing or speech. *(presentational speaking/writing)*
4. The learner is able to use the existential form "there is/are" to describe the daily weather. *(presentational speaking)*
5. The learner is able to correctly interpret some proverbs related to this topic and their significance to Swahili speakers and integrate the proverbs into written and spoken samples. *(presentational speaking/writing)*

The first three criteria focus on meaning and evaluate learner receptive and productive language skills in terms of the three modes of communication (interpretive, interpersonal, and presentational) as identified by ACTFL. Criteria 4 focuses on both a critical grammatical form appearing in the input provided by the teacher and authentic materials. Criteria 5 focuses on both the form and (cultural) meaning of proverbs connected to the topic/theme of the unit.

Often the focus on form or forms was part of the flipped classroom, that is, the course work at home in preparation for the actual class. The form-focused work was assessed in short quizzes; however, these quizzes evaluated learner mastery of the forms in isolation rather than in real, authentic, contextualized language. Therefore adding formal criteria to the rubric assessing the project-based work enabled the teacher to gauge whether these forms had actually been learned. Furthermore it opened a fruitful conversation between instructors of less commonly taught languages and the Michigan State University team on the role and place of focus on form(s) in proficiency-oriented instruction, on how grammatical forms can be assessed in alternative ways, and on alternative assessments (e.g., the use of tasks, projects, and portfolios for formative and summative purposes) in general.

Conclusions

In general terms, this chapter provides an example of how incorporating one core OACD principle and select OACD features can put OACD into practice in instruction in less commonly taught languages. Specifically it illustrates how the Less Commonly Taught Languages Partnership created several language-specific modules as well as an overall community of practice among teachers of less commonly taught languages across institutions of higher education. Instructors collaboratively developed innovative and flexible task-based and project-based teaching materials and assessments designed to raise learner language proficiency to an advanced level. By making these materials available as OER modules, teachers anywhere can build a curriculum that addresses learner needs and interests.

Study Questions

1. What kinds of pedagogical choices have you encountered that have helped or hindered the openness of instructional materials? In your experience what language proficiency approach (task-based language teaching, project-based language learning, or other) aligns best with OACD principles?
2. When designing materials for the classroom, how can one do reverse design without being authoritarian about curriculum design? Does this change by venue: if you are an administrator, part of a team, or a solo instructor? Outline your own situation, where you currently stand in terms of OACD materials and orientation on a scale from nothing at all to full OACD, and how you will go about reverse designing a revised curriculum with OACD at its core.
3. In working with pre-existing materials, what choices can instructors make to ensure learner needs and interests are addressed? How can learners help? How might in-service leaders, a research team, or program managers support you?

Notes

1. Editorial note: in some other chapters the terms *task-based instruction* and *project-based instruction* are used.
2. https://ncolctl.org/about/frequently-asked-questions/.
3. None of the participants are individually identified in the quotes to protect their privacy. Periodic interviews were conducted with all members of the working groups.
4. See www.copyright.gov for current copyright law, including what constitutes fair use of copyrighted materials in the classroom.
5. The teachers used the 2017 NCSSFL-ACTFL Can-Do Statements.

References

ACTFL (American Council on the Teaching of Foreign Languages). 2012. *ACTFL Proficiency Guidelines*. Alexandria: ACTFL.
Blumenfeld, Phyllis C., Elliot Soloway, Ronald W. Marx, Joseph S. Krajcik, Mark Guzdial, and Annemarie Palincsar. 1991. "Motivating Project-Based Learning: Sustaining the Doing, Supporting the Learning." *Educational Psychologist* 26, no. 3–4: 369–98.
Bryfonski, Lara, and Todd H. McKay. 2019. "TBLT Implementation and Evaluation: A Meta-Analysis." *Language Teaching Research* 23, no. 5: 603–32.
Charitos, Stephane. 2018. "The Future of Language Study in the U.S. Short-Term Crisis or Permanent Plight?" Presentation at the Shared LCTL Symposium, Rosemont, IL, September 2018.
Erlam, Rosemary. 2016. "'I'm Still Not Sure What a Task Is': Teachers Designing Language Tasks." *Language Teaching Research* 20, no. 3: 279–99. https://doi.org/10.1177/1362168814566087.
Johnson, Steven. 2019. "Colleges Lose a 'Stunning' 651 Foreign-Language Programs in 3 Years." 2019. *The Chronicle of Higher Education*, January 22, 2019. https://www.chronicle.com/article/colleges-lose-a-stunning-651-foreign-language-programs-in-3-years/.

Johnston, Bill, and Louis Janus. 2003. "Teacher Professional Development for the Less Commonly Taught Languages." Accessed August 1, 2019. https://files.eric.ed.gov/fulltext/ED479299.pdf.

Long, Mike. 2015. *Second Language Acquisition and Task-Based Language Teaching*. Malden: Wiley Blackwell.

Looney, Dennis, and Natalia Lusin. *Preliminary Report. Enrollments in Languages Other Than English in United States Institutions of Higher Education, Summer 2016 and Fall 2016: Preliminary Report*. Accessed August 1, 2019. https://www.mla.org/content/download/83540/2197676/2016-Enrollments-Short-Report.pdf.

Seaman, Julie E., I. Elaine Allen, and Jeff Seaman. 2018. *Grade Increase: Tracking Distance Education in the United States*. Accessed August 1, 2019. https://onlinelearningsurvey.com/reports/gradeincrease.pdf.

Skehan, Peter. 2014. "Limited Attentional Capacity, Second Language Performance, and Task-Based Pedagogy." In *Processing Perspectives on Task Performance*, edited by Peter Skehan, 211–60. Amsterdam: John Benjamins. https://doi.org/10.1075/tblt.5.

Vandommele, Goedele, Kris Van den Branden, and Koen Van Gorp. 2018. "Task-Based Language Teaching. How Task-Based Is It Really?" In *TBLT as a Researched Pedagogy*, edited by Virginia Samuda, Martin Bygate, and Kris Van den Branden, 165–97. Amsterdam: John Benjamins. https://doi.org/10.1075/tblt.12.07van.

Van den Branden, Kris. 2006. "Introduction: Task-Based Language Teaching in a Nutshell." In *Task-Based Language Education: From Theory to Practice*, edited by Kris Van den Branden, 1–16. Cambridge: Cambridge University Press.

Van Gorp, Koen, and Nora Bogaert. 2006. "Developing Language Tasks for Primary and Secondary Education." In *Task-Based Language Education: From Theory to Practice*, edited by Kris Van den Branden, 76–105. Cambridge: Cambridge University Press.

Wenger-Trayner, Etienne, and Beverly Wenger-Trayner. 2015. "Introduction to Communities of Practice." Accessed July 31, 2019. https://wenger-trayner.com/introduction-to-communities-of-practice/.

Wiley, David. n.d. "Defining the 'Open' in Open Content and Open Educational Resources." Accessed August 1, 2019. https://opencontent.org/definition/.

11

From Reading the News to Performing the News:
Using Oral Presentations as the Key Component of an OACD-Enabled Course

ROSSINA SOYAN

THE LANGUAGE FLAGSHIP PROGRAMS at US universities encourage learners in any major to develop professional-level skills in a critical world language. The programs are divided into two parts: Overseas Flagship programs that foster learner development to Superior (ILR 3) and beyond and US Domestic Flagship programs that work with learners at Novice Low—Advanced/Advanced High (ILR 0+—2/2+).

One of the great challenges in the domestic programs is to help learners move from the world of the self and immediate needs (Intermediate Low and Mid [ILR 1]) into the realm of topics related to current events Advanced (ILR 2), particularly in the presentational mode (ACTFL 2017). As a first step toward preparing learners for Advanced (ILR 2) topics, the Russian Flagship Program at Portland State University developed a sequence of three two-credit courses entitled "Globalization," which learners usually take simultaneously with Advanced Russian. In the Globalization courses the language input learners encounter is drawn mainly from current media, while oral presentations on media topics serve as the main task type for learner output.

The importance of oral presentations in a world language class for developing learners' communicative competence is undoubted (Al-Issa and Al-Qubtan 2010; Brooks and Wilson 2014; Miles 2009). A considerable amount of literature has been published on discrete aspects of oral presentations: scaffolding activities, such as analyzing videos of model or rehearsal presentations (Garcia-Pinar 2019; Mennim 2003; Okada, Sawaumi, and Ito 2017; Salem 2019); factors influencing oral language production (Kibler, Salerno, and Palacios 2014; Tian 2019; Yuan and Ellis 2003); and feedback and peer assessment (Otoshi and Heffernen 2008; Wang, Yu, and Teo 2018).

However, the research does not include many articles that focus on oral presentations as the primary building block in the architecture of a world language course. Murao (2019) addresses oral presentations as a summative, end-of-unit activity where learners prove their knowledge of the unit content, bringing to bear their own additional research on the topic under discussion. Similarly, Zhu (2019) offers a sixteen-hour training curriculum aimed at improving the delivery of oral presentations (pronunciation, tone, gestures) through various tasks. In each case, the integration of oral presentations into course design depends on learning objectives, curricular demands, learner needs, and class sizes. This chapter offers one more approach to using oral presentations as a building block of a world language course. Here, oral presentations are used as the key component of a course that implements principles of the OACD framework, particularly the absence of a textbook; the interchangeability of texts, tasks, and activities; ongoing learner involvement in the selection and delivery of content; and continual and systematic tailoring to learner needs.

General Description of the Globalization Sequence of the Portland State University Russian Language Flagship Program

The Globalization sequence consists of three two-credit courses taught over three successive ten-week terms in the academic year. By the end of the fall-winter-spring course sequence, learners produce and present paragraph-length discourse on multiple topics related to current events, thereby gaining experience in accomplishing an Advanced-level task in the presentational mode (read more on reverse design in Van Gorp et al., this volume). To achieve this goal the course is grounded in media texts, that is, print, audio, and video resources created by news agencies, including news blurbs, feature articles, interviews, and live news coverage. Learners read, discuss, and comprehend media texts in Russian and develop their global awareness and media literacy, which are features of Advanced (ILR 2) proficiency.

Each term of the Globalization sequence is comprised of three thematic modules that are selected by the Russian Flagship Program curriculum committee. Since at the beginning of the sequence learners have very limited previous exposure to media texts, the fall course focuses on concrete topics: media texts on global trends in food, holidays, and movies. In the winter term, current event topics dealing with politics, economics, and society are explored. In the spring term, the topics of health, environment, and Kazakhstan allow the course to serve as an initial orientation to a summer study abroad experience in Almaty. It must be emphasized that although module themes are predefined, media texts and activities within the modules are regularly updated, often chosen by teachers and learners in collaboration to reflect the interests of specific learner cohorts.

To ensure coherence within and between modules, transitions and threads are built into the course design (Stoller and Grabe 2017; for another example of coherence building within a modular course see Gregory, this volume). One main thread uniting the course sequence is the approach to the module themes: Similar events and trends around the world are compared through the lens of globalization. Parallel threads develop on their own throughout the academic year, following choices made by learners. For example, the 2019 winter term included a number of texts exploring the topic of protests—protests concerning the Moscow City Council elections, protests against the retirement age reform, and an online campaign for saving Siberian forests from fires.

How the Course Design of the Globalization Sequence Aligns with the OACD Framework

The Globalization sequence of the Russian Flagship Program can serve as an illustration of the OACD framework, particularly in how it is textbook-free and allows for interchangeable texts, tasks, and activities; ongoing learner involvement in the selection and delivery of content; and continual and systematic tailoring to learner needs. First, the sequence uses authentic, up-to-date media texts instead of a textbook. While the organization and scaffolding of news articles in a textbook are undoubtedly useful for both teachers and learners, such textbooks date quickly. Regularly updating media texts to cover recent events makes them more relevant to learners' experiences and better prepares them for conversations with peers from Russian-speaking countries. Second, the textbook-free curriculum fosters the use of interchangeable texts, tasks, and activities according to learner needs and interests.

Third, over the course of the academic year, learners have a growing say in the selection of specific topics for reading, discussion, and presentation within the course modules. Moreover learners select, on their own, specific news items for sharing in their in-class oral presentations over the year. In the fall and winter terms, the only limit for oral presentation topics is that learners must select recent media texts (i.e., preferably published within the last year) while in the spring term, an additional criterion is added: The news item must also feature Kazakhstan, the country many will visit for their summer study abroad term.

Fourth, continual and systematic tailoring to learner needs occurs through careful scaffolding of classroom activities, setting clear performance expectations, and providing detailed and individualized formative feedback. Learners receive grading rubrics for all the major assignments (oral presentations, essays), and the relatively small class size (five to ten learners per term) allows the teacher to spend a considerable amount of time helping all learners write and revise their texts through several drafts.

Scaffolding Activities Leading to In-Class Oral Presentations and End-of-Term Mock News Broadcasts

The main components of the Globalization sequence are (1) reading and discussion of media texts, (2) oral presentations in class, and (3) the culminating task in the format of a mock news broadcast. Working with media texts in the interpretive mode serves as the springboard for individual oral presentations in class, and oral presentations in class, in turn, help learners present the mock news broadcast. Thus the end-of-term mock news broadcast is just another performance in the string of presentations learners give to develop their oral proficiency (see Table 11.1). In the course of the academic year each learner gives approximately eleven oral presentations, ranging from

Table 11.1. Oral presentations within the globalization sequence

	Fall term	Winter term	Spring term	Total
In-class presentations	2	2	2	6
Mock news broadcast		3 (2 presentations in front of a more proficient group + 1 presentation at the Flagship assembly)	2 (dress rehearsal + presentation at the Flagship assembly)	5
Total	2	5	4	11

the lower-stakes in-class presentation to the higher-stakes end-of-term presentation where the learner presents to all the members of the Flagship program, both faculty and fellow learners.

Reading and Discussion of Media Texts

As the primary source of language input throughout the course, media texts are regularly accompanied by tasks typical for content-based instruction (Brinton and Snow 2017; Grabe and Stoller 2019; Stryker and Leaver 1997). Daily lesson plans are built around these texts.[1] Instruction is conducted exclusively in the target language, and all the materials are also provided in the target language.

While learners select topics they would like to explore each term, the teacher chooses specific texts for in-class discussions and creates a set of pre-reading and post-reading exercises for each text. Pre-reading exercises are aimed to introduce key vocabulary for a new topic and activate learners' background knowledge through speaking exercises. For example in a structured talk between Learner A and Learner B (Brandl 2008), learners work in pairs, each delivering two to three minutes of uninterrupted monologue to answer the questions related to the topic, while the other student in the pair serves as a listener. Speaking skills are also scaffolded through description of photos related to current events using the jigsaw format and retelling of short individual texts during the 4/3/2 speaking activity (Webb and Nation 2017).

Post-reading exercises consist of comprehension questions, paraphrasing and summarizing tasks, and more open-ended activities, such as responding to the text's notions by expressing opinions or writing response paragraphs based on prompts. A particularly important comprehension activity is having learners put parts of the text in the correct order since the teacher can thus draw learners' attention to how paragraphs are structured in the genre of media texts. Paying attention to paragraph structure in reading texts sets the stage for helping learners think about paragraph structure in their own production.

Although the main goal of this part of the course is understanding media texts, learners also start analyzing, synthesizing, and evaluating information; that is, they start developing higher-order thinking skills. Later, during their oral presentations, learners are asked to share their opinion on the news they have presented—why they chose the article and why it is important for the audience to hear the news. These questions push learners to reflect on their own and societal values and articulate them, which is sometimes the most memorable part of the presentation. The following sections give more detailed information about in-class oral presentations, in-class performance, grading, and mock news broadcast.

In-Class Oral Presentations

Preparation for Oral Presentations

In the beginning of the fall term, learners receive a set of preparatory materials for this task in Russian, including guidelines for creating oral presentations, a grading rubric, and a model text. In the model the main parts of the presentation (introduction, glossary, body, conclusion) are color coded, and transitions connecting parts and paragraphs are highlighted. Using the model text the teacher gives a sample oral presentation to learners so that they can see what is expected in their presentations of news items. Moreover various performance strategies (Reinhart 2013; Urban 2016) are discussed to help learners with their delivery.

Each learner signs up for a presentation on a specific date at the beginning of the term. Next learners choose a news article in Russian, reading the authentic text that contains authentic collocations and expressions related to the topic. Learners then write their own summary text following the structural elements highlighted in the teacher's model presentation. In this first draft, they are expected to paraphrase main ideas from the news article and adapt their text to the audience. Calibrating their paraphrasing for the audience requires them to rephrase expressions that may not be familiar to their classmates, and this reminds learners that oral presentations are not only about utilizing new vocabulary and syntax but also about sharing information that the audience can understand. Another goal of the presentations is to encourage learners to learn new words related to the topics they selected; they are therefore asked to share a glossed vocabulary list of up to five expressions with their English equivalents.

After the learner works independently, the teacher reviews draft 1 one week before the scheduled date to deliver the presentation. Learners receive detailed formative feedback following the rubric in Appendix A. The benefit of this feedback, however, is not only in its quantity but also in its place within the learning cycle (Brookhart 2017), which starts with draft 1 and ends with the performance (Figure 11.1).

Requiring that learners produce an audio recording of their revised text at least two days before they deliver it in class (Martin 2019, 1:05:47) solves a number of problems. The teacher can check that learners have paid attention to the written feedback and incorporated it into a new draft. The audio recording pushes learners to think about the oral delivery of their written text, and instructor feedback on the recording mainly focuses on features (stress, pronunciation, and intonation) that will help learners with their classroom performance.

In the fall term, learners generally struggle with writing several paragraphs and structuring their oral texts. By the winter and spring terms, the teacher's feedback on the first draft focuses on collocations and smaller grammar points. It is satisfying to see how each consecutive text becomes better structured and connected. Working on the same type of assignment and repeating the learning cycle (draft 1, revision, oral recording, live delivery) allows learners to improve with each successive presentation, making

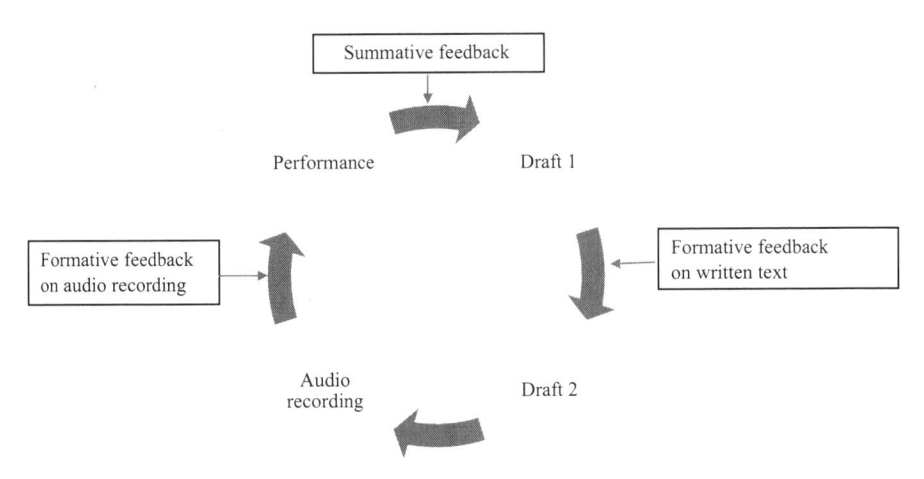

Figure 11.1. Oral presentation preparation cycle

it possible to reach a high standard of performance by the end of the academic year and make progress in proficiency.

In-Class Performance

Learners are asked to ensure that their presentations are approximately five minutes long. They are strongly encouraged to talk about, versus read, their text so that when delivering the presentation they can maintain eye contact with the audience. Since oral presentations are aimed at improving learners' unrehearsed oral control of news language, reading the prepared text would be counterproductive. Learners can use slides or notes to guide them. They are also encouraged to include numbers, key vocabulary, and expressions in their slides next to the photos related to their topic both to help with their performance and to aid their classmates' comprehension of the presentation.

Some may object that learner output during the oral presentation appears to be memorized performance, typical of Novice-level proficiency. However, considering the amount of work that goes into writing, revising, and delivering each presentation multiple times each term, learners actually gain significant experience with Advanced-level discourse over the course of the year. Moreover this type of performance develops proficiency in aspects of delivery that go beyond memory and automatization of linguistic forms and structures (rhythm of speech, gestures, and body language, etc.). The repeated task type, which pushes learners to produce Advanced-level output, can be compared to Rifkin's (2002) study of output-focused instruction, where learners in the experimental group moved from Intermediate mid/high to Advanced-level speaking proficiency through continuously practicing narration and reflecting on their output. A similar output goal runs through the Globalization sequence and informs the teacher's pedagogical choices.

After learner presents, their classmates, working in groups of two or three, are expected to come up with questions to ask the presenter. Each audience member also writes one or two sentences summarizing the main idea of the presentation and submits them to the teacher. This requirement motivates learners to listen carefully to the presentations (i.e., practicing Advanced listening skills) and work on writing and summarizing skills. It also provides the instructor feedback about how accessible the presentation was to the audience.

Grading

The requirements for successful completion of the task are adjusted from term to term. Generally the rubric for presentations emphasizes delivery, structure of the oral presentation, and time management skills (Appendix A). Content, grammar, and pronunciation, all important issues, are not included in the grade on the presentation since they are dealt with during the week preceding the oral presentation. If learners disregard these issues, they are asked to produce additional drafts and recordings. The presentation grade is accompanied by a short letter from the teacher highlighting the strengths of the presentation and areas for further work.

Culminating Task: Mock News Broadcast

The work on media texts culminates with two mock news broadcasts delivered to the whole Flagship community, the first time at the end of the winter term and the second at the end of the spring term (see Table 11.1). Work on the first mock news broadcast starts from week 3 of the winter term. Learners engage in collaborative learning—a feature of OACD, first discussing and agreeing on a country whose news they will present. They then gather facts about the country they have chosen to create a context for understanding news from that country. Each student signs up for one topic—geographical location, climate, population and official languages, political system, economic situation, famous events, famous people, and so on. This country profile, to which each student contributes one topic, goes through the same learning cycle (Figure 11.1) as other presentations and is delivered in front of a more proficient group. Then learners present the mock broadcast with the news from the country they have chosen twice—at the dress rehearsal and at the end-of-term assembly. As is evident, much class time is devoted to presenting to make learners feel confident about speaking on Advanced-level topics.

The mock news broadcast requires both teamwork and individual work. While learners prepare their texts individually and deliver them individually, they must negotiate all the other parts of the news broadcast, having chosen the country for the culminating task. First, they agree on the topics they are going to cover (politics, economics, society) and assign topics to presenters. Second, they choose in what order they are going to perform, who is going to open and close the news broadcast, and how transitions from one presenter to another are going to be worded. Third, they work on a single set of slides to support their presentations.

Countries for the mock news broadcast are usually former Soviet republics that still have news outlets publishing in Russian. At the end of three successive winter terms, mock news broadcasts were given on Armenia, Georgia, and Azerbaijan. The mock news broadcast at the end of the spring term is devoted to Kazakhstan.

Reflections: Preparation and Delivery of Oral Presentations in Other Instructional Contexts

The Globalization sequence of the Russian Flagship Program offers one approach to integrating oral presentations into course design. Depending on the number of learners and their proficiency level, interests, and needs, it is possible to imagine several ways in which the oral presentation preparation cycle can be either shortened or expanded.

For many learners who take the Globalization sequence, retaining information about their texts and delivering them orally are the most challenging points in the learning cycle. For whatever reason—intrinsic learner issues (performance anxiety, innate shyness, lack of preparation time, etc.) or task features (high vocabulary load, unfamiliar topic, etc.)—some learners tend to resort to reading their texts. For these learners delivering oral presentations can become an extremely frustrating task since they know they lose points for reading their presentation aloud rather than presenting it with or without notes.

To ameliorate this situation, it seems beneficial to offer a range of strategies to learners in response to the factors that impede their delivery. For performance anxiety there are delivery strategies (rehearsing text with disappearing words, picking a focal point in the room for presenting, being able to paraphrase if they forget a single word in their text, etc.). As for linguistic issues, helping learners balance the percentage of completely unfamiliar words in a presentation text and find substitutes for words that are difficult to pronounce is essential. Another strategy is helping learners to chunk their information into more manageable pieces. Increasing a focus on graphic organizers and introducing them to the learning cycle (see Figure 11.2) can help in this regard.

Graphic organizers contribute to the planning phase, that is, generating and organizing ideas and separating the idea generation process from the process of transforming these ideas into coherent paragraphs (Maamuujav, Krishnan, and Collins 2019). The visual representation of the text may help later during the performance, facilitating the process of retaining the content of paragraphs and transitions between them.

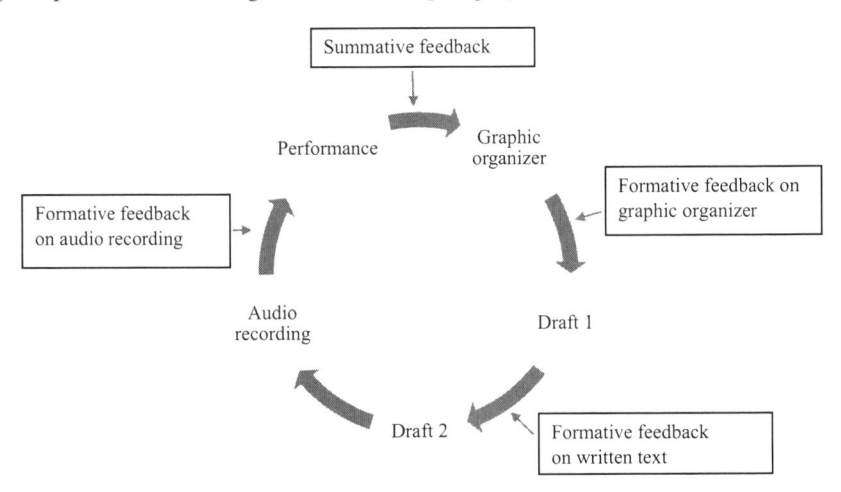

Figure 11.2. Revised oral presentation preparation cycle

Thus the graphic organizer should reflect the features highlighted in the rubric: audience, hook, glossary, text structure, news source, cohesive devices, opinion. It can look like a planning chart, a snowball, or a spider web.

An introductory lesson on oral presentations in the fall term can start with reading a news article at home and filling out a graphic organizer with the group in class. After the teacher has demonstrated how the graphic organizer should be used, learners can be asked to work in pairs or small groups and fill out another graphic organizer, and afterward they can read a new media text at home and fill out a graphic organizer on their own, following the model of gradual release of responsibility (Clementi 2020, 1:02:39; Krasner, this volume). Although expanding the oral presentation cycle and providing feedback on each graphic organizer may be too time-consuming in some contexts, this tool can be beneficial for smaller classes.

Conclusions

A course based on oral presentations can be adapted to various contexts. For example media texts can be replaced with texts on narrower topics, such as sustainability or the end of poverty. Depending on class size, the amount of feedback and length of the learning cycle can be shortened or lengthened (video recordings, reflections on delivery). A more proficient cohort of learners may need less scaffolding and less explicit guidelines. Moreover learners can be engaged to contribute to more aspects of the curriculum such as rubric creation (Weimer 2013) and the structure of the mock news broadcast. The Globalization sequence described in this chapter is just one of many possible manifestations of the OACD framework and content-based instruction.

It is difficult to elucidate specific effects of an OACD-enabled course on learners' oral proficiency testing results since learners usually take several language courses each term and not all learners take official oral proficiency interviews at the end of the course. However the repeated performances of paragraph-length speech on topics related to current events certainly provide multiple opportunities to perform Advanced (ILR 2) tasks. The assumption is that what is practiced in the classroom (e.g., paragraph-level speech) can be used to create language in new contexts during a proficiency test.

The ideas for combining program goals, learner interests, and learner needs with the OACD framework and content-based instruction as implemented in the Portland State University Globalization sequence may be valuable for others in designing courses for special curricular needs. The profession awaits further exploration of the application of OACD in multisection programs at the university level.

Study Questions

1. How would you adapt the oral presentation preparation cycle presented in this chapter to your own context? Would you want to? Why or why not? What kind of modifications would be necessary (content, scaffolding, assessment)?
2. If oral presentations are included in your course as an assessment measure, how do you scaffold this task? What have been the challenges in scaffolding? What have been the successes?

3. How might oral presentations be applied across courses, throughout programs, or at a departmental/institutional level to provide a form of force-multiplication in reaching more advanced levels of proficiency? Do a little research and outreach: what other programs are using oral presentations in similar ways (e.g., the Flagship Programs work interactively very often), and how can you work together for improvement to both programs?

Acknowledgments

I would like to thank Dr. William Comer, Dr. Anna Alsufieva, and Dr. Sergei Sychov for their encouragement and support throughout my three years of teaching the Globalization sequence.

Note

1. In a slight departure from the OACD definition, media texts are sometimes edited to better suit learners whose reading proficiency, especially at the start of the academic year, is only at Intermediate Low and Mid (IRL 1). These edits can include abbreviating very long texts, glossing key but unfamiliar words, and occasionally simplifying the syntax of a very long and complicated sentence.

Appendix A: Grading Rubric for Oral Presentations

Category and description	Max. points	Instructor's comments
1. SPEAKING DURING PERFORMANCE, NOT READING Minimal requirement: know your text and maintain eye contact with the audience	10 or 0 for the oral presentation	
Bonus: an excellent presentation (speech rate, volume, liveliness)	+ 2 points	
2. Comprehension by the audience (questions + written summaries after presentation)	2	
3. Oral presentation preparation (Draft 1—one week before the performance; audio recording—two days before the performance)	2	
4. Glossary (5 words or expressions useful for understanding the presentation)	2	
5. Text structure (introduction, main body, conclusion)	1	
6. Hook (Did you attract the audience's attention in the beginning of the presentation?) + Opinion (Did you share your own opinion at the end of the presentation?)	1	
7. News source, cohesive devices, closing sentence	1	
8. Presentation length (≈5 min)	1	
Total points	20 points + 2 bonus points	

References

ACTFL. 2017. "NCSSFL-ACTFL Can-Do Statements." https://www.actfl.org/resources/ncssfl-actfl-can-do-statements.

Al-Issa, Ali Said, and Redha Al-Qubtan. 2010. "Taking the Floor: Oral Presentations in EFL Classrooms." *TESOL Journal* 1, no. 2 (June): 227–46.

Brandl, Klaus. 2008. *Communicative Language Teaching in Action: Putting Principles to Work*. Upper Saddle River: Pearson Prentice Hall.

Brinton, Donna M., and Marguerite A. Snow. 2017. "The Evolving Architecture of Content-Based Instruction." In *The Content-Based Classroom: New Perspectives on Integrating Language and Content*, edited by Marguerite A. Snow and Donna M. Brinton, 2–20. Ann Arbor: University of Michigan Press.

Brookhart, Susan M. 2017. *How to Give Effective Feedback to Your Students*. Alexandria: Association for Supervision and Curriculum Development.

Brooks, Gavin, and John Wilson. 2014. "Using Oral Presentations to Improve Students' English Language Skills." *Kwansei Gakuin University Humanities Review* 19: 199–212.

Clementi, Donna. 2020. *Graphic Organizers: Visualize—Simplify—Connect*. ACTFL webinar. https://www.youtube.com/watch?v=g4tOAIRSjB0&list=PLh_cfDwS8mrsGfkQ5Tlbsd3GRHrgG7Ng9&index=17.

Garcia-Pinar, Aranzazu. 2019. "Getting Closer to Authenticity in the Course of Technical English." *English Language Teaching* 12, no. 11: 10–22. https://doi.org/10.5539/elt.v12n11p10.

Grabe, William, and Fredricka L. Stoller. 2019. "Reading to Learn: Why and How Content-Based Instructional Frameworks Facilitate the Process." In *Reading to Learn in a Foreign Language: An Integrated Approach to Foreign Language Instruction and Assessment*, edited by Keiko Koda and Junko Yamashita, 9–29. Oxon: Routledge.

Kibler, Amanda K., April S. Salerno, and Natalia Palacios. 2014. "'But Before I Go to My Next Step'": A Longitudinal Study of Adolescent English Language Learners' Transitional Devices in Oral Presentations." *TESOL Quarterly* 48, no. 2 (June): 222–51. https://doi.org/10.1002/tesq.96.

Maamuujav, Undarmaa, Jenell Krishnan, and Penelope Collins. 2019. "The Utility of Infographics in L2 Writing Classes: A Practical Strategy to Scaffold Writing Development." *TESOL Journal* 11, no. 2: e484. https://doi.org/10.1002/tesj.484.

Martin, Cynthia. 2019. "Russian Is Not Hard: How to Help Students Stop Worrying and Start Talking," Podcast interview with Natalie McCauley, December 12, 2019. https://www.teachrussian.org/Materials/1accd4e529acb278c5543524cc5c69e4/Russian-is-not-hard---how-to-help-stude?lang=ru#/().

Mennim, Paul. 2003. "Rehearsed Oral L2 Output and Reactive Focus on Form." *ELT Journal* 57, no. 2 (April): 130–38. https://doi.org/10.1093/elt/57.2.130.

Miles, Richard. 2009. "Oral Presentations for English Proficiency Purposes." *Reflections on English Language Teaching* 8, no. 2: 103–10.

Murao, Remi. 2019. "Cultivating Reading to Learn Skills in Fostering Oral Presentation Competence as an Essential Tool for Participating in an Increasingly Globalized Society." In *Reading to Learn in a Foreign Language: An Integrated Approach to Foreign Language Instruction and Assessment*, edited by Keiko Koda and Junko Yamashita, 84–110. Oxon: Routledge.

Okada, Yasuko, Takafumi Sawaumi, and Takehiko Ito. 2017. "Effects of Observing Model Video Presentations on Japanese EFL Learners' Oral Performance." *Electronic Journal of Foreign Language Teaching* 14, no. 2: 129–44.

Otoshi, Junko, and Neil Heffernen. 2008. "Factors Predicting Effective Oral Presentations in EFL Classrooms." *Asian EFL Journal* 10, no. 1 (March): 65–78.

Reinhart, Susan M. 2013. *Giving Academic Presentations*. Ann Arbor: University of Michigan Press.

Rifkin, Benjamin. 2002. "A Case Study of the Acquisition of Narration in Russian: At the Intersection of Foreign Language Education, Applied Linguistics, and Second Language Acquisition." *Slavic and East European Journal* 46, no. 3: 465–81. https://doi.org/10.2307/3220197.

Salem, Ashraf Atta M. S. 2019. "A Sage on a Stage, to Express and Impress: TED Talks for Improving Oral Presentation Skills, Vocabulary Retention and its Impact on Reducing Speaking Anxiety in ESP Settings." *English Language Teaching* 12, no. 6: 146–60. https://doi.org/10.5539/elt.v12n6p146.

Stoller, Fredricka L., and William Grabe. 2017. "Building Coherence into the Content-Based Curriculum: Six Ts Revisited." In *The Content-Based Classroom: New Perspectives on Integrating Language and Content*, edited by Marguerite A. Snow and Donna M. Brinton, 53–66. Ann Arbor: University of Michigan Press.

Stryker, Stephen, and Betty Lou Leaver, eds. 1997. *Content-Based Instruction in Foreign Language Education: Models and Methods*. Washington: Georgetown University Press.

Tian, Chunguang. 2019. "Anxiety in Classroom English Presentations: A Case Study in Korean Tertiary Educational Context." *Higher Education Studies* 9, no. 1: 132–43. https://doi.org/10.5539/hes.v9n1p132.

Urban, Tim. 2016. "Doing a TED Talk: The Full Story." *Wait but Why* (blog), March 2, 2016. https://waitbutwhy.com/2016/03/doing-a-ted-talk-the-full-story.html.

Wang, Bo, Shulin Yu, and Timothy Teo. 2018. "Experienced EFL Teachers' Beliefs about Feedback on Student Oral Presentations." *Asian-Pacific Journal of Second and Foreign Language Education* 3, no. 1: 1–13. https://doi.org/10.1186/s40862-018-0053-3.

Webb, Stuart, and Paul Nation. 2017. *How Vocabulary Is Learned*. Oxford: Oxford University Press.

Weimer, Maryellen. 2013. *Learner-Centered Teaching: Five Key Changes to Practice*. San Francisco: Jossey-Bass.

Yuan, Fangyuan, and Rod Ellis. 2003. "The Effects of Pre-Task Planning and On-Line Planning on Fluency, Complexity and Accuracy in L2 Monologic Oral Production." *Applied Linguistics* 24, no. 1: 1–27. https://doi.org/10.1093/applin/24.1.1.

Zhu, Wen. 2019. "10 Years vs. 16 Hours: An Effective Curriculum to Improve Chinese College Students' English Presentation Quality in Public." *English Language Teaching* 12, no. 9: 82–87. https://doi.org/10.5539/elt.v12n9p82.

12

Integrating Open Architecture Curricular Design in a Proficiency-Oriented, Content-Based Instruction Course in Korean

SANG YEE CHEON

THIS CHAPTER INTRODUCES *KOREAN Proficiency through Film* (KOR 480)—a proficiency-oriented, content-based film course for advanced learners of Korean at the University of Hawai'i at Mānoa's Korean Language Flagship Center. It describes how the use of a theme-based syllabus rather than a textbook, which is a key OACD principle, together with OACD features can increase flexibility in adapting to learner needs.

The University of Hawai'i at Mānoa's Korean Language Flagship Center and Its Undergraduate Korean Flagship Program

Since 2002 University of Hawai'i at Mānoa's Korean Flagship language and culture education program has been an integral component of the Language Flagship initiative, a federally sponsored program that promotes the growth of global language professionals—workers who easily transition from location to location due to their professional-level world language and culture proficiencies. The Korean Language Flagship Center, the first Korean language and culture education center in the United States, is dedicated to producing specialists with professional-level proficiency in Korean. The program began with nondegree post-BA programs for advanced language learners. In the fall of 2007, the post-baccalaureate program was transitioned into the Flagship MA program. An additional National Security Education Program grant was awarded to implement an undergraduate Flagship BA program as well, which was launched in the fall of 2008.

The Korean undergraduate program's Korean Flagship track (with BA and certificate programs) is designed for professional-level language training and thus focuses on areas of content specialization. This programmatic feature creates a requirement for continual and systemic tailoring to individual learner and cohort needs, making the Korean Language Flagship Center a natural context for OACD-based learning programs.

Korean Proficiency through Film, a Content-Based Course for Advanced Learners of Korean

Korean Proficiency through Film (KOR 480) is one of several content-based courses for learners at the Advanced level of proficiency at University of Hawaiʻi at Mānoa that integrate topics or themes and language skills. These courses offer learners the opportunity to increase their understanding of Korean culture while improving in the four language skills that are crucial for reaching higher levels of proficiency (Cheon 2007). The Korean Language Flagship Center thus modifies the content-based instruction model advanced by Brinton, Snow, and Wesche (2003) by combining content and language-skill instruction and changing topical domains each week, as well as including guest presentations by subject-matter specialists.

KOR 480 incorporates content-based with project-based instruction to raise Korean language proficiency and deepen knowledge of Korean culture, with an emphasis on writing and critical thinking about contemporary Korean history from 1945 to the present. Exposure to orally and visually authentic Korean film not only provides learners with rich cultural and sociopolitical information about Korea but also exposes them to vocabulary beyond the learners' current Advanced-level proficiency. By exposing them to culturally saturated texts (such as film) and engaging them in frequent discussion and feedback sessions, the course also creates opportunities for a more in-depth understanding of Korean culture, which is crucial to achieving professional-level proficiency.

Course Overview

The course is based on films that cover contemporary Korean history from 1945 to the present. Their content, including historical background and contemporary social issues, provides the topics or themes for reading and listening text selection and the starting point for all classroom activities. It is therefore important to select a coherent set of topics or themes, as they inform all aspects of the course. Seven to eight films are examined during the seventeen-week course, two of which are collaboratively selected by the teacher and learners, based in part on exit surveys of previous learners' preferred films.

The course meets once weekly for 150 minutes. With available class time concentrated into such a limited number of sessions, a flipped classroom approach enables the completion of course activities and attainment of learning objectives, managing precious classroom time to maximize interactive activities linked to the out-of-class reading, listening, and writing activities to reinforce and deepen learning. Learners watch seven films in class or individually outside of the classroom and complete content-based authentic reading and listening comprehension assignments at home based on the films, receiving feedback and comments from the teacher before class. On a weekly basis learners discuss, both as a whole class and in small groups, aspects of the films as well as the related reading and listening texts.

Once per semester each learner makes a fifteen- to twenty-minute presentation about a topic chosen by the learner that is connected to one of the films. The presentation is assessed following a rubric that includes success in explaining subject matter, PowerPoint presentation handouts, organization, content appropriateness and accuracy, and presentational attitude (such as posture or facial expression). Peer evaluation is also reflected in the score of the presenter's performance. The teacher assists learners with their presentational skills, grammar, and advanced vocabulary based on the weekly reading and listening materials.

Learners also write two three-page essays on topics chosen by learners and/or the teacher and a ten-page term paper (film review) in Korean.

At the end of the semester learners engage in one small group debate as part of a three-week-long Critical Thinking Skills Project. In the debate learners adhere to a debate protocol to focus on a topic chosen by the small group. During week 1 learners complete a critical thinking assignment where they provide their own opinions, based on research, on a provocative topic chosen by the teacher. In week 2 the teacher divides learners into four small groups, ensuring there is a mixture of stances, and a debate ensues. In week 3, the last day of the course, one speaker designated by each group presents to the entire class the summary of the pros and cons discussed and debated.

Class Schedule

Classroom time is segmented into the eight steps illustrated in Figure 12.1. The classroom format can vary depending on the topic or activities for the week. Some topics and activities are relatively difficult and require more time.

To maximize the rate of proficiency growth, KOR 480 emphasizes activities that integrate all four language skills—reading, listening, speaking, and writing—thus enabling them to reinforce one another. Table 12.1 shows examples of instructional activities in the four skills.

Throughout the course learners process reading texts and listening passages using higher-order thinking skills to manipulate content and produce innovative speech. To promote proficiency growth in *reading comprehension*, texts on selected topics are used to enhance understanding of content as well as for expanding active vocabulary and use of sophisticated grammatical expressions. Main points and key concepts from reading passages are covered in classroom review sessions facilitated by the teacher after learners have completed reading comprehension assignments outside of class. The teacher selects an initial set of reading texts used at the beginning of study of a particular film or topic. Learners can choose additional reading texts for subsequent classroom activities such as the presentation or debate.

To help learners develop proficiency in *listening comprehension*, they review media listening materials with specific questions on the same or similar topics to those presented earlier in connection with their out-of-class reading materials. These questions

```
        1. Teacher
        written
        feedback on
        assignments
  8.    before class    2.
  Teacher-led          Vocabulary
  wrap-up              test and
  discussion           review

                                    3.
  7.     Language and        Learner's oral
  Student-led    content (e.g.,    presentation,
  small group    ROK-US            Q&A session, and
  discussion     alliance)         peer evaluation

                                    4.
  6.                           Lecture by
  Listening                    instructor/
  assignment    5.             specialist
  review        Reading
                assignment
                review
```

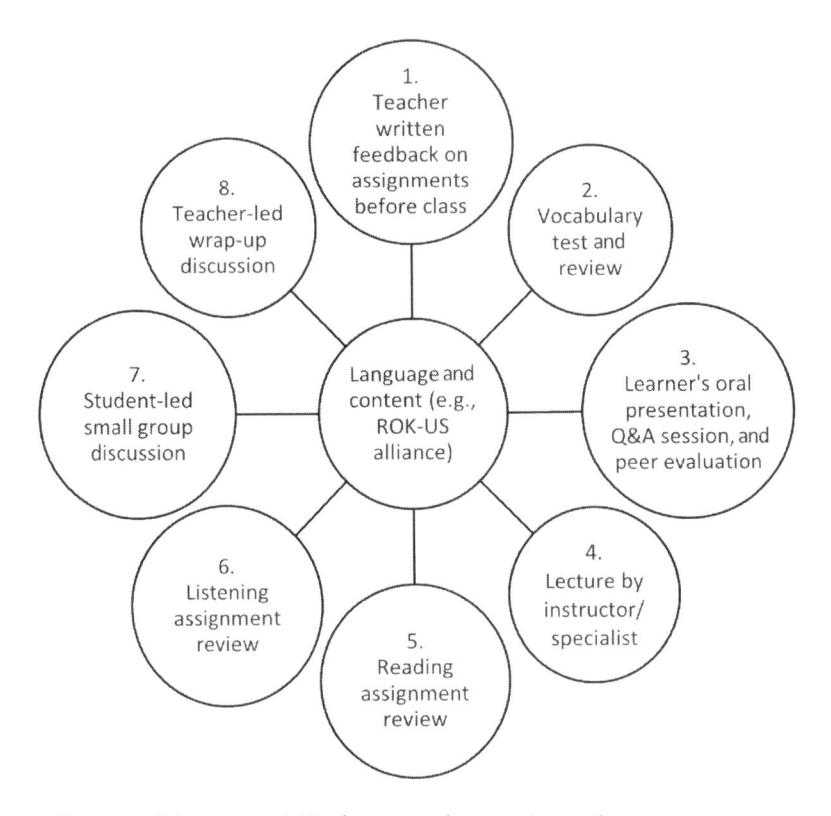

Figure 12.1. Sequence of classroom activities for content-language integration

engage both lower-order and higher-order thinking skills, ranging from simple yes-no questions to sharing opinions on the symbolic meanings of objects, for example the owls, full moon, and so on, in the film *Joint Security Area* or what they would have done in a similar situation. Presentations or lectures, delivered in the same manner as in Korean universities, followed by Q&A sessions, are conducted by the teacher or subject-matter specialists in order to expose learners to Korean culture and society as well as to improve listening skills. As with reading texts, the teacher selects the initial set of listening passages used at the beginning of study of a particular film or topic, and learners can find additional listening passages for subsequent classroom activities.

Oral presentations, weekly small group discussions in class, and one final small group debate at the end of the course offer learners the opportunity to develop proficiency in *speaking*. In weekly small group discussions learners collaborate on tasks such as analyzing a particular video clip, discussing a topic, or creating a story based on images provided by the teacher that require them to produce Korean within a group. The observable outcome is an analysis, a summary of ideas expressed, a story, or similar product. All participants within the group have distinct tasks or roles, including facilitator (managing discussion), recorder (taking notes for reporting), and reporter (presenting the summary of the group discussion). Roles are allocated without teacher

Table 12.1. Teaching Integrated Language Skills

	Comprehension	Production
Written form	Reading assignments to be done at home, followed by in-class review sessions to reinforce key vocabulary, grammatical expressions, and cultural concepts	Writing assignments to be done at home: short essays and a final term paper (a film review), with oral or written feedback from the instructor
Spoken form	Home or in-class listening activities, followed by in-class review sessions to reinforce key vocabulary, grammatical expressions, and cultural concepts	In-class speaking activities: oral presentations, weekly small group discussions, and a final debate, with instructor-provided oral feedback and comments

intervention, and all members are required to share their opinions. Afterward, the reporter shares the outcome with the entire class during the teacher-facilitated wrap-up session. The same topic is given to all groups, and all participants are able to compare their own discussion with other groups.

As described earlier, at the end of the course learners participate in a small group debate using a debate protocol to focus on a topic chosen by the group as part of the three-week long Critical Thinking Skills Project. The debate helps learners improve discourse-level speaking skills as they share ideas and opinions and give or receive feedback from peers. As in the weekly small group discussions, all participants in each group have distinct roles, including facilitator, recorder, reporter, checker, or wildcard (who can play the role of any missing member). On the last day of the course, during the teacher-facilitated wrap-up session, the reporter in each group presents a five-minute summary of the debate content to the entire class, and peers evaluate the presentation. This critical thinking skills group project is assessed through peer evaluation of group presentations.

Finally, to help learners develop proficiency in *writing*, teachers approach writing as a skill developed over time through experiencing and practicing various written genres, receiving product-based evaluation and feedback. Skills in academic and professional writing thus develop gradually through conscious effort and practice in composing, developing, and analyzing ideas. Learners can choose one of the two options for each short essay topic: (1) a topic they are interested in from the list of topics covered in class, or (2) a film from the list provided by the teacher related to the topic covered in class. The essay in option 2 is a film review, which is a similar but shorter version of the final critical writing assignment. The first essay is due at the end of week 5; the second is due at the end of week 12; and the third and final one is due at the end of week 17. Details of how the course promotes critical writing are discussed subsequently.

As stated earlier, the course is based on topics taken from contemporary Korean history from 1945 to the present, such as the lives and careers of four former presidents, the National Security Law, Korean War, ROK-US Alliance, May 16 military coup, assassination of President Park, Gwangju democratic uprising, and so forth,

Table 12.2. Grading Criteria

1.	Attendance and Participation	10%
2.	Four Vocabulary Tests (Vocabulary)	10%
3.	Ten Reading and Listening Assignments (Reading and Listening)	25%
4.	Critical Thinking Skills Project: Small-Group Debate (Speaking)	5%
5.	One Oral Presentation (Speaking)	10%
6.	Two Short Essays (Writing)	20%
7.	Final Term Paper: Film Review (Critical Writing)	20%
	Total	100%

and movies that cover or highlight the particular topic. Examples are *Joint Security Area* (2000), *The President's Barber* (2004), and *Peppermint Candy* (2000). Additional movies selected by learners based on their interests—*May 18* (2007), *A Taxi Driver* (2017), *The President's Last Bang* (2005), *Ode to My Father* (2014), and *1987* (2017)—are used.

Grading criteria for determining learner success are listed in Table 12.2.

In addition to summative assessments, ongoing informal formative assessment (Dababneh and Yuan, this volume) is practiced, in part through thorough educative feedback on writing assignments (where learners repeatedly revise versions based on feedback and comments), small group projects, presentations, and in-course summative assessments.

Integration of OACD in the Korean Proficiency through Film Course

The Korean Flagship goal of producing global professionals with Superior-level proficiency in a language critical to US competitiveness and security requires that learners exercise autonomy and exploit learning opportunities 24/7. That autonomy can be enhanced through the integration of OACD principles and features. One key OACD principle that informs Korean Proficiency through Film is the use of a theme-based syllabus rather than a textbook. This enables the teacher to freely change themes, films, introductory texts, and activities according to learner/cohort needs and new opportunities and in response to ongoing informal formative assessment integrated into the learning process. It also enables ongoing learner involvement with selection of content and activities and promotes learner and teacher creativity. The course aligns with proficiency-oriented learner-centered instructional approaches such as content-, project-, and scenario-based instruction, task-based instruction, as well as with transformative education philosophy (Campbell 2018, 2021). The national standards (The National Standards Collaborative Board 2015) inform all aspects of the course.

KOR 480 integrates a wide array of OACD features such as the use of unadapted authentic materials from Day 1, deliberate and continual use of the target language, project-based instruction and flipped classroom, and incorporation of collaborative learning. The following subsections discuss these aspects of the course in more detail.

Use of Unadapted Authentic Materials from Day 1

As suggested by the course title, Korean Proficiency through Film is based almost entirely on authentic materials. The main course material is comprised of full-length films concerned with contemporary Korean history or sociocultural issues from diverse perspectives. YouTube video materials are used for classroom activities like small group discussions or brainstorming. Reading comprehension assignments utilize newspaper articles and editorials from credible sources to improve critical reading skills.

Deliberate and Continual Use of the Target Language

The Korean Language Flagship Center incorporates various opportunities for learners to experience an immersion environment prior to their one-year overseas program. In principle all instruction is conducted in Korean, utilizing authentic materials in Korean. Learners use only Korean for their written assignments, oral presentations, in-class discussions, and debates.

Project-Based Instruction and Flipped Classroom

Project-based instruction and flipped classroom are used in the course to promote learner motivation and active engagement. Project-based instruction is grounded in a teaching approach that involves integration of knowing and doing (Markham 2011), in contrast to traditional teacher-led instruction. As Beckett and Slater (2005) state, in project-based instruction learners are exposed to language, content, and skills simultaneously, requiring them to be autonomous learners who actively participate in classroom activities related to real-world essential skills, including critical or creative thinking, interpersonal communication, and writing. KOR 480 includes a critical thinking skills project, described previously.

Flipped classroom is a blended learning model in which the conventional order of classroom activities and homework is flipped; learners study new course content on their own before coming to class, where they apply and work through the ideas they have encountered. In KOR 480 all assignments are given ahead of time and delved into in the following class. Class time is reserved primarily for target-language content-based lectures and for discussion and application of new information.

Incorporation of Collaborative Learning

Collaborative learning is "an educational approach that involves groups of learners working together to solve a problem, complete a task, or create a product" (Laal and Laal 2012, 491). Two examples of collaborative learning in KOR 480 are:

- weekly small group discussions, and
- small group debate (Critical Thinking Skills Project).

The small group discussions and debate, where learners work together in threes, fours, or fives, involve the exchange of ideas and opinions for the purpose of understanding the chosen topic. The debate involves the exchange of opposing views or opinions, for and against, through evidence and argument.

Development of Critical Thinking Skills
Critical writing is a process through which learners learn how to present their reasoning and evidence clearly and logically in written form (Smith 2020). Discussion sessions, debate sessions using a debate format, and writing assignments are also effective for developing critical thinking skills. Debate sessions promote these skills in spoken form. In KOR 480 tailored reading comprehension and writing assignments are used to foster critical thinking skills in written form. Learners choose one Korean film they would like to review after consultation with the teacher. Just like a book review, a film review consists of a brief plot summary, content analysis of the film, and detailed information about the film, including director, screenwriter, major actors, genre, thematic content, and so on. The film review includes assessment of the film's quality, stating general thoughts, impressions, and an implicit or explicit recommendation. Not everyone has the same opinion as the critic, and people have different personal film preferences. Therefore the critic should be able to present evidence, ideas, and theories in a logical way from diverse perspectives. All writing assignments, including the final writing assignment (film review), are given at the beginning of the semester. Feedback, which is critically important for significant improvement in writing skills, is provided by the teacher, concentrating on individual writing development and error correction. Learners can revise their writing assignment using feedback from the teacher.

Integration of Nonstandard Dialects and Integration of Formal and Colloquial Language
Highly proficient learners of Korean should be able to distinguish different levels of formality of language usage as well as regional dialectal differences. The importance of teaching colloquial language in Korean-language education has been largely overlooked by both teachers and researchers. In regard to nonstandard dialects or variants of Korean, the situation is even more dire. All Korean textbooks used in higher education are based exclusively on formal standard Korean. The impact of dialectal variation on learning and achievement has not received much attention even though approximately a quarter of the Korean population in South Korea (more than 13 million) speak the Gyeongsang dialects and more than five million people speak the Cholla dialects. Learners who find themselves in the Gyeongsang region will need some knowledge of the dialect to communicate in it with basic intelligibility.

Since *Korean Proficiency through Film* uses authentic materials, it is relatively easy to integrate nonstandard dialects and colloquial language in lesson plans. Films provide exposure to the various dialects of Korean, with a focus on colloquial rather than formal language.

Use of a Wide Variety of Listening and Reading Genres across the Full Spectrum of Social Media Platforms
Due to the development of diverse social media, many useful and reliable websites and social networking site platforms contain authentic reading and listening materials. Learners can share their work and communicate in and beyond the classroom

through various types of social media. YouTube is the primary social media platform utilized. Depending on how the video materials are used, learners are able to experience an immersive environment and obtain desired learning outcomes. YouTube videos show everyday life in Korea, real-time news, and presentations by experts on various topics. An advantage of YouTube over most social media platforms for purposes of language learning is the exposure it offers to a wide variety of content and native speaker accents using diverse dialects in addition to standard pronunciation of Seoul Korean.

Incorporation of Language Spoken by Two or More People with Ambient Noise, Grammatical Mistakes, or Fillers

One of the advantages of film as the main instructional material in a language classroom is that many scenes contain exchanges in natural settings. At times a brief script prepared by the teacher or learners can enable learners to review and discuss difficulties they encountered, how they resolved them, and more. It is important to use scripts judiciously, as overuse can create learner dependence and stunt listening comprehension development. Measured use of scripts can enhance outcomes in mastering subtle phonological (i.e., accentual, rhythmic, or intonational) and paralinguistic (i.e., facial expression, echoing, or body movement) aspects of native usage. An additional benefit is that learners can choose important scenes (using scripts) and can act out the chosen scenes in front of peers. Learners are encouraged to improvise the script, and they enjoy the spontaneous activity.

Top-Down and Bottom-Up Processing of Formal Presentations on Topical Domains Such as Politics, Economics, and History by High-Level Target-Language Speakers

KOR 480 covers the history of Korea since 1945, which includes sociocultural issues from various domains such as politics, economics, and sociology. In addition to the analysis of reading and listening texts described previously, a few formal guest presentations by high-level target-language speakers who are subject-matter specialists on course-related topical domains are given. For example, in the fall semester of 2020 guest presentations covered the following topics: (1) the ROK-US alliance, (2) history of the division of the Korean peninsula, (3) the International Monetary Fund (IMF) economic crisis, and (4) the *Yushin* Constitution of 1972. Depending on the availability of specialists, topics of guest presentations vary.

Discussion

Positive learner feedback reflects the importance of the role of the teacher as facilitator and, ideally, coach and advisor. Overall course ratings are high and learner comments are positive, with learners noting that the class was well organized and prepared. The following is randomly selected positive learner feedback submitted anonymously. Feedback about areas of concern is discussed afterward.

Critical Thinking Skills
1. The instructor made a class that challenged the students' language abilities and also challenged them to think critically, and that was what I appreciated the most about the class. Also, I think the teacher did a great job at scaffolding since I felt like I was really able to solidify the new vocabulary that we learned.
2. The instructor prepares the class well and gives a lot of opportunities to express our ideas.
3. The course is well organized and provides context and valuable history that makes you think.
4. This class gave me critical thinking skills to assess movies instead of just watching them. Now I enjoy movies on a different level.

Film Selection and Learning Korean through Film
1. I liked that the movie choices were films that I would not have seen otherwise. Two-thirds of them were actually enjoyable, too!
2. I think understanding the history through watching movies was important because it shows the application of Korean history.
3. Watching Korean film is valuable because it was fun way of learning Korean language and the history of Korean politics.
4. When I watched the movie *Peppermint Candy* before, I thought it was boring and did not make sense. Now it is one of my favorite movies.
5. Watching films made me feel a sense of accomplishment.
6. Even though I watched the movie *Joint Security Area* twice before, watching the film in class was something different from what I previously experienced.
7. I feel that the explanations and the section-by-section analysis of each movie provided a much deeper understanding of what exactly was going on in the movie.

Content-Based Instruction
1. I learned a lot about Korean politics, history, and culture through this class.
2. As someone who never learned about Korean political history, learning about the different presidents and the impact of politicians on the society and learning about what Korean nationals went through was valuable.
3. I was able to learn more about Korean history, film, society, and culture.
4. I struggled a bit with the new information, because it was historical and deep concepts. However I felt that I was ready to meet those challenges and that if I needed help I could ask for it.
5. I learned so much information on Korean political history and events such as the Gwangju Uprising.

Korean Language Use
1. I really like the zero-tolerance policy that the professor has for English in the classroom. Holding lectures in truly 100 percent Korean really helps me to lock my brain into Korean mode.

Balance between Formative and Summative Assessment through Feedback
1. The instructor always provided personal feedback for each assignment and helped me improve my performance in the class.
2. Quick and thorough feedback on assignments.
3. The instructor is well prepared for our course with appropriate home assignments each week and communicating with us closely with us throughout the semester.

Small Group Discussion and Debate
1. I think the group sessions were nice because I was able to share ideas with other students.
2. I found the in-class discussion content most valuable because it helped me looked deeper into the movie's content and context.

Some feedback suggested areas for improvement. Some learners felt that too much content was crammed into the single three-hour weekly class session. This resulted in the teacher exceeding the allotted class time, in a lengthy final paper, and in overly rapid talking by the teacher. Some learners wished the class could be longer. Also, the ten-page term paper in addition to more than ten assignments, tests, and the Critical Thinking Skills Project overwhelmed some learners. In the next course iteration the teacher will assign two three-page essays, three one-page impromptu in-class writing activities (which can be assessed formatively in a manner analogous to recall protocol or diagnostic assessment (Dababneh and Yuan, this volume), and a seven-page term paper instead of the current two three-page essays and one ten-page term paper.

The course model described here can be replicated, with appropriate modifications, in most instructional settings, including universities, community colleges, and high schools. The once-weekly 150-minute class format can be replaced with other schedules, for example three hourly sessions weekly, yielding a tradeoff of pros and cons. On the one hand, less time may be available in a single class session for a sequence of related interactions. In compensation there will be a more even alternation of class and out-of-class time, enabling more targeted preparation for each class session.

Conclusions
Curricula, assessments, and materials development at the Korean Language Flagship Center are all rooted in the content-based instruction approach to pedagogy (Cheon 2012). This chapter has examined how a core OACD principle—use of a theme-based syllabus rather than a textbook—and an array of OACD features have been successfully integrated into one such content-based instruction course, Korean Proficiency through Film. Based on learner feedback and teacher observation, integration of OACD has increased flexibility in adapting to learner needs. This flexibility has enhanced the learning experience overall, which has resulted in greater eagerness on the part of learners to engage with high-level culturally laden materials, including those incorporating regional and nonstandard language varieties.

In looking to future iterations of the course, increased learner involvement in the selection of materials is planned in order to further promote learner autonomy and proactivity. Currently the teacher selects the initial set of reading texts and listening passages used when beginning study of a new film or topic, but learners are free to choose reading texts and listening passages based on their interests for subsequent classroom activities.

Collaborative learning is an OACD feature that learners particularly liked. Course evaluations noted that the Critical Thinking Skills Project and other small-group-based work yielded meaningful learning outcomes through the collaboration that occurred during the small group discussions and debate. More opportunities for collaborative work, for example group presentations, are anticipated for the next iteration of the course.

Study Questions

1. How can you integrate a film component into your course, using some of the practices shared in this chapter?
2. In what ways (suggested by the chapter and by your own experience) can the advantages of a content-based instruction syllabus be enhanced by an open architecture curriculum design?
3. Korean is a category 4 (so-called "hard") language for native speakers of English. How do the features described in this chapter help make a hard language more accessible? How would they (not) be equally applicable to the language(s) you teach?

References

Beckett, Gulbahar H., and Tammy Slater. 2005. "The Project Framework: A Tool for Language, Content, and Skills Integration." *ELT Journal* 59, no. 2: 108–16.

Brinton, Donna M., Marguerite A. Snow, and Margorie B. Wesche. 2003. *Content-Based Second Language Instruction*. Ann Arbor, MI: University of Michigan Press.

Campbell, Christine. 2018. "Introduction." *Dialog on Language Instruction* 28, no. 1: 27–28.

Campbell, Christine. 2021. "Open Architecture Curricular Design." In *Transformative Language Learning and Teaching*, edited by Betty Lou Leaver, Dan Davidson, and Christine Campbell, 43–50. Cambridge: Cambridge University Press.

Cheon, Sang Yee. 2007. "Content-Based Language Instruction through Korean Film." *Korean Language in America* 12: 1–16.

Cheon, Sang Yee. 2012. "Culture Learning Curriculum for Advanced Learners of Korean." In *Innovations in Teaching Advanced Korean*, edited by Ho-min Sohn, Sang Yee Cheon, and Haejin E. Koh, 18–31. (*The Korean Language in America* 17). University Park: Penn State University Press.

Laal, Marjan, and Mozhgan Laal. 2012. "Collaborative Learning: What Is It?" *Journal of Procedia: Social and Behavioral Sciences* 31: 491–5.

Markham, Thom. 2011. "Project-Based Learning." *Teacher Librarian* 39, no. 2: 38–42.

Smith, Sheldon. 2020. "Critical Writing." Accessed September 23, 2020. https://www.eapfoundation.com/writing/critical/.

The National Standards Collaborative Board. 2015. *World-Readiness Standards for Learning Languages* (4th ed.). Alexandria: American Council on the Teaching of Foreign Languages.

13

Spiral-Like Design for Teaching Inflectional Languages at Novice Level in an OACD-Enabled Content-Based Course

MARIA BONDARENKO

THIS CHAPTER[1] DESCRIBES HOW spiral-like design can facilitate OACD-enabled content-based instruction for novice learners of highly inflected languages. The context is a week-long content-based instruction module within an eight-week intensive course for beginning learners of Russian. The instructor applied this approach by integrating techniques drawn from cognitive world language pedagogy to meet the needs of these novice learners.

The Challenge of Exploiting OACD with Novice Learners, Especially for Highly Inflected Languages

OACD supports many branches of the communicative language teaching paradigm, including task-, project-, scenario-, and content-based instruction (Campbell 2018; Corin 1997, 2021; Dababneh 2018; Derderian 2017; Leaver and Kaplan 2005; Lyu 2018). Its benefits are related primarily to the social-constructivist theory of knowledge acquisition (Introduction, this volume) and poststructuralist applied linguistics (Pavlenko 2002), where learning is understood not as a purely individual cognitive process but rather as a joint social activity. Recently Leaver and Campbell (2020) highlighted OACD's role as the design framework for an emerging transformative paradigm in language pedagogy.

To date, however, OACD has been effectively applied mostly at proficiency levels starting from 1+/Intermediate High (Krasner 2018). That is undoubtedly related to the cognitive challenges facing adults at early stages of language acquisition, especially for languages with complex morphological systems that differ typologically from learners' first language (e.g., Russian and most Slavic languages for English native speakers).

In such situations the development of fluency and accuracy requires acquisition of numerous morphological patterns (Krasner, this volume), a process that is facilitated by techniques drawn from cognitive language instructional practices (Germain 2017; Ullman and Lavelett 2018), some of which are outlined subsequently. Besides fluency and accuracy issues, Novice learners have difficulty attending simultaneously to form and meaning while processing input within meaning-based instruction (VanPatten 1996). Together these challenges can seriously restrict the use of OACD at lower proficiency levels. The question thus arises: can beginners learning a language like Russian enjoy the benefits of OACD?

Approaches to Overcoming the Challenge

Experiences to date suggest a variety of answers to this question. Some theoreticians recommend explicit teaching at initial stages of learning to build linguistic foundations for later implicit learning (Ellis 2005). In the same vein, Corin (1997, 2022) suggests an intensive pre-training to create schemata simulating (or at least approximating) those possessed by Novice learners in "conversion courses"—courses in which learners already possess some proficiency in a language typologically and genetically related to the target language. Campbell (2018) and Leaver and Campbell (2020) recommend OACD at the Intermediate and Advanced levels and accept the use of textbooks at the lowest levels.

Krasner (this volume) suggests a gradual transition from traditional linear scope-and-sequence to OACD through use of the gradual release of responsibility model. Her approach adapts communication-oriented textbooks to OACD settings utilizing input-oriented tasks that focus initially on receptive (listening and reading) skills so as to address the gap between receptive and productive skills in Novice learners. Krasner prioritizes internet-based genres and exploits both visual and auditory sensory channels, maximizing the efficiency of working memory through the process of constructing schemata, as defined by cognitive load theory (Sweller, Ayres, and Kalyuga 2011).

Demonstrating the inadequacies of traditional approaches to language proficiency growth that assume the inability to conduct content-based activities at beginner levels, Corin (2021) shows that all language task types—which he labels naming, description, narration, and argumentation—can be successfully performed at any level of language proficiency albeit on different text and language complexity levels. The progression from naming to argumentation can be reduced to weekly, daily, or even hourly cycles, a process that the author terms "vertical spiraling." Corin's (2021) approach supports early introduction of OACD within task-, project-, scenario-, and content-based instruction (see also Prabhu 1987, who recommends reasoning gap tasks for beginners).

Anticipating Corin's (2021) theoretical basis, Leaver and Kaplan (2005) describe an intensive elementary Czech course in which authentic materials only and a theme-based textbookless curriculum were successfully used from the very first hour thanks to elaborate application of task-based pedagogy. Authentic tasks (e.g., visa application), which often incorporated higher-order thinking skills, kept learners motivated and therefore allowed the introduction of more complicated grammar and vocabulary, atypical for elementary courses, in the order determined by authentic materials.

Spiral-Like Design to Facilitate OACD-Enabled Content-Based Instruction for Novice Learners

Successful implementation of OACD in novice-level language classrooms can be achieved by amalgamating principles of OACD with techniques (described subsequently) drawn from cognitive language pedagogy that address beginners' needs through "facilitating the internal processes of learning" (Richey, Klein, and Tracey 2011, 105). The spiral-like design described in this chapter aims to guide language development through selection, combination, recycling, drawing attention to form, and gradually enriched and expanded reproduction of language patterns within learners' zone of proximal development (Vygotsky 1978).

The most relevant trends in cognitive language pedagogy that support this spiral-like design include:

- *natural L2 learning theory* (Krashen 1981) supplemented by the output/intake hypotheses and awareness and feedback studies (Swain 1995; Nabei and Swain 2002);
- *focus-on-form approach* (Long 1998);
- *usage-based applied linguistics* (Wulff and Ellis 2018);
- research in individual cognitive styles and their language learning applications (Leaver, Ehrman, and Shekhtman 2005); and finally,
- various recommendations deriving from the *neurolinguistic approach* (NLA) to L2 instruction (Germain 2017).

While implementing OACD in novice-level L2 classrooms for highly inflected languages, this approach prioritizes the following *spiral-like design principles* (SDPs):

- (SDP1) *continuing diagnostics of linguistic needs* to ensure language recycling and comprehensive input;
- (SDP2) *cognates and linguistic tools for opinion support* (e.g., logical connectors and mental verbs) to enable reasoning gap tasks (Prabhu 1987; Corin 2021);
- (SDP3) *authentic simple textual and multimedia genres* to capitalize on learners' digital literacies and other skills and schemata (Bondarenko and Klimanova 2022; 2023);
- (SDP4) *spaced introduction of patterns from individual paradigms* (e.g., morphological forms of the same word, different declension models, rules, and exceptions);
- (SDP5) *exemplar-based learning* (Wulff and Ellis 2018) that encourages learners to focus on salient examples in which target lexicogrammatical patterns (Halliday 2013) are contextualized; the examples are then used as models;
- (SDP6) *"economic recycling of constructions"* (Ellis 2009, 15) drawing on corpus-informed L2 instruction (Samburskiy 2014);
- (SDP7) *double recycling*—"recycling of vocabulary and structures on the same theme in various contexts" to ensure "coherent transitions across themes" (Dababneh 2018, 18, 20) and spaced repetition;
- (SDP8) *input/intake as a cycle of multiple steps*, in accordance with the comprehensible input hypothesis (Krashen 1981) and levels of conceptualization principles (Stoller 2002);

- (SDP9) *circle of literacy (oral interaction-writing-reading) focused on teacher-learner oral dialog* to support oral input and modeling integrated in social contexts (Germain 2017, van Lier 2004); hypothesis and intake checking through oral output (Swain 1995); immediate corrective feedback (Nabei and Swain 2002); balanced development of oral, writing, and reading skills; and progression in increasing text-type complexity from short sentence to paragraph to extended text (Corin 2021; Germain 2017);
- (SDP10) *immediate oral corrective feedback in the form of recasting*—"reformulation of a previous erroneous utterance into a more target-like form" within a content-based, form-meaning-negotiation dialogue (Nabei and Swain 2002, 43);
- (SDP11) *"inherently repetitive tasks,"* in which "repetition is the means by which the activity goal is attained" (Gatbonton and Segalowitz 2005, 332) to support spaced repetition in meaningful contexts;
- (SDP12) *focus on form*—"briefly drawing students' attention to linguistic elements [...] in lessons whose overriding focus is on meaning" (Long 1998, 40), to facilitate the "experience of noticing [as] a necessary and sufficient condition for the conversion of input to intake" (Ellis 2005, 317);
- (SDP13) *metalinguistic activities* to synthesize acquired knowledge and support learners whose cognitive learning styles are based on reflective observation and abstract conceptualization (Leaver, Ehrman, and Shekhtman 2005); and
- (SDP14) *metacognitive discussions* that help learners take greater responsibility for the learning process (Oxford 2017; Wenden 1998) and thus promote learners' autonomy as one goal of transformative language learning and teaching (Leaver and Campbell 2020).

Bondarenko (in preparation) explores the (neuro)cognitive rationales of these principles.

Operationalizing Spiral-Like Design in an OACD-Based Intensive Course for Novice Learners of Russian

Learning Context

The OACD-based module described here was implemented in an elementary Russian class with ten participants in the 2019 Summer Intensive Language Program at the Middlebury Institute of International Studies in Monterey (2019 SILP MIIS). The eight-week program prioritized content-based instruction in immersive settings (twenty-five contact hours per week). The instructor (the author) developed an OACD-based curriculum with weekly theme-based modules. At the outset of the module presented here, learners had completed twenty-five contact hours and were at Novice Low (ILR 0+).

Defining Themes for a Weekly Theme-Based OACD Syllabus

The result of a needs analysis conducted via an open-ended online survey showed that learner interests about Russia revolved around two topics: food and Russian/former

SPIRAL-LIKE DESIGN FOR TEACHING INFLECTIONAL LANGUAGES

Soviet life and mentality from social, political, and cultural perspectives. Considering their linguistic skills (SDP1), for the second-week OACD module the instructor selected the theme *Жилищный вопрос в России* (The Housing Issue in Russia) encompassing the following learning units conducted over five days:

- U-1: Wealth and Poverty in Russia (introducing the course umbrella theme)
- U-2: Housing Phenomena: Kommunalka, Khrushchevka, Stalinka
- U-3: Kommunalka, Khrushchevka, Stalinka: History, Examples, Today's Issues
- U-4: Russian Oligarch Housing: Rublevka and Elite Apartments
- U-5: Conclusion: Housing Conditions and People's Mentality

This theme was closely connected to that of the previous and following weeks and ensured sequencing of thematic complexity through recycling of content and language (SDP6 and SDP7). Thus the second-week theme built on the content of the first week, which was organized around the theme *Мой дом—моя крепость* (My home—my fortress). By the end of the first week, learners were expected to produce a written text and maintain a conversation mostly based on description with basic elements of argumentation on the topic *Мой дом: что это значит для меня* (My home: what does that mean for me?). The following sample illustrates the expected language production:

> My name is. . . . I am American. . . . My family name is a typical Scottish. . . . That means that I have some Scottish blood. I speak/do not speak (a language). My parents, grandparents are from. . . . For me, "my house" means my country, my state, my city, my house, my favorite things (e.g., books, guitar), my hobbies, my family, my friends/neighbors, my pets, my language. My state (description). My family: I have a. . . . His/her/their name(s) is/are. . . . He/she/they live(s). . . . He/she/they work(s). . . . Our house (description). My room (description). I think I am a (non-)typical American because. . . . I (do not) like/have. . . . I think our family is a (non-)typical American family because. . . . I think my country, my state, my city is (not) a good place to live because. . . .

The second-week theme also introduced a thematic umbrella *Кому на Руси жить хорошо: бедность и богатство в России* (Who lives well in Russia: poverty and wealth in Russia), which encompassed interrelated themes to be addressed throughout the course.

Structure of OACD-Based Learning Units

Each unit of the module The Housing Issue in Russia was comprised of several discussion segments incorporating one or several reasoning, information, and basic opinion gap tasks. The tasks involved the use of authentic (or, in some instances, adapted) internet-based resources (e.g., statistical charts) facilitated by the inclusion of cognates and previously acquired linguistic patterns (SDP1, SDP2, and SDP3).

Each discussion was structured according to the traditional three-step task sequence—*pre-task*, *task implementation*, and *post-task* (Prabhu 1987)—interpreted in light of the *circle of literacy* (*oral interaction–writing–reading*), which emphasizes teacher-learner dialog with immediate corrective feedback (recasting) (SDP9 and SDP10). After the initial oral activity, learners collaboratively composed a text based on previous oral discussion and then read aloud the same or a more complex text to practice pronunciation and linguistic rules (SDP9).

In line with SDP12 and SDP13, the inter-task was introduced, a planned or spontaneous interruption of content-based instruction to raise learners' awareness of linguistic resources through a meaning negotiation conducted mostly in the target language ("Do you understand what the word X means? What is the opposite of X? How do you say X in English?"). In keeping with SDP13 and SDP14, the closure activity synthesized learning gain and stimulated reflection on learning experiences through metalinguistic and metacognitive discussions. Figure 13.1 presents the typical shape of units.

Content-Based Instruction Supported by the Inter-Task

The remainder of this section describes the first discussion within Unit 1 (Wealth and Poverty in Russia), illustrating the interplay between content-based instruction and inter-task segments. In the following descriptions, italics indicate discussion/dialog

II.1 PRE-TASK: ORAL DIALOG initiating a new set of tasks and a new circle of literacy

I.5 CLOSURE: Metalinguistic and metacognitive discussion aiming at synthesizing learning gain (both related to content and language) and reflecting on learning experience.

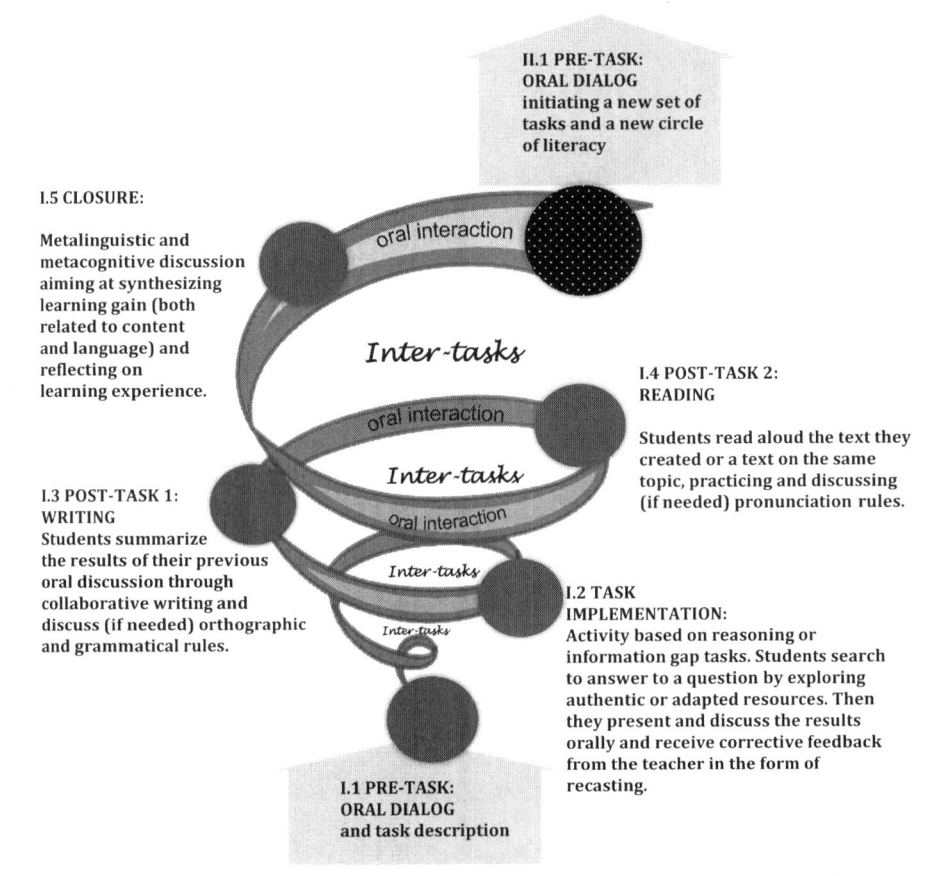

I.4 POST-TASK 2: READING Students read aloud the text they created or a text on the same topic, practicing and discussing (if needed) pronunciation rules.

I.3 POST-TASK 1: WRITING Students summarize the results of their previous oral discussion through collaborative writing and discuss (if needed) orthographic and grammatical rules.

I.2 TASK IMPLEMENTATION: Activity based on reasoning or information gap tasks. Students search to answer to a question by exploring authentic or adapted resources. Then they present and discuss the results orally and receive corrective feedback from the teacher in the form of recasting.

I.1 PRE-TASK: ORAL DIALOG and task description

Figure 13.1. The spiraled structure of typical unit discussions within OACD-based modules, with inter-tasks interspersed. The spiral proceeds from bottom (inside) toward the top (outside).

conducted in Russian. Newly presented words (cognates and words built from the same roots as previously known words) and other words that will be the focus of discussion are presented in brackets in Russian with transliteration. Underscoring indicates suffixes that will be a focus of discussion.

I. Pre-task (task description). Conducted entirely in Russian through teacher-led discussion supported by visual aids. The instructor reviews previously learned language while modeling new language that builds on existing language, including new words built from already-known roots and suffixes, and leveraging cognates (SDP1, SDP2, SDP6, and SDP7):

> At home [*Дома, doma*] you wrote a text [*текст, tekst*] on the topic [*тема, tema*] "My home" [*Мой дом, moĭ dom*]: what does that mean for me? You/We Americans [*американцы, amerikantsy*] and your/our home — that is America [*Америка, Amerika*]. Today we have a new topic [*новая тема, novaĭa tema*]. It is also "home," but in a new perspective [*в новой перспективе, v novoĭ perspektive*]. It is the Russian perspective [*российская перспектива, rossiĭskaĭa perspektiva*]. The Russian Federation [*Российская федерация, rossiĭskaĭa federatsiĭa*] is a large, beautiful, and interesting country [*страна, strana*]. Russian people [*россияне, rossiĭane*] live there. Russia [*Россия, Rossiĭa*] — that is their home. How do they live? Good? Bad? My first question: what do you think, is there poverty [*бед<u>ность</u>, bed<u>nost'</u>*] in Russia? Do you know/understand what the word *бед<u>ность</u>* [*bed<u>nost'</u>*] means?

Thus, learners discovered the meaning of new words directly from the question prompting argumentation (discussion with opinion support, SDP12), while the question "Do you understand the word..." opened a natural form-meaning negotiation and metalinguistic dialogue integrated into a content-oriented discussion without interrupting the flow of the discussion (SDP13).

The inter-task, conducted entirely in Russian, focuses on reviewing "adjective + noun" agreement and the prepositional case of nouns in *-ия* (*-iĭa*) (*Россия, Rossiĭa—в России, v Rossii*), but also on new vocabulary, supported by visual aids that show contrasting vocabulary items and word structure (suffixes; Figure 13.2): poor and rich home/man/city/region [*бедный и богатый дом/человек/город/регион, bednyĭ i bogatyĭ dom/chelovek/gorod/region*], poor and rich country [*бедная и богатая страна, bednaĭa i bogataĭa strana*]; poorness (i.e., poverty) [*бед<u>ность</u>, bed<u>nost'</u>*] — richness (i.e., wealth) [*бога<u>тство</u>, boga<u>tstvo</u>*]; *-<u>ость</u>* [*-<u>ost'</u>*] is an abstract suffix [*абстрактный суффикс, abstraktnyĭ suffiks*], *-<u>ство</u>* [*-<u>stvo</u>*] is also an abstract suffix.

Continuation of instructor-led discussion in Russian: "What do you think [*Как вы думаете, Kak vy dumaete*], is there poorness (poverty) in Russia? Are there poor people [*бедн<u>ые</u> люди, bedn<u>ye</u> lĭudi*]? Are there rich people [*богат<u>ые</u> люди, bogat<u>ye</u> lĭudi*] in Russia?" An expected answer: "I think/I know that [*Я думаю/Я знаю, что, Ĭa dumaĭu/Ĭa znaĭu, chto*] in Russia there is poorness (poverty) and richness (wealth), poor people and rich people. I don't know." If errors occur, the teacher provides corrective feedback in the form of recasting "Do I understand well, you want to say..." (SDP10). In this discussion, conducted entirely in Russian, a simple pattern for supporting opinion—*I think/I know that*—is practiced (SDP2).

The inter-task draws attention to "adjective + noun" agreement in the plural (a recently introduced pattern): rich and poor people [*богат<u>ые</u> и бедн<u>ые</u> люди, bogat<u>ye</u> i*

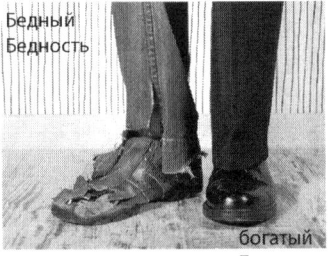

Figure 13.2. Visual support for introducing Russian analogs of the words *poor, rich, poorness* (i.e., poverty), *richness* (i.e., wealth)

bednye liudi]. The discussion is conducted in Russian (*Какая это форма? Почему тут -ые? What form is it? Why is it -yie?*).

Continuation of instructor-led discussion in Russian: "Do you want to know [*Вы хотите знать, Vy khotite znat'*] the facts [*факты, fakty*]? I want [*Я хочу, Ia khochu*] to! I want to know the facts, what the statistics [*статистика, statistika*] say. Do you (also) want to?" An expected answer modeled by the teacher: "Yes, I (also) want to know the facts." The usage of the verb "to want" [*хотеть, khotet'*], introduced in only two forms as a contextualized lexicogrammatical pattern, implements spaced introduction of items from the same paradigm (SDP4) and exemplar-based teaching (SDP5). Throughout the activity, these patterns have been practiced on many occasions: "Do you want to say (within recasting), Do you want to read? Do you want to write?"

The inter-task focuses on the verb "to want" [*хотеть, khotet'*] in two basic forms ("I want, You want").

Continuation of instructor-led discussion in Russian: "Excellent! If we want [*мы хотим, my khotim*] to know the facts, then we need to look at the statistics from the internet [*из Интернета, iz Interneta*]. Look at the figure [*график, grafik*] (Figure 13.3).

II. Task implementation. Working in pairs, learners analyze the authentic chart (Figure 13.3), while the teacher intervenes to help with exploring its content and language: "Are those new or old statistics? Do you understand what the words *зарплата, зарплата в день, больше чем, меньше чем* (wage, wage per day, more/less then) mean? What do the colors (red, grey, pink) on the chart mean?"

The inter-task focuses on new vocabulary (*salary, salary per day, color, red, orange, pink, more than, less than, how much, ten, thirty, forty, fifty*) and grammar patterns (genitive plural in *-ов [-ov]* introduced as lexicogrammatical patterns: "how many percent/dollars [*сколько процентов/долларов, skol'ko protsentov/dollarov*]."

Learners answer the initial question about the existence of poverty in Russia based on statistical data, while the instructor scaffolds their production through guiding questions and corrective feedback through recasting. An expected answer: "Yes, there is poverty in Russia. The statistics say that there are poor people in Russia (How many? More than 40 percent). They have a small salary, less than 10 dollars per day." The instructor can redirect the conversation toward learners' experience through the following questions: "Tell me please, 10 dollar per day, is it a lot or little in America? Is it

SPIRAL-LIKE DESIGN FOR TEACHING INFLECTIONAL LANGUAGES 185

ЗАРПЛАТА В ДЕНЬ ($)

В МИРЕ

- МЕНЬШЕ $2 — 15%
- БОЛЬШЕ $50 — 7%
- $20-50 — 9%
- $10-20 — 13%
- $2-10 — 56%

В мире есть бедность.
А в России?
Как вы думаете,
в России есть бедность?

В РОССИИ

- ОЧЕНЬ БЕДНЫЕ
- МЕНЬШЕ $3.5 — 6%
- БОЛЬШЕ $35 — 7%
- $20-35 — 16%
- $3.5-10 — 37%
- $10-20 — 34%

БЕДНЫЕ

6% + 37% + 34% = 77 %
$0-20 В ДЕНЬ:
БЕДНЫЕ И ОЧЕНЬ БЕДНЫЕ

Figure 13.3. Wages across various population segments in Russia
Source: Солидарность, Деньги к деньгам. February 17, 2018. https://www.solidarnost.org/articles/Den_gi_k_den_gam.html. Used with permission.

a lot or little for you? What is the minimum wage per day in America, in your state, in your city? What is a 'normal' wage (if you are a student, if you have a family)?"

Then the instructor introduces a new set of similar questions within a similar task (SDP11) related to richness (i.e., wealth) in Russia and suggests that learners explore in pairs recent Forbes data available on the internet to select the names of the first two or more Russian billionaires in the top fifty. Learners come back with the answers while the teacher scaffolds the oral discussion.

III. Post-task (writing). With the teacher's assistance learners write a summary of their findings using collaborative writing. They take turns writing down in a collaborative online document what others suggest, and then edit the text to make it coherent, correct mistakes, and give it a title (alternative: learners write in pairs and peer review each other's texts). Here is a sample of such a written production in English translation:

Big Paradox

Statistics say that in Russia there are poor people, more than 40 percent. They have very small salaries, less than 10 dollars per day. But statistics from the internet also say that there are very rich people in Russia. For example, in the Forbes rating, there are Russian billionaires and oligarchs. They are all men. They have very big salaries. The leader (in the first place) is. . . . That is a big paradox: very rich and very poor people live in Russia. Post-Soviet Russia today is a country of contrast. We think there are social problems in Russian . . .

The inter-task focuses on all grammatical and spelling rules and logical connectors that occur in the text.

IV. Post-task (reading). Learners read aloud the composed text or a new one suggested by the teacher with some new elements. If pronunciation errors occur, the teacher models the pronunciation and discusses phonetic rules.

V. Closure (meta-linguistic and metacognitive discussion). In the final stage learners make a list of vocabulary words and patterns they have used during the activity. At this time any questions related to the content, language, and pedagogical aspects of the activity can be discussed in the first language.

Outcomes and Lessons Learned

The experience described previously implementing OACD-based content-based instruction in a beginning language classroom demonstrates that this is feasible. Supported by spiral-like design, these novice learners experienced benefits associated with content-based instruction and OACD, including learning a language with a complex morphology through collaborative exploration (including elements of research, analysis, and argumentation) of complex topics of interest to learners.

The same design principles have been successfully reproduced by the author in the same and different learning settings. Within the 2019 SILP MIIS, learners resumed their investigation of poverty and wealth within a new research-based project on Russians' economic status, salaries, and cost of living. They also explored their second topic of common interest—food—through evaluation of Russian shopping-basket prices compared to Russian salaries. Between 2016 and 2021, at the University of Montreal, many OACD-based modules on similar or different topics have been used in large (up to thirty learners) first- and second-semester Russian language classrooms within semester-by-semester language programs in nonimmersive settings (three hours per week).

Evidence of novice learners' success in content-based learning comes from teacher observations of classroom performance, feedback within metacognitive discussions, performance in proficiency tests, and appreciation surveys. By the end of the 2019 SILP learners demonstrated the expected level of proficiency (ranging from Novice High [ILR 0+] to Intermediate Low to Mid [ILR 1]) and expressed appreciation for the quality of both the learning experience and instructional approach. Although none had been exposed to content-based instruction previously, they demonstrated readiness for such an experience.

A major limitation of this study is that it includes no comparative examination of whether the novice learners exposed to OACD performed better or took control of their learning more quickly than with traditional approaches. Future research on this topic, including longitudinal study, is needed.

Important lessons from challenges that arose during implementation included the understanding that the "openness" of OACD was related not only to curricula based on learners' interests and linguistic patterns introduced in the order of their appearance in authentic materials but also to the open-endedness of classroom activities. In the beginning of a well-prepared OACD module, the teacher can have only a general idea about the final product and how the module will be implemented. Based on ongoing observation of learners' performance and their emotional and cognitive state, the teacher must be ready to modify the scenario "on the fly," slow down or accelerate the pacing, introduce additional inter-task segments, or challenge learners with additional questions.

Conclusions

This chapter has focused on the use of spiral-like design to facilitate OACD-enabled content-based instruction for novice learners of highly inflected languages like Russian. Proficiency level and linguistic characteristics of the target language do shape the way in which OACD can be implemented at this level. The OACD principle that learners participate in the selection of meaningful content limits control over the order in which linguistic patterns are introduced. To meet novice learners' needs, language monitoring techniques grounded in research into human cognition, such as those introduced in the spiral-like design, can be integrated into the OACD framework. Thus the author's experience implementing OACD in Russian language instruction at low proficiency levels supports the claim for a holistic sociocognitive imperative, arguing that "highly effective pedagogy requires viewing language and language learning as both cognitive and social phenomena" (Touth and Davin 2016, 149). Spiral-like design, which integrates sociocultural approaches with others keyed to the cognitive machinery of language learning, facilitates the transformative experience within a holistic—both cognitive and social—perspective in beginning Russian language classes.

Study Questions

1. Analyze your Novice-level curriculum. In what ways is it informed by sociocultural learning theory? Where it does not, identify where it might benefit from some minor adjustments.
2. What challenges do you foresee in implementing OACD in your courses? How might you meet those challenges?
3. Identify the ways in which your course is and is not spiraled and how you might take greater advantage of this approach.

Note

1. This chapter would never have been possible without the invaluable collaboration of Dr. Vita V. Kogan, coordinator of the Russian language program at the 2019 Summer Intensive Language Program of Middlebury Institute of International Studies at Monterey, CA, USA.

References

Bondarenko, Maria. In preparation. "Spiral-like Design for Communicative L2 Teaching at Low Proficiency Levels: Principles and Rationales."
Bondarenko, Maria, and Liudmila Klimanova. 2022. "Pathways to Digital L2 Literacies for Text-Based Telecollaboration at the Beginner Level." In *Enhancing Beginner-Level Foreign Language Education for Adult*

Learners, edited by Ekaterina Nemtchinova, 149–66. New York: Routledge. https://doi.org/10.4324/9781003058441.

Bondarenko, Maria, and Luidmila Klimanova. 2023. "The Dialogic Conception of Beginning L2 Writing Via Social Networking and Telecollaboration." In *Technology in Second Language Writing: Advances in Composing, Translation, Writing Pedagogy and Data-Driven Learning*, edited by Jingjing Qin and Paul Stapleton, 114–32. New York: Routledge.

Campbell, Christine. 2018. "Introduction to Proceedings of the Actualizing Open Architecture in the Classroom." *Dialog on Language Instruction* 28, no. 1: 27–28.

Corin, Andrew. 1997. "A Course to Convert Czech Proficiency to Proficiency in Serbian and Croatian." In *Content-Based Instruction in Foreign Language Education: Models and Methods*, edited by Stephen B. Stryker and Betty Lou Leaver, 78–104. Washington, DC: Georgetown University Press.

Corin, Andrew. 2021. "Foreign Language Learning Efficiency: Transformative Learning in an Outcomes-Based Environment." In *Transformative Language Learning and Teaching*, edited by Betty Lou Leaver, Dan E. Davidson, and Christine Campbell, 51–60. Cambridge: Cambridge University Press.

Corin, Andrew. 2022. Kurikulum sa otvorenom arhitekturom za učenje srpskog i drugih jezika u SAD. *Naučni sastanak slavista u Vukove dane* 51: 17–27.

Dababneh, Reem. 2018. "The Scenario-Based Syllabus for the Post-Basic Arabic Program at the DLIFLC." *Dialog on Language Instruction* 28, no. 1: 13–26.

Derderian, Ani. 2017. "Designing for Teaching and Learning in an Open World: Task Supported Open Architecture Language Instruction." *International Journal of Adult Vocational Education and Technology* 8, no. 3: 55–67.

Ellis, Nick. 2005. "At the Interface: Dynamic Interactions of Explicit and Implicit Language Knowledge." *Studies in Second Language Acquisition* 27: 305–52.

Ellis, Nick. 2009. "The Psycholinguistics of the Interaction Approach." In *Multiple Perspectives on Interaction in SLA: Second Language Research in Honor of Susan M. Gass*, edited by Alison Mackey and Charlene Polio, 11–40. London: Routledge.

Gatbonton, Elizabeth, and Norman Segalowitz. 2005. "Rethinking Communicative Language Teaching: A Focus on Access to Fluency." *The Canadian Modern Language Review/La Revue canadienne des langues vivantes* 61, no. 3: 325–53.

Germain, Claude. 2017. *The Neurolinguistic Approach (NLA) for Learning and Teaching Foreign Languages, Theory and Practice*. Cambridge: Cambridge Scholars Publishing.

Halliday, Michael. 2013. *Halliday's Introduction to Functional Grammar*. 4th ed. London: Routledge.

Krashen, Stephen. 1981. *Second Language Acquisition and Second Language Learning*. Oxford: Pergamon.

Krasner, Irene. 2018. "Open Architecture Approach to Teaching Russian as a Foreign Language." *ACTR Letter* 45, no. 2: 1–5.

Leaver, Betty Lou, and Cristine Campbell. 2020. "The Shifting Paradigm in Russian Language Programs from Communicative Language Teaching to Transformative Language Learning and Teaching." In *Art of Teaching Russian*, edited by Evgeny Dengub, Irina Dubinina, and Jason Merrill, 247–62. Washington, DC: Georgetown University Press.

Leaver, Betty Lou, Madeline Ehrman, and Boris Shekhtman. 2005. *Achieving Success in Second Language Acquisition*. Cambridge: Cambridge University Press.

Leaver, Betty Lou, and Masha M. Kaplan. 2005. "Task-Based Instruction in U.S. Government Slavic Language Programs. In *Task-Based Instruction in Foreign Language Education: Practices and Programs*, edited by Betty Lou Leaver and Jane Willis, 47–66. Washington, DC: Georgetown University Press.

Long, Michael. 1998. "Focus on Form in Task-Based L2 Teaching," *University of Hawai'i Working Paper in ESL* 16, no. 2: 35–49.

Lyu, H. T. 2018. "Learning through Discussions in a High-Level Language Course." *Dialog on Language Instruction* 28, no. 1: 65–72.

Nabei, Toshiyo, and Merrill Swain. 2002. "Learner Awareness of Recasts in Classroom Interaction: A Case Study of an Adult EFL Student's Second Language Learning." *Language Awareness* 11, no. 1: 43–66.

Oxford, Rebecca. 2017. *Teaching and Researching Language Learning Strategies: Self-Regulation in Context*. 2nd ed. London: Routledge.

Pavlenko, A. 2002. "Poststructuralist Approaches to the Study of Social Factors in Second Language Learning and Use." In *Portraits of the L2 User*, edited by Vivian Cook, 277–302. Clevedon: Multilingual Matters.

Prabhu, N. S. 1987. *Second Language Pedagogy*. Oxford: Oxford University Press.
Richey, Rita, James Klein, and Monica Tracey. 2011. "Conditions-Based Theory." In *The Instructional Design Knowledge Base: Theory, Research and Practice*, edited by Rita Richey, James Klein, and Monica Tracey, 104–28. London: Routledge.
Samburskiy, Denis. 2014. "Corpus-Informed Pedagogical Grammar of English: Pros and Cons." *Procedia—Social and Behavioral Sciences* 154: 263–67.
Stoller, Frederika. 2002. "Content-Based Instruction: A Shell for Language Teaching or a Framework for Strategic Language and Content Learning?" https://carla.umn.edu/cobaltt/modules/strategies/stoller2002/stoller.pdf.
Swain, Merrill. 1995. "Three Functions of Output in Second Language Learning." In *Principle and Practice in Applied Linguistics: Studies in Honour of H.G. Widdowson*, edited by Gruy Cook and Barbara Seidlhofer, 124–44. Oxford: Oxford University Press.
Sweller, John, Paul Ayres, and Slava Kalyuga. 2011. *Cognitive Load Theory*. New York: Springer.
Touth, Paul, and Kristin Davin. 2016. "The Sociocognitive Imperative of L2 Pedagogy." *The Modern Language Journal* 100: 148–68.
Ullman, Michal, and Jarrett Lovelett. 2018. "Implications of the Declarative/Procedural Model for Improving Second Language Learning: The Role of Memory Enhancement Techniques." *Second Language Research* 34, no. 1: 39–65.
van Lier, Leo. 2004. *Ecology and Semiotics of Language Learning. A Sociocultural Perspective*. Boston: Kluwer Academic Publishers.
VanPatten, Bill. 1996. *Input Processing and Grammar Instruction in Second Language Acquisition*. Norwood: Ablex.
Vygotsky, Lev. 1978. *Mind in Society: The Development of Higher Psychological Processes*, edited by Michael Cole, Vera Jolm-Steiner, Sylvia Scribner, and Ellen Souberman. Cambridge: Harvard University Press.
Wenden, Anita. 1998. "Metacognitive Knowledge and Language Learning." *Applied Linguistics* 19, no. 4: 515–37.
Wulff, Stefanie, and Nick Ellis. 2018. "Usage-Based Approaches to SLA." In *Bilingual Cognition and Language: The State of the Science across Its Subfields*, edited by David Miller, Fatih Bayram, Jason Rothman, and Ludovica Serratrice, 37–56. Amsterdam: John Benjamins.

Part 5
Learning Assessment, Program Evaluation, and Program Management in an OACD Context

14

Open Architecture Curricular Design as an Enabler of Diagnostic Instruction[1]

REEM DABABNEH AND RONG YUAN

OTHER CHAPTERS IN THIS volume (Chapter 1, Wang) have noted the role of OACD in enhancing intermediate- and advanced-course proficiency outcomes in the School of Resident Education (RE) of the Defense Language Institute Foreign Language Center's (DLIFLC) Directorate of Continuing Education during the years 2006–2019. This chapter narrows the focus to OACD's role as an enabler of *diagnostic instruction* as a key contributor to the outcomes achieved.

Throughout this period a guiding principle within the Directorate of Continuing Education was "to teach, not to the schedule, but to learner needs" (Alanazi, personal communication, May 23, 2023) through what was known as *diagnostic instruction*. The term refers to the concept that every well-designed instructional activity is an opportunity for teachers and learners to assess ongoing learning and adapt in reaction to that assessment.

This chapter describes the implementation of diagnostic instruction in the School of Resident Education at the Directorate of Continuing Education,[2] providing examples of two types of formative assessment: daily informal formative assessment drawn from curricular activities (scenarios, preparatory activities, translation, writing, etc.) and formalized formative assessment: *diagnostic assessment* (DA), *online diagnostic assessment* (ODA), and *recall protocol*.[3]

The Distinction between Summative and Formative Assessment

Instruction and assessment were once viewed as separate entities in world language education. Traditionally learners were assessed outside the learning process through testing events requiring them to demonstrate mastery of specific learned content or competencies. As language assessment practices evolved, teachers began to question this bifurcation.

Over the past four decades testing specialists have pondered to what extent assessment can be "educative," informing learners about their strengths and weaknesses and preparing them for the next level of learning (Wiggins 1998). In the field of second language acquisition, the advent of task-based instruction and the national standards in the 1990s signaled a more conscious integration of instruction with assessment, and in 2004 Lantolf and Poehner (2004) proposed "dynamic assessment" as a way to further fuse the two.[4] More comprehensively Garza (2021) has suggested multitiered assessments that reflect teaching and focus on catching language proficiency in action as it is performed in the classroom, using the same modalities and formats demonstrated in class activities and projects.

Progressively academic dialogue on assessment has turned toward the notion of formative assessment as a learning-oriented alternative to summative assessment, the latter traditionally test-based. Formative assessment is clearly distinguished from summative assessment in the literature. Bachman (1990) presents the following distinction:

> In the language testing literature, FA [Formative Assessment] is usually contrasted with Summative Assessment [SA] on the grounds that the former is intended to feed back into the teaching and learning process while the latter reports on the outcomes of learning. (60–61)

More recently, Clementi (2022) posited: "Any well-designed classroom activity is formative assessment," in the sense that the activity "enables," or "provides a basis for" assessment.

In 2010 the American Council on the Teaching of Foreign Languages issued a practitioner's guide to developing assessments that offers a definition of formative assessment and summative assessment, with helpful examples of each:

> Formative assessment ranges from quick learning checks to activities guiding students to more independent use of language.... In summative assessment, students demonstrate to themselves and their teacher that they can apply the lessons learned, the skills acquired, and the knowledge gained in the unit of instruction. This is when students produce language on their own and show what they are able to do as a result of the instruction. Summative assessment is a new application of the individual elements of vocabulary and grammar assessed at the formative level. Through summative assessment, students showcase the level of proficiency acquired. (Sandrock 2010, 62–64)

This characterization of summative assessment reflects a qualitative evolution away from the typically discrete-point, decontextualized achievement-type summative tests of earlier times. The forms of learner activity referred to by Sandrock as being useful for summative assessment could be equally utilized for formative assessment. The foregoing references thus suggest a convergent trend between summative assessment and formative assessment, including integration of both more fully into the learning process.

Overview of Formative Assessment
Origins
Formative assessment as a concept was first introduced by Scriven (1967), then quickly adopted and expanded by Bloom (1968) and subsequent publications (Allal and Lopez 2005). As summarized by Black and William (2009), formative assessment aims to do

the following, in this sequence: (1) establish where the learners are in their learning, (2) establish where they are going, and (3) establish what needs to be done to get them there.

Most researchers consider formative assessment to be deeply rooted in social constructivism. According to this theory, the learning process engages learners in multidimensional interactions through which they actively construct new knowledge from knowledge they already possess, improving their metacognitive skills and self-regulating their learning in the process (Greenfield 2009).

The practice of formative assessment was equally inspired by Vygotsky's concept of zone of proximal development (Vygotsky 1934/1978), which is the zone where a learner can, with the aid of a mentor who engages the learner in mediation, make a leap of progress to the next level of development, transferring what has been internalized through mediation beyond the immediate task to other tasks. The zone of proximal development allows practitioners to assess the gap between learners' current attainment level and the optimal learning objectives for the next phase of learning. Learners and mediators work together within the learner's zone of proximal development to achieve improvement in language performance and/or proficiency. Usually teachers provide scaffolding to learners, adjusting instruction to facilitate attainment of learning objectives. Diagnostic assessment (including tailored learning plans; see subsequent discussion), online diagnostic assessment, and recall protocol are formalized assessments teachers can use when assessing learner zone of proximal development.

Teacher and Learner Roles

The roles of teacher and learner are equally pivotal during formative assessment. Teachers, whether informally during instruction or through formalized protocols, assess learners' current levels of performance and/or proficiency and provide scaffolding to help advancement. They also assess learning styles, strategies, and similar. Learners, for their part, come to understand their own learning and eventually to self-regulate it, conducting self-assessment and adjusting learning strategies in order to move forward toward learning objectives (Black and William 1998).

Educative Value

After reviewing experimental and quasi-experimental research and several meta-analyses, Black and William (1998) concluded that formative assessment enhances learning outcomes, in contrast to summative testing, the latter having a limited and often unintended effect on learning. Improved learning outcomes through the use of formative assessment have also been reported by Trumbull and Lash (2013). As explained by Leaver (2022), the most visible short-term benefit of formative assessment may be achieved by learners at the "cusp" of a proficiency level—that is, "a level of proficiency that is not quite at the next level but that exhibits most of the identifiers of the next level" (Leaver 2022, 71). Formative assessment helps identify specific "missing pieces" that will enable the learner to cross the cusp to the next base proficiency level.

OACD as the Enabler of Diagnostic Instruction

OACD serves as an enabler for exploiting formative assessment, creating flexibility that enables an instructional process continuously informed by formative assessment to adapt in response to it in real time. This is possible because every instructional activity enables instructors and learners to assess ongoing learning even in the absence of formalized formative assessment protocols. Immediate exploitation of continuous formative assessment, in turn, enables a reduction of in-course testing and maximization of learning time. An instructional process in which formative assessment is utilized in this way came to be termed *diagnostic instruction* following the introduction of OACD in the School of Resident Education and other Directorate of Continuing Education programs in 2006. In practice diagnostic instruction included two types of formative assessment:

- Daily informal formative assessment that "fed back" observations of curricular activities such as scenarios, preparatory activities, and others into the teaching and learning process (as per Bachman's definition above)
- Periodic formalized formative assessment through recall protocol, diagnostic assessment (including follow-up through tailored learning plans), and online diagnostic assessment.

Diagnostic instruction, a key component of OACD at the Directorate of Continuing Education, contributed to a striking improvement in overall proficiency results, particularly in the School of Resident Education, where the objectives of the intermediate and advanced courses in the School of Resident Education were Advanced High (ILR 2+) and Superior (ILR 3), respectively, in listening and reading. The stated entrance requirements in both skills for the intermediate course were Advanced (ILR 2) and Advanced High (ILR 2+) for the advanced course. Between 2008 and 2013, for which a comparison is available for 850 intermediate- and advanced-course students (Leaver and Campbell 2015), graduation attainment rose from 50 percent to just over 80 percent, with close to 60 percent exceeding graduation requirements, even though not all incoming students met the stated entrance requirements. In 2013 one of every fifteen individual exit-test results (L, R, or S) was a 3+ or 4. (See Chapter 1 for more examples of proficiency results.)

Diagnostic Instruction through Informal Formative Assessment

It is important to understand the context in which informal formative assessment occurred. From 2006 through 2019 the School of Resident Education specialized in teaching intermediate and advanced courses designed to enhance proficiency in Arabic, Chinese, Korean, Persian-Farsi, Russian, Spanish, and several other languages. These courses initially ran four (Spanish) to twelve (Modern Standard Arabic, Chinese Mandarin, Korean) months, six hours daily, five days per week. (See previous discussion for the course proficiency objectives and the entry proficiency requirements.) Prior to the introduction of OACD, many learners failed to achieve these proficiency levels.

OACD was introduced in 2006 as the framework for course curricula in the School of Resident Education and other schools at the Directorate of Continuing Education. The School of Resident Education syllabi, especially in later years, were often comprised of weekly units with one broad theme, often split into four daily subthemes with a culminating project or scenario on the fifth day (Corin 2021). Weekly end-of-unit activities were preceded by a series of tasks designed to generate a smooth build-up to execution of the culminating scenario or project.

To enhance the connection between instruction and assessment, the School of Resident Education attempted to weave informal formative assessment into every activity. The goal was to create an approach to assessment that was maximally integrated into the learning process, with tailored learning plans based initially on diagnostic assessment results, but subsequently also utilizing formative assessment derived from recall protocol or informally through learning activities.

Scenarios

Scenarios became one of the most efficient tools for promoting the type of agile learning easily supported in the OACD environment while generating rich input for informal formative assessment during all of their phases.[5] Scenarios provided simulated real-life contexts for meaningful, language-appropriate communication in various, often high-level cultural situations. They also created opportunities to enhance learner autonomy and sharpen learners' critical thinking. Scenarios required role players to handle the different responsibilities of "group work, role assignment, identification of objectives and problems, negotiation of solutions, discussion and prioritization of recommendations, consensus making, consolidation of recommendations, preparation of written documents, and presentation of recommendations" (Dababneh 2018, 19).

Scenarios thus provided a rich source of evidence for assessing language comprehension, performance skills, sociocultural competencies, and more, because they required participants to listen, read, speak, and write about the topics they have been studying throughout the week. As learners grew in knowledge and skills, teachers withdrew from center stage, allowing learners to take the lead in managing the planning and conduct of the scenario.

The schedule on the day of the culminating scenario was typically organized to permit learners to work in the morning in groups researching, filtering, or classifying information and arranging material they had collected independently or in groups on previous days. The afternoon was devoted to role-playing and feedback from both learners and teachers. Observation, note-taking, and feedback exchange were tools used to ensure that every interaction became a learning opportunity.

Scenarios depend on feedback for efficacy (Xiao and Yang 2019). Significant and frequent opportunities for feedback and troubleshooting occurred during the planning and performing of scenarios. The feedback reflected an assessment of strengths and shortcomings in both process and product, guided by assessment rubrics that highlighted key skills and competencies characterizing particular stages or levels of performance.

Preparatory Activities

The week-long preparation for culminating scenarios included numerous creative tasks and analyses of texts germane to the various subtopics. Because of their open-ended nature, these tasks, like the scenarios to which they contributed, provided ongoing opportunities for informal formative assessment.

Analysis of texts provided by instructors to introduce individual subtopics of the main theme offered opportunities for formative assessment, varying from simple comprehension questions, filling out graphic organizers and similar, up to deep analysis of all levels of a text. During analysis, gaps in learning would be exposed and addressed.

Abundant opportunities for informal formative assessment arose naturally in the course of tasks and research related to the various subtopics contributing to the culminating scenario. Much of this work was carried out in small groups or individually, requiring learners to cross-brief one another on what they had learned. Such peer teaching was an ongoing activity throughout the week. As has been noted anecdotally by generations of teachers, the ability to teach material to others provides a potent check of one's own comprehension and performance skills, further deepened by feedback, whether offered directly or implicitly through listener questions or (mis)understanding. This process of peer teaching with feedback, repeated from week to week, was especially important for incremental proficiency growth.

Scenarios and assessment rubrics (e.g., for creating brochures or winning debates) were often developed jointly by learners and teachers. Ongoing learner-teacher dialogue and oral questioning; learner-generated activities, including quizzes for peers; and other forms of active learner involvement contributed to assessments being motivational and educative. The goal was a continuous cycle of formative assessment and feedback while building gradually toward an end-of-week culmination, with this process repeated week after week.

Translation and Writing

Translation and other writing activities provided especially effective formative assessment opportunities for intermediate- and advanced-course learners, whose focus had to extend beyond word-level equivalencies to achieve their proficiency objectives. Translation into English, for example, much like recall protocol (see subsequent discussion), can reveal a great deal about learners' challenges in understanding nonexplicit aspects of meaning such as authorial attitude, emotional tone, cultural references, and allusions. Other opportunities for formative assessment were provided by target-language writing tasks that often arose naturally in the course of tasks or scenarios—summarizing articles or composing texts to express and support opinion related to task/scenario objectives and receiving feedback from peers and teachers. Sentence and paragraph structure could reveal how learners processed language and where fossilizations might be taking place; vocabulary and phraseology could reveal knowledge gaps. Teachers used these samples to track progress and advise accordingly. Learners were also encouraged to keep personal journals.

Such writing activities have special value for formative assessment in an OACD context. Beyond offering assessment opportunities integrated into content-based learning, they also provide documentary support for continuous teacher-learner negotiation to assess and address needs, which could include modification of the curriculum.

Finally, and crucially, assessment of learners' linguistic and sociocultural competencies is only one purpose of informal formative assessment. Another often more difficult task is to assess learning style and sensory preferences, personality profiles, motivations, strategic competencies, tolerance of ambiguity, and other personal characteristics that can profoundly affect individual learning and group dynamics. All of these factors can, and often do, create a need to adapt learning design and activities.

In a perfect world informal formative assessment would suffice for all of the needs identified. In the real world, assessing especially the latter more subjective aspects of learners' profiles through observation alone requires training and experience beyond what many instructors possess. This circumstance provides one of the most cogent reasons for formalized formative assessment processes.

Diagnostic Instruction through Formalized Formative Assessment
Diagnostic Assessment

Diagnostic assessment (DA) has been widely applied at DLIFLC for many years. In the School of Resident Education, it was a mandated component of every intermediate and advanced course. Corin and Entis (2022, 97) state that diagnostic assessment "arose at DLIFLC out of the practice of providing formative feedback based on immediate recall protocol . . . and learning styles beginning around 1989" in several basic programs.[6]

Diagnostic assessment arose from the ever-present need to take all possible measures to improve job-relevant proficiency without extending training time. By tuning in to individual learner challenges, errors, preferred learning styles, and so forth, proficiency enhancement could theoretically be achieved more quickly. Anecdotally diagnostic assessment accomplished just that.

By 1998 diagnostic assessment had evolved into a three-skill diagnostic interview conducted by two native-speaker diagnostic assessment specialists, who would present authentic listening and reading material and elicit a ratable sample in listening comprehension, reading comprehension, and speaking (Cohen 2003). Selection of materials required establishing the ILR level of texts based on criteria similar to those used to establish the ILR level of a ratable speech sample (Child 1998). DA specialists used a set of texts, each rated at a specific ILR level, with associated comprehension questions, adapting the interview depending on the proficiencies demonstrated by learners. The specialists' goals were to obtain a proficiency rating and to identify specific gaps or weaknesses that learners needed to address in order to achieve the next level of global language proficiency, focusing on those within their immediate grasp (Corin and Entis 2022).

Diagnostic assessment ultimately came to consist of three stages: pre-interview data collection, three-skill interview, and post-interview follow-up. As practiced in the School of Resident Education, pre-interview data collection included:

- a biographical questionnaire about relevant aspects of the learner's life history;
- information about personality type through a test using Jung's (1929) archetypes, cognitive style through the E&L Cognitive Styles Construct instrument (Ehrman and Leaver 2002), sensory preferences through the Barsch Learning Style Inventory (Barsch 1991), and motivations through the Motivated Strategies for Learning Questionnaire (Pintrich et al. 1991), with results displayed in chart form, constituting an approximate learner profile subject to updating based on observation and consultation with the learner; and
- an L2 writing sample typically on a topic related to the learner's life history or future plans, composed without the use of linguistic reference materials.

The writing sample suggested an opening level for the three-skill interview and some areas to be probed during elicitation. The three-skill interview provided information about language acquired and being acquired. Follow-up included the drafting of a tailored learning plan (discussed subsequently).

Diagnostic assessment is generally conducted at key junctures in learning, such as the end of the second semester of a three-semester sequence, after a significant learning event like an immersion, approaching course completion to identify areas for last-minute intervention, at the start of an intermediate or advanced course to pinpoint incoming target-language proficiencies, or in response to observed learning difficulties. In the School of Resident Education, diagnostic assessment was conducted at the start of courses to establish a proficiency baseline and enable creation of a tailored learning plan, at mid-course, and near course completion. Diagnostic assessment was also conducted before and after an immersion.

Online Diagnostic Assessment
Beginning in 2006, not long after the Directorate of Continuing Education language training detachments were first established at the job locations of many language specialists, an informal push began to deliver diagnostic assessment to hundreds of learners simultaneously or in situations where a diagnostic specialist was not available, often for less commonly taught languages. At that time DLIFLC was making major advances in distance learning and computer-based instruction. It was only natural that an online form of diagnostic assessment—online diagnostic assessment—would evolve. Online diagnostic assessment assessed proficiency levels and assisted with establishing learning plans (see subsequent discussion) but was not informed by personal observation of learners' circumstances or learning styles, making diagnostic assessment preferable where available. As of this writing, online diagnostic assessment in more than twenty languages is available at https://oda.dliflc.edu.

Recall Protocol
In recall protocol learners are presented with a written or oral text and asked to write down what they remember. The early users of recall protocol in language acquisition came from the field of German: Elizabeth Bernhardt and Charles James. In her dissertation, cited in Bernhardt and James (1987), Bernhardt used recall protocol to understand the psychology of reading comprehension development, including physiology, such as eye movements. James followed Bernhardt's model in researching the acquisition of listening skills.

Recall protocol was applied at DLIFLC in the former School of Slavic Languages beginning in 1989 but differed from the application described by Bernhardt and James. While the latter used recall protocol for data collection during research, the former used it to inform teaching. For that reason the DLIFLC protocol allowed learners extra passes through listening materials and extra time with reading, the point being to pinpoint processing challenges, not memory of content. Teachers would then look for patterns of error, such as confusion caused by grammatical constructions not present in learners' native language. In the School of Resident Education, in addition to language processing barriers, recall protocol checked developing sociocultural competencies and issues of fossilization. Recall protocol can also serve to increase learner confidence because of its emphasis on what learners understand versus what they miss.

The following process was used:

1. Learners read or listen to a text without using dictionaries or asking questions, focusing on what they understand.
2. They then write complete, meaningful sentences describing everything they understood. The recall protocol is written in English to differentiate misunderstandings caused by lack of target-language vocabulary and so forth from mere copying of vocabulary or constructions not understood.

Learners are allowed to repeat the reading and listening multiple times.

Information gleaned from recall protocol illuminates language processing and informs tailoring of instruction. For example in Arabic and Slavic languages, non-English syntax may interfere with processing lexemes and morphemes already acquired. Recall protocol will usually reveal this barrier: the doer of the action might be confused with the receiver in non-subject-verb-object languages. Likewise some tense forms may not have been internalized, and the learner might report a planned future action as having already occurred. Problems with mood can be discerned. Recall protocols can also pinpoint gaps in particular lexical domains (political, historical, scientific, etc.) as well as unfamiliarity with vocabulary and phrases associated with registers not regularly encountered in the classroom. The teacher can then direct learning activities to problem areas. Learners may no longer experience certain language processing barriers once they have been revealed to them, for example by a few sets of sentences showing how changing word order affects meaning in the target language. Lexical deficiencies can point to topics and text types for inclusion in the curriculum.

Tailored Learning Plans

In the School of Resident Education, learners worked with their teachers at the beginning of a course to devise tailored learning plans (Leaver 2003) reflecting information from the diagnostic assessment pre-interview data collection and needs that surfaced during the three-skill interview. This information was used by both learner and teacher to inform instruction in language and for improving learning strategies. As the course progressed, the Learning Plan was modified based on learner-teacher dialogue about challenges and opportunities as they arose. Teachers listened to learner suggestions for improvement and negotiated with them a formal or implied learning contract—an acknowledgement of expectations and codependent responsibilities. The learning plan timeline listed the attainment of concrete outcomes. Learner and instructor reviewed and renegotiated the plan monthly.

Co-construction of the learning plan and frequent review and modification fostered ownership and trust. Learners participated in setting goals, determining action, identifying tools and resources, evaluating progress, and planning success. Empowering learners in this way enhanced their eagerness to learn and willingness to venture out of their comfort zones.

Discussion

OACD-enabled diagnostic instruction informs learners' and teachers' efforts to continuously adjust (fine tune) near-term goals and the means to achieve them. In the School of Resident Education experience, use of informal and formalized formative assessment together resulted in more rapid proficiency enhancement than would have been possible through instruction alone or instruction plus one or another single form of formative assessment. Ongoing constructive feedback from all these sources increased knowledge, fostered language awareness and self-reflection, stimulated self-directed learning, and boosted confidence. Most importantly it enabled teachers and learners to exploit the flexibility afforded by OACD to modify learning processes to meet immediate needs and exploit opportunities.

Evidence from School of Resident Education programs for the effectiveness of various forms of formative assessment individually, or even in combination, is anecdotal. From the initial introduction of OACD in 2006, all forms of formative assessment described in this chapter were simultaneously in use, making it difficult to differentiate their effects. The most persuasive evidence is rather for their combined effect, indicated by the statistical evidence cited previously.

The various forms of formative assessment examined in this chapter can be applied with varying degrees of difficulty in all instructional environments, including K-12 and both larger and smaller college or university programs. Informal formative assessment should of course be a regular component of every world language course, limited only by instructors' individual skills. Professional development to enhance these skills is doubtless most readily available in larger programs that can afford to employ professional development specialists to work with instructors. Recall protocol is applicable in any instructional environment and requires little training in excess of normal professional development. Diagnostic assessment, a powerful tool for highly detailed formative assessment, does require training for effective implementation (Corin and Entis 2022), preferably including periodic norming to ensure accurate assessment of proficiency levels. Following one DLIFLC model, school districts or institutions of higher learning could identify one person per language to become a diagnostic assessment specialist, who could then familiarize peers with diagnostic assessment and its benefits, and perhaps work initially with learners identified as having difficulties.[7]

Conclusions

The techniques for OACD-enabled diagnostic instruction described in this chapter are by no means the only ones available or imaginable. The possibilities for inventive instructors are unlimited. The primary limiting factor to the systematic and continuous application and exploitation of formative assessment through diagnostic instruction is rigidity (vs. openness) of curricular design. The success achieved by many School of Resident Education students following the introduction of OACD and diagnostic instruction in 2006 suggests that their combined effect can indeed lead to enhanced learning outcomes.

Study Questions

1. Examine the assessments you currently use. Identify the nature of each: formative or summative. What is each providing you that you need in your course and for your learners?
2. Can your summative assessments be replaced by formative assessments? Consider the reason for them (e.g., grading, institutional requirements). Are these requirements immutable, or can some kinds of formative assessment replace them?
3. Given the resources (training, time, experience) needed to develop an understanding of diagnostic assessment as well as to make it an underpinning for diagnostic instruction, prepare a plan, with goals and timelines, to move toward diagnostic instruction by obtaining the resources and gradually introducing diagnostic instruction into your course.

Notes

1. This chapter has been approved for public release by the Defense Language Institute Foreign Language Center's Public Affairs Office. For verification please email mpao@dliflc.edu. Contents of this chapter are not necessarily the official views of the Defense Language Institute Foreign Language Center, nor are they endorsed by the Department of the Army, the Department of Defense, or the US government. All third-party products and materials featured in the chapter remain the intellectual property of their respective authors or originators. Use of outside materials is done under the fair use copyright principle, for educational purposes only. The content of this chapter is the sole responsibility of the author(s).
2. During these years, the Directorate of Continuing Education had four divisions, sometimes called schools, all of which used formative assessment. The choice to present examples from the School of Resident Education arises out of the authors' leaderships positions there and hence greater familiarity with its programs. The School of Resident Education was disbanded in 2019 as part of an institutional reorganization but is now being reconstructed in 2024.
3. Program descriptions reflect their status of the time of writing; the nature of DLIFLC programs, particularly diagnostic assessment, have varied over time, given changing needs and requirements of the military services, and may currently differ in small or large details at the time this book is released. Readers interested in current details should query the authors for an update.
4. In 2004 Lantolf and Poehner published "Dynamic Assessment of L2 Development: Bringing the Past into the Future," where they outline "Dynamic Assessment" (DA) as a developmental approach to assessment and instruction derived from Vygotsky's theory of the zone of proximal development. They posit that "DA distinguishes itself from other approaches to assessment by insisting that mediation of the examinee's performance prompts, hints, leading questions etc.—during the assessment procedure is crucial to understanding his/her abilities and for promoting development during the assessment process itself" (49). They further assert: "Dynamic assessment integrates assessment and instruction into a seamless, unified activity aimed at promoting learner development through appropriate forms of mediation that are sensitive to the individual's (or in some cases a group's) current abilities. In essence, DA is a procedure for simultaneously assessing and promoting development that takes account of the individual's (or group's) zone of proximal development (ZPD)" (50). Sternberg and Grigorenko (2001) use intervention during *dynamic testing* to teach learners how to perform better. While dynamic assessment and dynamic testing share some commonalities with *diagnostic assessment* (described previously), they nevertheless differ from it distinctly.
5. For examples of scenario topics, see Dababneh 2018. For an example of a weekly module with culminating scenario, see Corin 2021. Wang (this volume) describes a three-day project or scenario in the School of Resident Education Chinese Mandarin Program.

6. The School of Resident Education was formed later, as part of an institutional reorganization circa 2000.
7. Those interested in learning more about the process for becoming a DA specialist can write to campbell-languageconsultants@gmail.com.

References

Allal, Linda, and Lucie Mottier Lopez. 2005. "Formative Assessment of Learning: A Review of Publications in French." In *Formative Assessment: Improved Learning in Secondary Classrooms*, 241–64. Paris: Organisation for Economic Co-operation and Development.
Bachman, Lyle F. 1990. *Fundamental Considerations in Language Testing*. Oxford: Oxford University Press.
Barsch, Jeffrey. 1991. *Barsch Learning Styles Inventory*. Novato: Academic Therapy Publications.
Bernhardt, Elizabeth, and Charles James. 1987. "The Teaching and Testing of Comprehension in Foreign Language Learning." In *Proficiency, Policy and Professionalism in Foreign Language Education*, edited by Diane W. Birckbichler, 65–81. Lincolnwood: National Textbook Company.
Black, Paul, and Dylan William. 1998. "Assessment and Classroom Learning." *Assessment in Education: Principles, Policy & Practice* 5, no. 1: 7–74.
Black, Paul, and Dylan William. 2009. "Developing the Theory of Formative Assessment." *Educational Assessment, Evaluation and Accountability* 21, no. 1: 5–31.
Bloom, Benjamin S. 1968. "Learning for Mastery." Reprint from *Evaluation Comment* 1, no. 2. Accessed August 13, 2023. https://eric.ed.gov/?id=ED053419.
Child, James R. 1998. "Language Skill Levels, Textual Modes, and the Rating Process." *Foreign Language Annals* 31, no. 3: 381–91.
Clementi, Diane. 2022. Curriculum Design Workshop. American Council on the Teaching of Foreign Languages Conference. Boston, MA.
Cohen, Bella. 2003. *Diagnostic Assessment at the Superior-Distinguished Threshold*. Salinas: MSI Press.
Corin, Andrew. 2021. "Foreign Language Learning Efficiency: Transformative Learning in an Outcomes-Based Environment." In *Transformative Language Learning and Teaching*, edited by Betty L. Leaver, Dan E. Davidson, and Christine Campbell, 51–60. Cambridge: Cambridge University Press.
Corin, Andrew, and Sergey Entis. 2022. "Protocol-Based Formative Assessment: Evolution and Revolution at the Defense Language Institute Foreign Language Center." *Journal of Distinguished Language Studies* 8: 95–115.
Dababneh, Reem. 2018. "The Scenario-Based Syllabus for the Post-Basic Arabic Program." *Dialog on Language Instruction* 28, no. 1: 18–27.
Ehrman, M., and B. L. Leaver. 2002. E & L Learning Style Questionnaire v. 2.0. http://www.cambridge.org/resources/0521837510/2127_Leaver%20learning%20styles%20test.DOC.
Garza, Thomas Jesus. 2021. "#39. Assess High-Level Production the Way We Teach High-Level Production." In *Practices That Work: Bringing Learners to Professional Proficiency in World Languages*, edited by Thomas Jesus Garza, 195–99. Hollister: MSI Press.
Greenfield, P. M. 2009. "Linking Social Change and Developmental Change: Shifting Pathways of Human Development." *Developmental Psychology* 45, no. 2: 401–18. https://doi.org/10.1037/a0014726.
Jung, Carl Gustav. 1929. *Psychologische Typen*. Olten: Walter-Verlag.
Lantolf, James P., and Matthew E. Poehner. 2004. "Dynamic Assessment of L2 Development: Bringing the Past into the Future." *Journal of Applied Linguistics* 1, no. 1: 49–72.
Leaver, Betty Lou. 2003. *Individualized Learning Plans for Very Advanced Learners of Foreign Languages*. Salinas: MSI Press.
Leaver, Betty Lou. 2022. "On the Cusp: Zone of Proximal Development Grids to Guide Formative Assessment." *Journal of Distinguished Language Studies* 8: 69–93.
Leaver, Betty Lou, and Christine Campbell. 2015. "Experience with Higher Levels of Proficiency." In *To Advanced Proficiency and Beyond: Theory and Methods for Developing Superior Second Language Ability*, edited by Tony Bown and Jennifer Bown, 3–22. Washington, DC: Georgetown University Press.
Pintrich, P., D. A. F. Smith, T. Garcia, and W. McKeachie. 1991. *A Manual for the Use of the Motivated Strategies for Learning Questionnaire (MSLQ)*. Ann Arbor: National Center for Research to Improve Post-Secondary Teaching and Learning (University of Michigan). http://files.eric.ed.gov/fulltext/ED338122.pdf.

Sandrock, Paul. 2010. *The Keys to Assessing Language Performance: A Teacher's Manual for Measuring Student Progress.* Alexandria, VA: ACTFL.

Scriven, Michael. 1967. "The Methodology of Evaluation." In *Perspectives of Curriculum Evaluation*, edited by Ralph W. Tyler, Robert M. Gagné, and Michael Scriven, 39–83. Chicago: Rand McNally.

Sternberg, Robert, and Elena Grigorenko. 2001. *Dynamic Testing.* Cambridge: Cambridge University Press.

Trumbull, Elise, and Andrea Lash. 2013. *Understanding Formative Assessment: Insights from Learning Theory and Measurement Theory.* San Francisco: WestEd. https://www.wested.org/online_pubs/resource1307.pdf.

Vygotsky, Lev. 1934/1978. *Mind in Society: The Development of Higher Psychological Processes.* Cambridge, MA: Harvard University Press.

Wiggins, Grant. 1998. *Educative Assessment: Designing Assessments to Inform and Improve Student Performance.* San Francisco: Jossey-Bass.

Xiao, Yangyu, and Min Yang. 2019. "Formative Assessment and Self-Regulated Learning: How Formative Assessment Supports Students' Self-Regulation in English Language Learning." *System*, 81, 39–49. https://doi.org/10.1016/j.system.2019.01.004.

15

An Open Architecture Approach to Program Evaluation in a Language Learning Setting

WENDY ASHBY

THE OPEN ARCHITECTURE (OA) classroom is decidedly constructivist in its approaches to both learning (see also Bondarenko, this volume) and learning assessment (Dababneh and Yuan, this volume). As such it relies on just-in-time, point-of-need instruction to accommodate varied learning approaches, learner interests, and language proficiency profiles, resulting in learning programs that are constantly being constructed by both instructors and learners (Gregory, this volume). The curricular resequencing and continual content renewal that this produces—hallmarks of *open architecture curricular design* (OACD)—reflect broader trends in approaches to L2 instruction, course design, and learning assessment over the past several decades.

This evolutionary process necessitates a corresponding shift in approaches to program assessment and evaluation toward what may be termed *open architecture program evaluation* (OAPE). OAPE is an optimized tool for assessing the "continuous, recursive and divergent process [of] created... constructions" (Guba and Lincoln 2003, 263) while maintaining acceptable levels of summative academic quality control. It rests on buy-in from all participants and strives for continual improvement through (1) continual and systematic tailoring to program mission, vision, circumstances, and needs; (2) input of all stakeholders in the selection, design, implementation, and analysis of evaluative processes and program improvement measures; and (3) ongoing generation of meaningful and actionable recommendations for change—conversations traditionally limited to five-year re-accreditation requirements. These characteristics of OAPE correspond closely to definitional principles of OACD-based learning programs, including continual and systematic tailoring to individual learner/cohort needs and ongoing learner involvement in the selection and delivery of content and design or direction of activities. OAPE represents an inevitable response to the broader developmental trends in world language education. This chapter will discuss OAPE as an open architecture approach to L2 program evaluation.

OAPE: Assessment, Measurement, and Evaluation

While forward-looking, OAPE is strongly anchored in the current generation of program evaluation and accreditation best practices that ask language programs to engage in "ongoing, collegial, self-reflective dialogue about the continuous improvement of student learning and institutional processes [by regularly] assess[ing] progress toward . . . stated goals and mak[ing] decisions . . . in a . . . systematic cycle . . . based on analyses of both quantitative and qualitative data" (Association for the Accreditation of Community and Junior Colleges 2020). Despite the developmental intent of the periodic (re-)accreditation process, it has historically tended to morph into a results-driven, external value judgment of program effectiveness (Norris 2006). This grew from a developmental trajectory that initially emphasized quantification and an "unfortunate tendency to conflate assessment and measurement" (Norris 2006, 578). Thus program measurement was pressed into duty as a means of "yield[ing] information regarding worthiness, appropriateness, goodness, or validity" (Sullivan 2006, 591) for external stakeholders.

More recent approaches define assessment as "a general term that includes the full range of procedures used to gain information about student learning" (Linn and Gronlund 2000, 31), measurement as "the process of obtaining a numerical description of the degree to which an individual possesses a particular characteristic" (Linn and Gronlund 2000, 32), and evaluation as "the value judgments made based on assessment and measurement" (Sullivan 2006, 591). Evaluation, so construed, "allow[s], indeed encourage[s], inclusion of a vast range of artifacts that are best approached qualitatively [thus not] . . . limit[ing] ourselves to only those outcomes that are readily measurable, [lest] we produce a list of trivial behaviorist indicators" (Wright 2006, 594). Thus deconstructed, evaluation can be formative and summative, linking process and product while valuing both qualitative and quantitative results (Brown 2004).

The Parallel Trajectories of Instructional and Program Evaluation Practices in Language Learning: Evolution toward OACD and OAPE

From World War II to the present, educational psychology, social scientific program evaluation, and second language acquisition (SLA) have developed on parallel arcs from behaviorism through cognitivism to constructivism. This has encompassed four "generations" of educational program evaluation (Kiely and Rea-Dickins 2005), and the evolution of language teaching methods from grammar translation through audiolingualism, natural approaches mimicking first language acquisition, communicative/sociolinguistic approaches, to integrated post-methodologies. Initially language learning borrowed its evaluation standards from the social sciences (Spolsky 2000). As second language acquisition grew into its own academic discipline, L2-specific evaluation measures and practices emerged (Norris and Watanabe 2011).

Behaviorist Language Teaching and First-Generation Educational Program Evaluation

Postwar audiolingual instructional methods for language learning were grounded in behaviorist educational psychology, positing learning as a product of operant conditioning and success the result of reinforced, habitual correct utterances and error avoidance. Large-scale educational evaluation consisted of "primarily summative (product oriented) and accountability-driven focus on the measurement of outcomes" (Norris and Watanabe 2011, 4693). Resulting first-generation evaluation activities were couched in number reporting as measurements of success. Numbers of faculty with terminal degrees, majors, minors, graduation rates, grad school acceptance, library books, standardized test scores, and so on (Wright 2006) were painstakingly recorded. In language programs this approach dovetailed well with methodologies based on highly controlled language input and production, allowing easy quantification of tangible outcomes that tracked grammar-based syllabi.

Cognitivist Language Teaching and Second-Generation Educational Evaluation

In the 1970s cognitivist educational-psychological approaches that celebrated error as an integral part of learning through hypothesis testing gained traction. Cognitivism birthed second-generation educational evaluation practices based on qualitative, process-driven approaches (Cain and Cronbach 1982) that included "new designs and data-collection methods, from survey research to observations and interviews" (Norris and Watanabe 2011, 4695). As language teaching methodology shifted from demanding correctly produced utterances to empowering multiple competencies (Stern 1983) — communicative (Savignon 1972; Canale and Swain 1980; Hall 1999), sociolinguistic (Hymes 1972), and ethnocultural (Oxford 1994; Saville-Troike 1983) — the overall evaluative climate in language learning shifted from quantification to more holistic measures of program development (Kiely and Rea-Dickins 2005).

Constructivist Language Teaching and Third-Generation Educational Evaluation

Constructivist educational psychology emerged in the late 1990s, positing that active learners co-create knowledge in highly individualized, self-directed, asynchronous, adaptive, nonlinear teaching environments. Consequently, third-generation program evaluation looked to language programs' unique histories as context for their decision-making, policy development, and program improvements (Kealy and Rea-Dickens 2005). Language teaching methods prized learner-centered (Jourdain 1998) ethnographic encounters with target cultures and language speakers. They emphasized self/other-reflection, problem solving, discourse ability (Kramsch 1989), and dialogic approaches (Peck 1992). Thus successful language programs were those that enabled language learners to navigate a "socially-situated cycle of enquiry, dialogue, and action" Kiely 2009, 99).

Open Architecture Language Teaching and Fourth-Generation Educational Evaluation

While constructivist educational psychology remained foundational to fourth-generation program evaluation (Kealy and Rea-Dickens 2005), its distinction lay in performativity. No longer employing evaluation as a means of gaining endorsement via longitudinal accreditation cycle judgements of external stakeholders, fourth-generation evaluation constitutes a continuous, self-directed, internally evolving process of "improving current programs, encouraging innovations, and then evaluating each innovation's effectiveness [with] the key step [being] systematic gathering of information for sustained improvement" (Light 2004, 224). Instead of serving external stakeholders, it primarily "seeks to find out how different aspects of the program work ... [and provides] ... a deeper understanding of the processes of teaching and learning that occur" (Richards 2001, 289).

OAPE is an illuminative, constructivist process whereby internal stakeholders co-create a self-defined, bottom-up, formative dialog on qualitative progress indicators (Stecher and Davis 1996) in order to obtain user-oriented data for L2 program decision-making going forward (Brown 2004). While generated from fourth-generation evaluation premises employed in the service of user-informed, summative end products for long-cycle accreditation purposes, OAPE represents an intensified elaboration of these processes as a necessary response to and corollary of OACD-based learning, which encourages ongoing learner involvement in the selection and delivery of content and design or direction of activities. Choice of themes, texts, tasks, and activities is based in part on teacher-learner negotiation, with all parties contributing to the drafting and ongoing revision of aspects of the curriculum. In the case of OAPE the distinguishing hallmarks are continual, cyclic formative assessment in support of OACD's highly recursive curricular and materials modification processes (Van Gorp, Heidrich Uebel, and Giupponi, this volume), as well as its unprecedented degree of bottom-up, hands-on L2 faculty and support personnel participation in pursuit of ongoing improvement (Oded and Oded, this volume).

Operationalizing OAPE-Informed Program Review at DLIFLC

Although fully optimized OAPE remains aspirational, a participatory (Alderson and Scott 1992) self-evaluative annual program review (Pawson and Tilley 2014) process approaching this goal was implemented in 2006 in the Defense Language Institute Foreign Language Center's (DLIFLC) Directorate of Continuing Education.[1] In 2014 DLIFLC's Evaluation and Standards Division was tasked to initiate an analogous process across the much more populous initial language acquisition programs (called "basic programs") in 2014. This was part of a comprehensive response necessitated by the Pentagon's decision to increase the basic program proficiency objective for listening comprehension, reading comprehension, and speaking from Advanced/Advanced/Intermediate High (ILR 2/2/1+) to Advanced High/Advanced High/Advanced (ILR 2+/2+/2).

This OA-driven annual evaluation process rested on four simple pillars imposed by upper-level leadership. Specifically, the self-guided, internally performed language program review needed to address syllabus, curriculum, learner performance, and instructor performance. Each program then selected its own quantitative and qualitative artifacts (Arias, Maturana, and Restrepo 2012) and presented them along with contextualizing information for assessing program strengths and weaknesses. In the Directorate of Continuing Education, the audience was typically the associate provost and other directorate leaders, whereas basic program processes tended to involve larger gatherings of deans, chairs, and program managers. In both contexts the review process culminated in a self-directed list of prioritized "due outs"—program improvement tasks that managers and faculty endeavored to complete by the next evaluation round.

In the larger basic program context, once this internal stakeholder process was complete, all gathered materials, discussion results, and due outs were made available to external stakeholders and other interested parties via public fora regularly attended by DLIFLC senior leadership, other language program personnel, and instructional support organizations. These personnel could clarify content and results, point out gaps, and make other concerns known. Program-internal information users retained full control of the manner in which their challenges and progress were represented to external entities, allowing "the pattern of actual attitudes and activities within the program [to] determine the lines of enquiry which shape[d] the data collection, and the hypotheses tested in the analysis of these data" (Kiely and Rea-Dickins 2005, 45). This not only favored an evaluative focus on internal reflection and discussion but also supported a culture in which even smaller-scale, short-cycle, solution-focused "postmortems" for individual courses became commonplace in response to emerging challenges (Oded and Oded, this volume).

DLIFLC's Office of Standardization and Academic Excellence had aspired to integrate OAPE into its longitudinal Association for the Accreditation of Community and Junior Colleges accreditation cycle during the period 2015–2017 to ensure the obligatory five-year institutional re-accreditation processes would both inform and be informed by individual programs' annual program review processes. It was hoped these approaches could "force multiply" one another to generate a truly innovative, ongoing, maximally integrated program improvement process, birthing what could be characterized as a fifth generation of program evaluation practice. At the time these aspirations were eclipsed by the operational demands of other activities (Andrew R. Corin, personal communication).

Best Practices and Resources for Conducting an OAPE in a Language Learning Setting

OAPE, as indicated previously, represents an extension of fourth-generation program evaluation. As such OAPE evaluations should be grounded in internal and external stakeholder trust (Kealy and Rea-Dickens 2005) gained through program-fair, realistic, best-practice-driven (Pawson and Tilley 2014) activities that are clearly "utility-focused, feasibility-conscious, propriety-oriented, and accuracy-based" (Patton 2008, 17). Utility-focused evaluation ensures generated information is useful by answering pertinent stakeholder questions. Evaluations that neglect internal and external stakeholder input to identify program needs, form questions, collect/interpret data, and make change recommendations are often poorly supported (Lang 2006a). They risk becoming "misguided, academic exercises [the findings of which are] ignored, criticized or resisted because they do not address anyone's particular questions" (Joint Committee on Standards for Educational Evaluation 1994, 25). Feasibility-conscious evaluators use time and resources as judiciously as possible to minimize program disruptions while ensuring adequate resources for necessary activities. Propriety-oriented evaluations build credibility through ethical data gathering and storage to protect the safety, dignity, and welfare of human subjects. Finally accurate program evaluation rests on timely, appropriate release of correct, unbiased data to affected parties in a comprehensible, relevant format (Norris 2006).

The steps for conducting such a program-fair "big" evaluation (i.e., one analogous to or aligned with cyclic five-year re-accreditation requirements) are (1) develop and describe program goals and identify key evaluation points, (2) define desired outcomes and develop evaluation questions, (3) develop an evaluation process, (4) collect data, (5) analyze gathered information, and (6) provide information to interested audience(s) (Westat 2002). It is critical that the L2 OAPE coordinator operate within a gradual release of responsibility model (Krasner, this volume) to help the program identify a range of internal and external stakeholders (students, instructors, administrators, end users, etc.) and employ them effectively from outset of *each* of these six stages (Yarbrough, Shulha, Hopson, and Caruthers 2011).

In an actual re-accreditation review process, a program's freedom is constrained to some extent by the accrediting agency's specific standards and substandards. Within a smaller-scale annual program review with due outs, as was carried out in the Directorate of Continuing Education at DLIFLC over a twelve-year period, the idealized form may be approached more closely. To the extent that the process becomes routinized, as was the case in the Directorate of Continuing Education, some of these steps can be actuated less formally—reviewed and reconsidered rather than addressed *ab ovo*, thus reducing the burden on program personnel. The recursiveness that is a feature of OAPE can thus be achieved in a way that is both feasible and sustainable. In the Directorate of Continuing Education experience, the annual program review process initially met with resistance from some program administrators and faculty. Over time, as the process became routinized, support for OPAE grew within the individual language programs for the opportunity it provided to showcase accomplishments, seek solutions to challenges in a supportive context, and generally to maintain situational awareness of all matters relating to the program's development (Oded and Oded, this volume).

Stage One: Defining Language Program Goals and Key Evaluation Points

After identifying and engaging stakeholders, an effective OAPE coordinator in a language learning setting can pose framing questions to help them identify unique program evaluation needs. How does their program function within the wider language learning profession as well as within the institution and community? Who are their end users, and what are their expectations? What aspects of their program do they need the data to illuminate? What other aspects of the program do they hope to illuminate? Framing questions should be "largely internal to the programs, resulting in high participation and ownership" (Norris 2006, 582). Once large-scale needs are established, the OAPE coordinator in a language learning setting can assist participants in prioritizing evaluation areas. The Association of Departments of Foreign Languages has prepared a comprehensive checklist of useful language and literature program evaluation categories (Association of Departments of Foreign Languages 2009a) and a guide for external reviewers (Association of Departments of Foreign Languages 2009b) that can be useful for helping language program stakeholders determine their goals and meaningful data points.

Stage Two: Generating Outcomes-Based OAPE Questions in a Language Learning Setting
The evaluation coordinator is instrumental in guiding stakeholders to formulate useful, specific, program-driven evaluation questions. While fourth-generation evaluation is self-defined and open-ended, an OAPE coordinator in a language learning setting should nevertheless remind stakeholders that "in well-conceived educational programs, student learning outcomes serve as the touchstone for curriculum development, instructional practice, student advancement and achievement, and, to be sure, program evaluation and improvement" (Norris 2006, 577). Stakeholders will find it helpful to frame evaluation questions within a larger discussion of their eventual usefulness in accreditation processes that ask language programs to demonstrate how they are utilizing evidence of student learning to make program decisions. Thus questions that illuminate how learning outcomes are tied to program processes (Byrnes 2008), curricular content/revision, (Cachey 2014), overlooked areas of need, (Carsten-Wickham 2008), effectiveness of articulation across and between language levels (Windham 2008), and student performance relative to national standards (Matthews and Hansen 2004) are particularly fruitful.

OAPE coordinators in a language learning setting can point stakeholders to common professional standards for language learning as the derivational basis for self-evaluation questions. The *World-Readiness Standards for Learning Languages* (2015, 4th ed.) have demonstrated high levels of reliability and validity for language and culture learning (Clifford 2016; Surface and Dierdorff 2003). For English as a second language OAPE coordinators, the Standards for English Language Programs and Institutions used by the Commission on English Language Program Accreditation (CEA 2019) can prove useful. The Modern Language Association website (https://www.mla.org/Resources) contains several publications outlining properties of successful language programs and considerations for evaluating literary studies outcomes. The National Standards in Foreign Language Education Project, National Council on the Accreditation of Teacher Educators, and Interstate New Teacher Assessment and Support Consortium all have useful standardized professional metrics that can inform language teacher training program evaluation.

Stage 3: Helping Internal Stakeholders Map Their OAPE Process in a Language Learning Setting
Once a comprehensive set of evaluation questions is agreed upon, the OAPE coordinator in a language learning setting can guide internal stakeholders as they devise a timeline and execution plan for a "systematic collection and analysis of information necessary to improve a curriculum, assess its effectiveness and its efficiency, and determine participants' attitudes within the context of a particular institution" (Brown

1995, 227). Some useful guiding questions include: How much time can the department spend on evaluation activities? Are there other large-scale projects or needs that require resources? How will disruptions caused by evaluation processes be handled? Who is available to conduct evaluation activities? Will there be additional compensation or duty releases for those individuals? What if faculty, learners, or end users resist evaluation efforts? How will participation requests from overlooked stakeholders be managed? Is there enough expertise in the department to handle evaluation activities, or is external expertise required? What effect if any will external personnel have on processes and outcomes? Well-conceived needs, wants, and contingency plans provide the foundation for effective stakeholder participation (McAlpine and Dhonau 2007) and ultimate acceptance of the program evaluation results.

Stage 4: Collecting Language Program Data

It is not uncommon for stakeholders to want to jump straight into data generation and analysis. An OAPE coordinator in a language learning setting contributes to a better evaluation by encouraging stakeholders to complete the first three steps mindfully before turning their attention to data. Ideally existing program data and artifacts should be used instead of those generated specifically for evaluative purposes for two reasons. It streamlines the data collection process and creates a tangible motivation for developing a regular collection practice. While stakeholders may ask a coordinator to take over data collection as a perceived "expert," a program-fair evaluation approach helps internal stakeholders identify and strengthen their own data-gathering procedures that "establish multiple points of view, identify the unique logic of the program, and determine the relative importance of issues identified in the preliminary stage of data collection" (Kawamura, Dassier, and Costner 2006, 42).

Indeed the lasting contribution of an effective OAPE coordinator in a language learning setting is to help internal reviewers "recognize that knowledge of the program to be evaluated resides in a coherent representation (and one that is acceptable to those involved) of what the program is, how it operates, who it serves, and how well it serves its function" (Kawamura Dassier, and Costner 2006, 39). Some questions to help stakeholders identify and source their unique program narrative materials include: Who does the language program serve? What projects are learners involved in? How has the program engaged with the wider community? What connections have been established or strengthened with native target language speakers? Who is using the language in their lives/jobs after graduation? How do learners feel about their language learning experience? These can be used in conjunction with more traditional quantitative measures such as proficiency exam results, retention numbers, persistence data, and so forth to paint a rich, comprehensive language program picture.

Stage 5: Analyzing OAPE Data from a Language Learning Setting

Once data are gathered, the OAPE coordinator in a language learning setting can help internal stakeholders analyze it in ways that best answer the language program's self-identified, context-driven (Hargreaves 1989), content-specific (Costner 2006) questions. At this stage, "multiple assessment methodologies are called upon to meet multiple intended uses for assessment information, and the specific form of any given assessment issues from its use" (Norris 2006, 582). While OAPE in a language learning setting leans toward the qualitative, the OAPE coordinators can remind stakeholders that quantitative data is both acceptable and useful in support of overall program narratives where appropriate. In some cases quantitative data may be the only indicator of an area needing further inquiry and/or illuminative qualitative contextualization. Data triangulation creates a clearer, stronger, and more accurate program narrative for use by both internal and external stakeholders.

Stage 6: Communicating OAPE Results from a Language Learning Setting to External Stakeholders

Ideally OAPE results from a language learning setting should be shared and discussed openly and comprehensively while adhering to best practices for data and human subject protection. The evaluation coordinator can help internal stakeholders be sure their reports portray the language program in a way they agree on before more formal reports are generated and made accessible. Once released reports should ideally contain front matter (cover, executive summary, conceptual framework, research questions, and methodology); profile (program overview, milestones, goals/objectives, curriculum, student enrollment); extracurricular instruction (individualized, study abroad, distance learning); evaluation (synthesized data on how instruction is evaluated by learners, peers, and other stakeholders); focus group results (strengths, weaknesses, and suggestions); faculty interviews; proficiency tests (learner performance on external and internal measures); and conclusion (summary, conclusion, references, and appendices) (Birckbichler 2006).

Once complete the OAPE coordinator in a language learning setting can either present contents to external stakeholders or assist internal stakeholders to engage external stakeholders effectively and diplomatically, encouraging ownership of evaluation results and reinforcing future stakeholder participation in their own evaluative processes (Kawamura et al. 2006). While framing their own language program story, internal evaluators "let [external] stakeholders know the results..., provide qualitative and quantitative documentation about the program, place a program in its institutional context and show how it fits in a wider context, summarize strengths and weaknesses of the program, and offer specific recommendations [that] allow all stakeholders to... understand the context in which recommendations have been made" (Lang 2006b, 105). Whether part of informal troubleshooting, course postmortems, annual program reviews, or formalized cyclical accreditation evaluation, an ethnographic approach is preferred because it "aims not only to represent the voices of stakeholders of the program but also to encourage these same stakeholders to start documenting their own voices so that the examination of the program can continue after the evaluation is formally completed."

Conclusions: Benefits of an OA Approach to Program Evaluation in a Language Learning Setting

OAPE in a language learning setting is grounded in qualitative, formative, process-based, bottom-up, forward-looking ethnographic approaches to a world language program's ongoing internal professional development narrative. Its recursive, evolving nature provides a necessary response to OACD developments and a pedagogically and historically supported framework for stakeholder-based, narrative reflection on continuous program improvement. It enhances the utility function foundational to evaluative best practices by encouraging ownership and buy-in from L2 teachers needed to sustain cultures of ongoing self-evaluation.

In practice OAPE "check[s] for the presence of a functioning, effective assessment process and reward[s] programs on the basis of [demonstrated] improvement in student learning" (Wright 2006). It celebrates storytelling about how self-generated, ongoing improvement processes add educational value instead of "proving" excellence to outsiders. Bottom-up involvement of the evaluated has given rise to more differentiated and better triangulated data collection tools (Llosa and Slayton 2009) and solidified systematic formative self-evaluation as foundational to effective longitudinal, summative external evaluation cycles (Norris 2006). Undoubtedly the more direct participation of the evaluated in formulating, conducting, and using their own evaluations (Kiely and Rea-Dickins 2005; Norriset al. 2009; Watanabe, Norris, and Gonzáles-Lloret 2009) can result in improvements in L2 assessment, measurement, program review, and evaluation processes.

Study Questions

1. OA language program evaluation tenets are decidedly qualitative. Is a quantitative L2 OAPE framework possible? If so, what does that look like?
2. Could language programs exploit OAPE as a means of avoiding commonly accepted performance and proficiency standards, thus hiding failures? How can this be avoided?
3. The Covid-19 pandemic has accelerated the processes of OACD's evolution. Do you envision a similar acceleration of possible OAPE processes in language learning or other disciplines?

Note

1. At that time, the Directorate of Continuing Education's mission encompassed instruction at upper levels of proficiency, programs for deployed language professionals, and language for special-purposes programs taught either at remote military bases or by distance learning.

References

Alderson, Charles, and Mike Scott. 1992. "Insiders, Outsiders and Participatory Evaluation." In *Evaluating Second Language Education*, edited by Charles Alderson and Alan Beretta, 25–27. Cambridge: Cambridge University Press.

Arias, Clara, Liliana M. Maturana, and Maria I. Restrepo. 2012. "Evaluation in Foreign Language Learning: Towards Fair and Democratic Practices." *Lenguaje* 40, no. 1 (June): 99–126.

ADFL (Association of Departments of Foreign Languages). 2009a. "Checklist for Self-study for Departments of Foreign Languages and Literatures." *ADFL Bulletin* 40, no. 2–3 (Winter–Spring): 144–53.

ADFL (Association of Departments of Foreign Languages). 2009b. "ADE Guide for External Reviewers." *ADFL Bulletin* 40, no. 2–3 (Winter–Spring): 138–43.

AACJC (Association for the Accreditation of Community and Junior Colleges). 2020. "Guide to Institutional Self Evaluation Improvement." https://accjc.org/wp-content/uploads/Guide-to-Institutional-Self-Evaluation-Improvement-Peer-Review_Jan2020.pdf.

Birckbichler, Diane. 2006. "Rationale for Foreign Language Program Evaluation." In *Evaluating Foreign Language Programs: Content, Context, and Change*, edited by Diane Birckbichler, 118–22. Columbus: The Ohio State University Foreign Language Center.

Brown, James D. 2004. "Language Program Evaluation: A Synthesis of Existing Possibilities." In *The Second Language Curriculum*, edited by Robert K. Johnson, 222–41. Cambridge: Cambridge University Press.

Brown, James D. 1995. "Language Program Evaluation: Decisions, Problems and Solutions." *Annual Review of Applied Linguistics* 15 (March): 227–48.

Byrnes, Heidi. 2008. "Owning Up to Ownership of Foreign Language Program Outcomes Assessment." *ADFL Bulletin* 39, no. 2–3 (Winter–Spring): 28–30.

Cachey, Theodor. 2014. "Reframing Assessment: Innovation and Accountability Between the Global and the Local." In *Issues in Language Program Direction: Innovation and Accountability in Language Program Evaluation*, edited by Nicole Mills and John Norris, 230–44. Boston: Cengage Learning.

Cain, Pamela S., and Lee J. Cronbach. 1982. "Toward Reform of Program Evaluation: Aims, Methods, and Institutional Arrangements." *Contemporary Sociology* 11, no. 5 (September): 537–38.

Canale, Michael, and Merrill Swain. 1980. "Theoretical Bases of Communicative Approaches to Second Language Teaching and Testing." *Applied Linguistics* 1, no. 1 (Spring): 1–47.

Carsten-Wickham, Belinda. 2008. "Assessment and Foreign Languages: A Chair's Perspective." *ADFL Bulletin* 39, no. 2–3 (Winter–Spring): 36–43.

Clifford, Ray. 2016. "A Rationale for Criterion-Referenced Proficiency Testing." *Foreign Language Annals* 49, no. 2 (Summer): 224–234.

Commission on English Language Program Accreditation (CEA). 2019. "CEA Standards for English Language Programs and Institutions." https://cea-accredit.org/images/2019_doc_and_handbooks/2019_CEA_Standards.pdf.

Costner, Kelly M. 2006. "Content Specific Approaches to Program Evaluation." In *Evaluating Foreign Language Programs: Content, Context, Change*, edited by Diane Birckbichler, 15–28. Columbus: The Ohio State University Foreign Language Publications.

Guba, Egon G., and Yvonna S. Lincoln. 2003. *Fourth Generation Evaluation*. Newbury Park: Sage Publications.

Hall, Joan K. 1999. "The Communication Standards." In *Foreign Language Standards: Linking Research, Theories, and Practices*, edited by June K. Phillips and Robert M. Terry, 15–56. Lincolnwood: National Textbook Company.

Hargreaves, Peter. 1989. "Tailoring the Evaluation to Fit the Context." In *The Second Language Curriculum*, edited by Robert K. Johnson, 222–41. Cambridge: Cambridge University Press.

Hymes, Dell. 1972. "On Communicative Competence." In *Sociolinguistics: Selected Readings*, edited by John B. Pride and Janet Holmes, 269–93. Harmondsworth: Penguin Books.

Joint Committee on Standards for Educational Evaluation (JCSEE). 1994. *Program Evaluation Standards: How to Assess Evaluations of Educational Programs*. Thousand Oaks: Sage.

Jourdain, Sarah. 1998. "Building Connections to Culture: A Student-Centered Approach." *Foreign Language Annals* 31, no. 3 (October): 439–450.

Kawamura, Hiroaki, Jean-Louise Dassier, and Kelly M. Costner. 2006. "Program Evaluation as Ethnography." In *Evaluating Foreign Language Programs: Content, Context, Change*, edited by Diane Birckbichler, 39–62. Columbus: The Ohio State University Foreign Language Publications.

Kiely, Richard. 2009. "Small Answers to the Big Question: Learning from Language Programme Evaluation." *Language Teaching Research* 13, no. 1 (January): 99–116.

Kiely, Richard, and Pauline Rea-Dickins. 2005. *Program Evaluation in Language Education*. New York: Palgrave Macmillan.

Kramsch, Claire. 1989. "New Directions in the Study of Foreign Languages." *ADFL Bulletin* 1, no. 21 (Fall): 4–11.

Lang, Yong. 2006a. "Communication: An Essential Tool in Program Evaluation." In *Evaluating Foreign Language Programs: Content, Context, Change*, edited by Diane Birckbichler, 29–36. Columbus: The Ohio State University Foreign Language Publications.

Lang, Yong. 2006b. "Effective Reporting." In *Evaluating Foreign Language Programs: Content, Context, Change*, edited by Diane Birckbichler, 105–11. Columbus: The Ohio State University Foreign Language Publications.

Light, Richard J. 2004. *Making the Most of College: Students Speak Their Minds*. Cambridge: Harvard University Press.

Linn, Robert L., and Norman E. Gronlund. 2000. *Measurement and Assessment in Teaching*. Upper Saddle River: Prentice-Hall.

Llosa, Lorena, and Julie Slayton. 2009. "Using Program Evaluation to Inform and Improve the Education of Young English Language Learners in US Schools." *Language Teaching Research* 13, no. 1: 35–54.

Matthews, Tom, and Cheryl M. Hansen. 2004. "Ongoing Assessment of a University Foreign Language Program." *Foreign Language Annals* 37, no. 4 (December): 630–640.

McAlpine, David D., and Stephanie S. Dhonau. 2007. "Creating a Culture for the Preparation of an ACTFL/NCATE Program Review." *Foreign Language Annals* 40, no. 2 (May): 247–59.

Norris, John M. 2006. "The Why (and How) of Assessing Student Learning Outcomes in College Foreign Language Programs." *Modern Language Journal* 90, no. 4 (Winter): 576–583.

Norris, John M., John M. Davis, Castle Sinicrope, and Yukiko Watanabe. 2009. *Toward Useful Program Evaluation in College Foreign Language Education*. Honolulu: University of Hawai'i at Mānoa National Foreign Language Resource Center.

Norris, John M., and Yukiko Watanabe. 2011. "Program Evaluation." In *The Encyclopedia of Applied Linguistics*, edited by Carole A. Chapelle, 4693–98. New York: Wiley-Blackwell. Oxford, Rebecca. 1994. "Teaching Culture in the Language Classroom: Toward a New Philosophy." In *Georgetown University Roundtable on Languages and Linguistics*, edited by James E. Alatis, 26–45. Washington: Georgetown University Press.

Patton, Michael Q. 2008. *Utilization-Focused Evaluation*. Thousand Oaks: Sage.

Pawson, Ray, and Nick Tilley. 2014. *Realistic Evaluation*. Los Angeles: Sage.

Peck, Jeffrey M. 1992. "Toward a Cultural Hermeneutics of the 'Foreign' Language Classroom: Notes for a Critical and Political Pedagogy." *ADFL Bulletin* 23, no. 3 (Spring): 11–17.

Richards, Jack C. 2017. *Curriculum Development in Language Teaching*. Cambridge: Cambridge University Press.

Savignon, Sandra J. 1972. *Communicative Competence: An Experiment in Foreign Language Teaching*. Philadelphia: Center for Curriculum Development.

Saville-Troike, Muriel. 1983. "An Anthropological Linguistic Perspective on Uses of Ethnography in Bilingual Language Proficiency Assessment." In *An Ethnographic/Sociolinguistic Approach to Language Proficiency Assessment*, edited by Charlene Rivera, 131–36. Avon: Multilingual Matters.

Spolsky, Bernard. 2000. "Language Testing in The Modern Language Journal." *Modern Language Journal* 84, no. 4 (Winter): 536–552.

Stecher, Brian M., and W. Alan Davis. 1996. *How to Focus an Evaluation*. Newbury Park: Sage.

Stern, Hans H. 1983. "Toward a Multi-Dimensional Foreign Language Curriculum." In *Foreign Languages: Key Links in the Chain of Learning*, edited by Robert J. Meade, 120–46. Middlebury: Northeast Conference on the Teaching of Foreign Languages.

Sullivan, Joann H. 2006. "The Importance of Program Evaluation in Collegiate Foreign Language Programs." *Modern Language Journal* 90, no. 4 (Winter): 590–593.

Surface, Eric A., and Erich C. Dierdorff. 2003. "Reliability and the ACTFL Oral Proficiency Interview: Reporting Indices of Interrater Consistency and Agreement for 19 Languages." *Foreign Language Annals* 36, no. 4 (December): 507–19.

Watanabe, Yukiko, John M. Norris, and Marta Gonzáles-Lloret. 2009. "Identifying and Responding to Evaluation Needs in College Foreign Language Programs." In *Toward Useful Program Evaluation in College Foreign Language Education*, edited by John M. Norris, John M. Davis, Castle Sinicrope, and Yukiko Watanabe, 5–58. Honolulu: University of Hawai'i at Mānoa, National Foreign Language Resource Center.

Westat, Joy. 2008. *The 2002 User-Friendly Handbook for Project Evaluation*. Washington, DC: National Science Foundation Division of Research, Evaluation and Communication.

Windham, Scott. 2008. "Redesigning Lower-level Curricula for Learning Outcomes: A Case Study." *ADFL Bulletin* 39, no. 2–3 (Winter–Spring): 31–35.

Wright, Barbara D. 2006. "Learning Languages and the Language of Learning." *Modern Language Journal* 90, no. 4 (November): 593–597.

Yarbrough, Donald B., Lyn M. Shulha, Rodney K. Hopson, and Flora A. Caruthers. 2011. *The Program Evaluation Standards: A Guide for Evaluators and Evaluation Users*. Joint Committee on Standards for Educational Evaluation. Thousand Oaks: Sage.

16

Implementing Open Architecture Curricular Design at the Classroom and Department Level[1]
Lessons from a Ten-Year Experience

YANIV ODED AND ILKNUR ODED

THIS CHAPTER DESCRIBES CONCEPTUAL shifts that transformed the DLIFLC Hebrew Department during its ten-year experience with *open architecture curricular design* (OACD) and practical lessons from that experience at two levels: (1) classroom, where OACD was implemented by individual teachers within small teaching teams, and (2) department (eighteen teachers, organized into four teams, teaching nine sections of six students each[2]), where OACD became the unifying framework for guiding course development and instruction.

The two levels are interdependent. Writing about educational reform, Glickman, Gordon, and Ross-Gordon (2010) introduce the metaphor of a fractal, "a geometric shape that is similar to itself at different scales" (411). Like midsized tree branches that are "remarkably similar in shape to the larger branches from which they come . . . schools reveal self-similarity in different scales" (411–12). Similarly, teacher-student interactions in the classroom tend to be analogous to supervisor-teacher (dean-chair, district-school, etc.) interactions: learner autonomy depends on teacher autonomy, collaborative learning starts with collaborative teaching, and Open Architecture (OA) in the classroom relies on OA at the program or department level. In other words change at the level of the teacher or small instructional team is dependent in part on the broader operational culture and educational philosophy that pervade all levels of the organization.

Background to the Introduction of OACD at the Classroom Level in the Hebrew Department at DLIFLC

The Defense Language Institute Foreign Language Center (DLIFLC) is the Department of Defense's primary language and culture instructional facility. To enhance graduates' proficiency following the events of September 11, 2001, DLIFLC decreased its teacher-to-student ratio to 1:3 (2006–2009), introduced new technologies, and worked to improve curriculum and faculty training. Furthermore, a new final test was developed—the Defense Language Proficiency Test (DLPT) version 5 (DLPT5)—which relies solely on authentic materials, including unedited listening passages, as was the case with the Defense Language Proficiency Test, version 4. One important distinction between the two versions is that Version 5 contained listening passages that were not re-recorded for inclusion in the instrument. DLIFLC's graduation requirement remained Advanced/Advanced/Intermediate High (ILR 2/2/1+) (listening/reading/speaking), but its new objective required that at least 76 percent of graduates attain at least Advanced High (ILR 2+) in listening and reading on the Defense Language Proficiency Test, version 5, and Advanced (ILR 2) in speaking on the Oral Proficiency Interview. However, upon introducing the Defense Language Proficiency Test, version 5, exit testing results across DLIFLC dropped rather than improved and remained below the Advanced High/Advanced High/Advanced (ILR 2+/2+/2) objective of 76 percent. As of 2019 about 70 percent of basic program graduates attained Advanced/Advanced/Intermediate High (ILR 2/2/1+) but fewer than 30 percent achieved Advanced High/Advanced High/Advanced (ILR 2+/2+/2).

In 2009 Defense Language Proficiency Test, version 5, was introduced into the Hebrew Department. While other languages were seeing high failure rates on the instrument (almost 40 percent in some programs) and about 20 percent production of Advanced High/Advanced High/Advanced (ILR 2+/2+/2), the first Hebrew class to take the DLPT5—HE109 graduated with 100 percent attainment of Advanced High/Advanced High/Advanced (ILR 2+/2+/2) of all students who took the test. Similar results were achieved the following year also by HE110, which was taught by the same teaching team. The following section examines the role of OACD in enabling this success.

Instructional-Curricular Initiatives in HE109

The saying goes that "the person who invented the stick was not the smartest or the strongest; that person just needed it the most." This applies to the exploration of new instructional paths in the Hebrew Department; the innovations that led ultimately to the department's transformation based on OACD were born of necessity.

In 2008–9 the looming Defense Language Proficiency Test, version 5, was creating stress for teachers and learners alike. In addition to the innovations described previously, the new test eliminated low-level short passages and included Advanced High and Superior (ILR 2+ and 3) passages that were longer and more challenging than the instructional content used in the department at the time. Awareness of high failure rates in other programs further exacerbated concerns.

Instructional materials in the year-long Hebrew Basic Program included two textbooks for the first and second semesters and nonauthentic teacher-prepared materials

IMPLEMENTING OACD AT THE CLASSROOM AND DEPARTMENT LEVEL

for the third (final) semester. Since department tests aligned with prior Defense Language Proficiency Test versions, there was no structured way to assess learner readiness for the Defense Language Proficiency Test, version 5. An important factor was the composition of the team charged with leading the first class to take the Defense Language Proficiency Test, version 5—a single section of six students. The team consisted of two new teachers hired in 2007, one of them (one of the authors) having been selected as team leader[3] only in 2008.

Though it had limited experience, this teaching team also had limited investment in existing practices. This made it fertile ground for instructional-curricular experimentation, which started in 2008 and evolved throughout 2009 and 2010. The experimentation was not carefully planned and organized and yielded a wide array of disconnected initiatives. However it did have a clear twofold rationale. First since teachers no longer knew substantially more than learners about the final test (teachers being familiar with performance trends from the old test), the learner-teacher relationship became more egalitarian and learner-centered. Learners became partners and teammates in the instructional process, and teachers consciously shared both decision-making and content development with them (see Gregory 2022 in this volume on self-sequenced modularity). Second since the final test was an unknown (which meant that teachers could not "prepare" students for it), the focus of instruction inevitably became more proficiency-oriented. Partially joking, both teachers admitted that "the only trick we now have for Defense Language Proficiency Test preparation is for learners to learn Hebrew."

These two factors—learners as partners with teachers and a strong proficiency orientation—translated into strong learner engagement in, and control of, the learning process (i.e., self-direction and learner autonomy) as well as heightened awareness of the learning process and their role in it (i.e., metacognition). Several of the challenges/opportunities created by the Defense Language Proficiency Test, version 5, and the manner in which they were addressed illustrate these developments:

- Loss of predetermined vocabulary lists: Learners were tasked with constructing lists of key terms by topic (e.g., terms needed to understand Advanced (ILR 2) texts on economics). They shared their lists with classmates, agreed on one list, then continuously added definitions and links to these terms as the course progressed. In this way they created personal dictionaries (Echevarría and Short 2013).
- Absence of appropriate practice and assessment materials: Learners received basic training in identifying the level of texts and writing comprehension questions. They were then tasked with constructing practice materials for the class and explaining their rationale for the questions and answers.
- Absence of authentic, high-level instructional materials: Learners were trained in basic lesson design and then tasked with finding materials, facilitating lessons, and assigning homework.

The curriculum development solutions described previously were not isolated instances in a generally teacher-centered curriculum but part of a developmental trend that played out over the course of the program. The practice of peer-self-assigned homework, for example, started with teachers providing homework options to choose from (individually and as a class). They then asked learners to propose homework assignments for teacher approval. Finally teachers gave learners the freedom to engage in self-study without preapproval as long as they shared their work with the class. Learner delivery of lessons was similarly scaffolded. As Krasner 2022 points out in this volume, OACD can be gradually introduced from the outset of instruction.

Regarding research and presentation projects, before 2009 the common practice had been to assign such projects only to third-semester learners (after they supposedly reached a high enough proficiency level). Often learner products were of low quality due to lack of experience with authentic materials and the research process. In 2009 learners were assigned projects beginning in the first semester. Initially they researched and presented in English on topics related to Israel. As the program progressed, projects were done in Hebrew on topics relating to the United States. Toward the end of the program learners researched and presented in Hebrew on key societal issues in Israel today (see Soyan, this volume, on the importance of oral presentations for language proficiency).

Both practices—teaching or delivery of course content by learners and self-assigned homework—were introduced by the students themselves in the context of a class activity named "The Trial," an initiative by and for learners in which they put Israel "on trial" for its practice of pre-emptive military strikes. Learners formed groups, gathered and researched evidence (i.e., self-assigned homework), and constructed a trial-like lesson format (opening statements, presentation of evidence, cross examinations). The initial fifty-minute lesson evolved into a two-week module covering warfare, history, economics, international law, and ethics. At one point, three days into the trial, learners decided that the teacher—one of the authors—could not serve as an impartial judge and opted to facilitate the lesson themselves. For the next week and a half the teacher's role was limited to that of invited witness and language resource.

At the time these instructional-curricular initiatives were unfolding, information about OACD as a concept was not yet available to DLIFLC faculty (see Chapter 1 in this volume; Corin 2020a, 2020b). After the initial successes of 2009 and 2010, teachers, students, and DLIFLC leadership scrutinized the initiatives in an attempt to understand and share what was being done across the institute. One popular concept at the time was that of the *net generation/digital natives*. It has subsequently been critiqued by some scholars (Bennett, Maton, and Kervin 2008; Hargittai 2010; Thomas 2011; Vaidhyanathan 2008) and its popularity has waned. At the time, however, many at DLIFLC framed this Hebrew Department endeavor as building a digital-native curriculum, presumably because many of its curricular initiatives relied heavily on Web 2.0 tools and concepts (i.e., tools that build on user-generated content and participation). For example:

- Using Google Sites, each learner developed a personal website for setting learning goals and implementing self-selected learning projects. Learners also developed and maintained a collaborative class website for sharing and managing class projects.

- Learners were tasked with building an online presence within the target culture complete with blogging, active participation in chat rooms, and news talk-backs.
- Each learner contributed to Wikipedia pages in Hebrew and created at least one new Wikipedia page (e.g., a page about the learner's hometown), which required working with Israeli content editors.
- Many learner-directed projects relied on online authoring tools for generating both group and individual projects, such as preparing a class news broadcast (see Soyan, this volume) and video blogging.
- Within lessons, learners projected and manipulated content on the classroom Smartboard from their laptops and worked synchronously with various Web 2.0 tools such as Google Docs, Lino, and Prezi to develop and share content.

Thus when discussing and reporting about the Hebrew team's accomplishments, (e.g., Lamar 2011) the project was framed as a technology initiative. Its real impetus, however, was pedagogy, not technology, and its goals were learner ownership of course content and participation in (rather than learning about) Israeli culture. In presentations by Hebrew students and teachers, they referred to it as the student-directed and virtual immersion programs.

The academic success of the first Hebrew classes to take the Defense Language Proficiency Test, version 5, in 2009 and 2010—HE109 and the following year HE110, with their teacher-learner co-constructed programs—thus generated institutional interest and rapid, albeit superficial, expansion. The key emphasis was on how to replicate and expand the initiative, and it soon became the victim of its own success. Learner-generated projects deemed successful were misguidedly turned into teacher-mandated assignments, and even within the Hebrew Department such a simple initiative as the learner-generated vocabulary project was turned by some teachers into a mandatory vocabulary list. This misapplication was rooted in a misunderstanding of the driving forces behind the innovations and their epistemological framework. This misunderstanding can help explain why inconsistent adaptations (2010–2015) across the Hebrew Department of the instructional initiatives that had been used in HE109 and HE110 yielded mixed results, with Advanced High/Advanced High/Advanced (ILR 2+/2+/2) scores hovering around 50 percent.

In 2016 however the instructional initiatives and overarching OACD framework used in HE109 and HE110 were systematically implemented across the Hebrew Department and yielded notable improvements. From 2016 to 2019 Advanced High/Advanced High/Advanced (ILR 2+/2+/2) exit testing results in the Hebrew program increased from 68.8 percent in 2015 to 81.5 percent in 2019; the percentage of Hebrew students graduating with Superior/Superior/Advanced (ILR 3/3/2) rose from 37.5 percent in 2015 to 59.3 percent in 2019, and the average academic disenrollment remained about 5 percent per year compared to an institute-wide average of 13.5 percent. The following three sections explore the conceptual basis and practical implementation of this department-wide innovation, as well as the challenges that were encountered.

Conceptual Shifts at the Department Level
Three conceptual shifts enabled the Hebrew Department's transformation into an OACD-based program:

1. From a focus on compliance to a commitment to continuous improvement as the primary approach to program development
2. From a narrow framework of instructional design to a wider system of *human performance improvement*
3. From a repetitive to a competitive orientation in the educational leadership

From Compliance to a Commitment to Continuous Improvement
A key pillar of many human resource models is the development of employee commitment. Compliance is about working according to externally imposed control systems, while commitment is internalized, leading to proactivity and employee motivation. As Senge (2006) notes, "[T]he committed person brings energy, passion, and excitement that cannot be generated if you are only compliant" (221). Within the educational reform literature, notions of teacher and learner commitment, as opposed to compliance, have been gaining more prominence in recent years (Kellie 2010; Debard and Kubow 2002).

Compliance and commitment to continuous improvement are not mutually exclusive. Teachers do need to follow certain regulations and requirements. However, requirements are merely a starting point; motivation and ownership depend on continuous commitment. As for how to generate such commitment, Senge suggests "[Y]ou cannot force commitment.... Your primary influence is the environment you create" (cited in Bernhardt 2018, 1). This focus on *environment* provides a link to the next conceptual shift.

From Instructional Design to Human Performance Improvement
Human performance improvement, also known as *human performance technology*, is a field of study and practice that aims to "achieve, through people, increasingly successful accomplishments that are valued by all organizational stakeholders"—that is, "valued accomplishment through people" (Stolovitch 2018, 122). While instructional design focuses on the design and development of learning solutions, human performance improvement/human performance technology maintains "that in many cases the best solution to a learning or performance problem may not involve instruction . . . a non-instructional solution may be a better remedy" (Reiser and Dempsey 2007, 133). For example instead of extensive training on how to complete a certain administrative process, the focus should be on simplifying that process.

Among the first to reach this conclusion was Gilbert, who concluded that "the key focus of any organizational intervention should not be people's learning but people's ability to perform their job better and the benefits that such improved or enhanced performance could bring to their organization" (Oded and Su 2010, 49). According to Gilbert (2007) "all behavioral components of performance—have two aspects of equal importance: a person with a repertory of behavior (P) and a supporting environment (E)" (81). Accordingly, "we can change performance in one of two ways: by modifying the behavior repertory itself or by modifying the environment" (97). He continues, "[T]he environment is easier to manipulate than people's repertoires" (86), and it yields clearer and longer lasting effects. Simply put facilitating OACD is best achieved not via extensive trainings but by establishing a learning and working environment that is aligned with OACD. This conclusion, which recalls the fractals metaphor, provides a link to the third conceptual shift.

From Repetitive to Competitive Orientation in the Educational Leadership

Repetitive-competitive continuums have been defined and utilized in various contexts. Repetitive refers to a mindset or deliberate orientation that is focused on doing more/better with what was already achieved. Competitive refers to a mindset or orientation that is focused on finding new ways for doing new things. The underlying transformative conceptualization of these terms is not foreign to educational environments. The very goal of transformative learning, according to Mezirow (1990), is to enable one to "explore alternative perspectives, transform old ways of understanding, and act on new perspectives" (p. 18). Building on Mezirow (1990), Kegan (2009) succinctly distinguished between informative and transformative learning. Informative learning is "aimed at increasing our fund of knowledge, at increasing our repertoire of skills, at extending already established cognitive structures" (42). In transformative learning, on the other hand, "we do not only form meaning, and we do not only change our meanings; we change the very form by which we are making our meanings" (44–45).

The two orientations are pertinent to a discussion of three facets of organizational functioning: (1) daily operations, (2) disposition toward change, and (3) tolerance for failure:

a. Within a repetitive orientation daily operations are managed hierarchically and problems are escalated vertically to supervisors. Supervisors within such an orientation allocate specific times for "important" issues while spending most of their time on "urgent" matters.[4] Within a competitive orientation decisions relating to daily operations are delegated, and problems are dispersed horizontally across organic teams. Supervisors within such an orientation allocate specific times for addressing "urgent" matters, such as answering emails between 6 and 7 a.m., but devote the majority of their time to facilitating "important" new initiatives.
b. Within a repetitive orientation, change is largely viewed as a challenge to be managed; it is approached with caution, and speed and variety are carefully controlled to mitigate risk. Within a competitive orientation, change is viewed through the prism of opportunities to be seized. Moving fast in a decentralized manner and with multiple beta solutions is both valued and viewed as a key mechanism for risk mitigation.
c. Within a repetitive orientation, tolerance for failure is limited; failure is avoided even at the cost of limiting innovation. Within a competitive orientation, small-scale failures in the context of multiple decentralized initiatives are accepted as an inevitable byproduct of trying new things, taking calculated risks, and fostering innovation.

Neither orientation is "good" or "bad," and both, albeit in different doses, can be found in most organizations. Tolerance for failure, speed, and variety of change, and supervisors' involvement and time allocation are governed by an array of factors, including legal and ethical considerations. School principals and even classroom teachers may astutely embrace a more repetitive orientation in some aspects of their work while choosing a more competitive posture for others. The crucial point is that the choice should be conscious and principled, based on benefits, risks, and goals. Here the authors maintain that for OACD to flourish, supervisors need to shift purposefully toward a more competitive orientation.

OACD Implementation at the Department Level

This section describes the Hebrew Department's transformation into an OACD-based program through its embrace of the conceptual shifts described previously. Because there is abundant literature on facilitating the first two shifts (from compliance to commitment and from instructional design to human performance improvement/human performance technology), the focus here will be on the shift from repetitive to competitive orientation based on the three facets listed earlier.

Daily Operations and Fostering Organic Teams

While DLIFLC relies on hierarchical structures—department chairs and subordinate team leaders—the Hebrew Department's orientation was toward building a team of leaders. Teacher and team autonomy—a crucial prerequisite for learner autonomy according to Little (1995, 178) and Glickman, Gordon, and Ross-Gordon's (2010) concept of "fractals" in education—was codified to include autonomy in selecting content, scope, and sequence. A two-year limit was set for Hebrew team leaders, and the selection of new leaders, as well as new employees, is now done jointly by teachers and the department chair. Peer observations and mentoring were established as primary means for ongoing professional development in tandem with nonevaluative chair walkthroughs (Downey et al. 2010), where the primary focus is on reflective interaction. A team feedback component was added to all teaching award nominations, tying professional recognition to collegiality and teamwork. Teaching teams engage in systematic teacher swapping to enhance department-level cohesion and foster idea-sharing across teams.

To strengthen interpersonal relationships and enhance cohesion and collaboration (i.e., to build social capital), an end-of-month team building and training event was instituted at which teachers spend time together and share new ideas (Van Gorp et al. in this volume extend this idea to cross-institutional teacher collaboration). These team events/meetings have four key characteristics:

- They are conducted mid-day, replacing an instructional period, and not at the end of the day when teachers are less energized.
- While these meetings usually include important decision-making on both academic and administrative matters, their focus is on consensus building, not voting and trading, on "unity, not unanimity" (Parker 2006, 666).
- While teachers attend these meetings, learners are afforded the opportunity and responsibility to lead community-of-learners events where they teach each other, engage in community building, and discuss new initiatives.

- Several times every year, faculty and learners meet together to share and discuss current initiatives and challenges.

Disposition toward Change (Speed and Variety)

Whereas the traditional curriculum in the Hebrew Department relied on textbooks complemented by supplementary materials, the situation is now reversed, with the curriculum relying on decentralized authentic content complemented by textbook snippets. The year-long program currently utilizes segments of one textbook during the first semester. Goals and topics covered in class and tests are discussed jointly by teachers and learners, and each class charts its own path for reaching its goals. Hence the initiatives discussed in the first section of this chapter are not a representative sample or model for the whole department, but one path out of many.

To further foster innovation, traditional and more cumbersome models such as ADDIE (Analyze, Design, Develop, Implement, Evaluate)[5] (Branson et al. 1975; Watson 1981) were replaced with *rapid prototyping design*, which "relies on continuous usability testing of prototypes" (Oded and Su 2010, 54). Involving all stakeholders (learners, teachers, team leader, chair) in prototype testing not only mitigates concerns but also creates a sense of shared ownership, thus enhancing buy-in. New projects are also no longer called *pilots* (a term used for leadership-driven interventions, which subsequently become mandatory if deemed successful) but *initiatives*, resulting in a plethora of decentralized initiatives—most originating with teachers—with far less office politics. To ensure quality control and to balance individual-team desiderata, new initiatives must be supported by at least one team member and learners, as assessed by sensing sessions (with the chair and/or team leader) and surveys.

Tolerance for Failure

No one, and no organization, wants to fail. Failure aversion, however, can stymie innovation, which necessitates taking calculated risks and accepting—even embracing—failure as a byproduct of innovation and an opportunity to learn. The key issue is that of scale. While small-scale decentralized ventures can produce versatile solutions that can later be disseminated, *small-scale* failures can be mitigated, and risks can be constrained. Hence even within organizations that are more prone to a repetitive orientation, a certain level of risk-taking is necessary for success. Put differently, risk aversion is itself a risk that may lead to failure. While we should not reward for trying and failing—"[a] system that rewards people for their behavior (e.g., hard work, knowledge, motivation) without accounting for accomplishment encourages incompetence" (Stolovitch 2018, 124)—neither should we punish or equate failing with being a failure.

Challenges Encountered When Implementing OACD

DLIFLC is generally disposed toward a repetitive orientation, due in part to the size and complexity of its operation (e.g., the need to maintain comparable accountability across all language programs, schools, departments, and classes). Accordingly hierarchical decision-making is common. Enabling variety and speed in initiatives is challenging, at times even prohibited by military or government regulations. While innovation is possible, tolerance for failure is low due to national security considerations (e.g., the need to meet stakeholders' manpower requirements) and the considerable financial investment involved in training each military language professional. Nevertheless two key factors have enabled the Hebrew Department (and other small programs at DLIFLC) to maintain its competitive orientation. Hebrew was a small "noncritical" language program with only one department (about fifty students). Hence innovations are easier to implement than in larger programs and less likely to cause apprehension on the part of DLIFLC leadership. Moreover the Hebrew Department has become one of the top-performing basic programs at DLIFLC—and the program reached 74 percent attainment of the Advanced High/Advanced High/Advanced (ILR 2+/2+/2) objectives (with many students scoring Superior/Superior [ILR 3/3] in both listening and reading).

Concerns regarding faculty (eighteen people) were threefold: resistance, working with faculty with varying levels and types of experience and skills, and balancing individual versus team needs and desires. Resistance from faculty members was in fact minimal. A few seasoned teachers did worry about the program's direction and reliance on untested materials. However the combination of working in teams, systematic mentoring with peer observations, and routine department discussions and professional development events, where requirements and operational boundaries were clearly explained, alleviated the first two concerns. In fact teacher professional development proved a crucial element in fostering informed teacher autonomy. As for balancing individual versus team needs and desires, requiring teachers to garner teammates' support for new initiatives while making award nominations dependent on peer input (i.e., maintaining team cohesion while controlling for unhealthy competition) has yielded both ongoing professional development and more balanced initiatives. Three notable lessons were that:

1. collaboration did not limit innovation but rather enhanced it;
2. even seemingly less effective initiatives did not fail (as measured by grades and learner feedback) due to strong learner-teacher commitment to the initiatives; and
3. not having "all our eggs in one basket" changed our view of success and failure. When one has a plethora of small-scale decentralized initiatives, as long as no initiative fails terribly, one succeeds.

Some learners, particularly those with analytical learning styles (who generally prefer step-by-step learning, facts, and direct instruction; Messick 1976), initially criticize the absence of textbooks, clear scope and sequence, and structured centralized grammar instruction. These criticisms become particularly pronounced when transitioning to the second semester (week 20) and exclusive reliance on authentic content. Quarterly learner surveys show that as the program progresses and learner control of content and homework increases, criticisms diminish. Three initiatives that were particularly helpful in alleviating learner concerns were the establishment of a self-study repository with learner/teacher-developed content, peer-mentoring, and the learner-led community of learners events.

Conclusions

OACD has transformed the Hebrew Department into a perpetual educational startup at both the classroom and department levels. Within this startup learners and teachers in every class continually invent and co-construct their own unique learning paths with consistent outstanding results. Challenges do occur, and neither teachers nor learners consider the system perfect. Nevertheless it has yielded significantly enhanced learning outcomes, and teachers and learners generally remain engaged and committed to improving the process.

Study Questions

1. Looking at the three facets of organizational functioning discussed in this paper—daily operations, disposition toward change, and tolerance for failure—where would you place yourself and your organization on the continuum from repetitive to competitive orientation? What significance does that have should you choose full implementation of OACD? What steps would you need to take to get from where you are today to a future where OACD is fully implemented?
2. Implementing OACD at the department level almost inevitably yields some tensions between individual preferences and skill sets and those of colleagues. How might such tensions be manifested in your teaching context? How might you address them?
3. Does OACD particularly align more with a proficiency approach? As an administrator or faculty developer (in-service leader, etc.), how do you approach faculty and colleagues who opt to use more of grammar-based or cognitive approaches within an OACD framework?

Notes

1. This chapter has been approved for public release by the Defense Language Institute Foreign Language Center's Public Affairs Office. For verification please email mpao@dliflc.edu. Contents of this chapter are not necessarily the official views of the Defense Language Institute Foreign Language Center, nor are they endorsed by the Department of the Army, the Department of Defense, or the US government. All third-party products and materials featured in the chapter remain the intellectual property of their respective authors or originators. Use of outside materials is done under the fair use copyright principle, for educational purposes only. The content of this chapter is the sole responsibility of the author(s).
2. One team consisted of eight teachers teaching four sections; two teams consisted of four teachers, each teaching two sections; and one team consisted of two teachers teaching one section.
3. A "team leader" at DLIFLC is a coordinator of team activities and weekly schedules, not a supervisor.
4. Covey (1990/2016) suggests a matrix of intersecting "urgent" and "important" axes for how managers spend their time. *Urgent* matters that they cannot avoid can be important (finding a substitute teacher when someone is absent unexpectedly) or not important (answering a phone call asking for program information). *Important* matters may not be urgent, yielding lasting results though they take longer to accomplish (e.g., planning). Some tasks may be neither important nor urgent.
5. Although ADDIE (Analyze, Design, Develop, Implement, Evaluate) has appeared in many government programs, including DLIFLC, mostly in the last decade, the model first appeared in 1975 as a creation of the Center for Educational Technology at Florida State University, which quickly spread into the US armed forces and still dominates in many military training programs today.

References

Bennett, S., K. Maton, and L. Kervin. 2008. "The 'Digital Natives' Debate: A Critical Review of the Evidence." *British Journal of Educational Technology* 39, no. 5: 775–86.

Bernhardt, Victoria, L. 2018. *Data Analysis for Continuous School Improvement*. New York: Routledge.

Branson, R. K., G. T. Rayner, J. L. Cox, J. P. Furman, F. J. King, and W. H. Hannum. 1975. *Interservice Procedures for Instructional Systems Development*. Vols. 1–5. TRADOC Pam 350–30. Ft. Monroe: US Army Training and Doctrine Command.

Corin, Andrew R. 2020a. "Open Architecture Curriculum and Transformative Language Learning Revisited. Part 1. The Relationship between Open Architecture Curricular Design and Transformative Language Learning." *ACTR Letter* 46, no. 3–4 (Spring-Summer): 1–2, 4–5.

Corin, Andrew R. 2020b. "Open Architecture Curriculum and Transformative Language Learning Revisited. Part 2. Toward a Constrained Definition of OACD." *ACTR Letter* 47, no. 1 (Fall): 1–2, 4.

Covey, Stephen. 1990/2016. *The 7 Habits of Highly Effective People*. Miami: Mango Publishing.

Debard, Robert, and Patricia K. Kubow. 2002. "From Compliance to Commitment: The Need for Constituent Discourse in Implementing Testing Policy." *Educational Policy* 16, no. 3: 387–405.

Downey, Carolyn J., Betty E. Steffy, William K. Poston, Jr., and Fenwick W. English. 2010. *Advancing the Three-Minute Classroom Walk-Through: Mastering Reflective Practice*. Thousand Oaks: Corwin Press.

Echevarría, J., M. E. Vogt, and D. Short. 2013. *Making Content Comprehensible for Elementary English Language Learners: The SIOP Model*. Boston: Allyn & Bacon.

Gilbert, T. F. 2007. *Human Competence: Engineering Worthy Performance*. Hoboken: Wiley.

Glickman, Carl D., Stephen P. Gordon, and Jovita M. Ross-Gordon. 2010. *SuperVision and Instructional Leadership: A Developmental Approach*. New York: Pearson.

Hargittai, E. 2010. "Digital Na(t)ives? Variation in Internet Skills and Uses among Members of the 'Net Generation'." *Sociological Inquiry* 80, no. 1: 92–113.

Kegan, Robert. 2009. "What 'Form' Transforms?: A Constructive-Developmental Approach to Transformative Learning." In *Contemporary Theories of Learning: Learning Theorists . . . in Their Own Words*, edited by Knud Illeris, 35–52. New York: Routledge.

Kellie, Terry. 2010. "Compliance, Commitment, and Capacity: Examining Districts' Responses to No Child Left Behind." *Planning and Changing* 41, no. 1–2: 80–109.

Lamar, Brian. 2011. "If You Can't Take DLIFLC to Israel, Bring Israel to DLIFLC." *Globe* 34, no. 1: 23.

Little, David. 1995. "Learning as Dialogue: The Dependence of Learner Autonomy on Teacher Autonomy. *System* 23, no. 2: 175–81.

Messick, S., ed. 1976. *Individuality in Learning*. San Francisco: Jossey-Bass.

Mezirow, Jack. 1990. "How Critical Reflection Triggers Transformative Learning." In *Fostering Critical Reflection in Adulthood: A Guide to Transformative and Emancipatory Learning*, edited by Jack Mezirow, 1–20. San Francisco: Jossey-Bass Publishers.

Oded, Yaniv, and Bude Su. 2010. "Streamlining Administrative Procedures at the Defense Language Institute: The Strategic Impact Model in Action." *Performance Improvement Quarterly* 23, no. 2: 47–69.

Parker, Glenn M. 2006. "What Makes a Team Effective or Ineffective?" *Organization Development*, edited by Joan V. Gallos, 656–80. San Francisco: Jossey-Bass.

Reiser, R., and J. Dempsey. 2007. *Trends and Issues in Instructional Design and Technology*. Upper Saddle River: Pearson Merrill Prentice Hall.

Senge, Peter M. 2006. *The Fifth Discipline: The Art & Practice of The Learning Organization*. New York: Crown Business.

Stolovitch, Harold D. 2018. "The Development and Evolution of Human Performance Improvement." In *Trends and Issues in Instructional Design and Technology*, edited by Robert A. Reiser and John V. Dempsey, 122–31. New York: Pearson.

Thomas, M. 2011. *Deconstructing Digital Natives: Young People, Technology, and the New Literacies*. New York: Routledge.

Vaidhyanathan, S. 2008. "Generational Myth: Not All Young People Are Tech-Savvy." *Chronicle of Higher Education* 55, no. 5: B7–9.

Watson, Russell. 1981. *Instructional System Development*. Paper presented to the International Congress for Individualized Instruction.

List of Contributors

Wendy Ashby (PhD, University of Arizona, second language acquisition and teaching) has served as a German/ESL instructor, faculty/curriculum developer, and program evaluator for the Departments of Defense and State and postsecondary institutions. She currently works in Academic Affairs at Cochise College and owns L2 Matters Consulting. drwashby@gmail.com

María Bondarenko (PhD, Russian State University for the Humanities) is a Russian and French L2 instructor, instructional designer, and lecturer in L2 education affiliated with the University of Montreal (Canada) and the University of Heidelberg (Germany). Her research interest is the cognitive approaches to L2 teaching, beginner L2 pedagogy, and Russian verbs of motion. maria.bondarenko@umontreal.ca

Christine Campbell (PhD, Purdue University) is president of Campbell Language Consultants and professor emerita of the Defense Language Institute Foreign Language Center, where she served as associate provost of two directorates. She is former president of the American Association of the Teachers of Spanish and Portuguese (AATSP) and recipient of its 2020 Distinguished Leadership Award. campbelllanguageconsultants@gmail.com

Kueilan Chen (PhD, linguistics, University of Illinois, Urbana-Champaign) is the immersion specialist for Chinese Mandarin immersion programs and professor of Chinese at the Defense Language Institute Foreign Language Center. For thirty years, she has been active professionally, regularly presenting at national and government-sponsored conferences. She is president of the International Language and Culture Foundation. kueilan.chen@dliflc.edu

Sang Yee Cheon (PhD, linguistics, University of Hawai'i at Mānoa) is associate professor of Korean and director of the Korean Language Flagship Center at the University of Hawai'i at Mānoa. Her primary research focuses on cultural competence and language proficiency related to the curricular improvement of the Korean Flagship undergraduate degree program. scheon@hawaii.edu

Andrew R. Corin (PhD, University of California, Los Angeles) is professor emeritus, DLIFLC, most recently associate provost and director of the Office of Standardization and Academic Excellence. Previous position include research officer, International Criminal Tribunal for the Former Yugoslavia; adjunct associate professor of Slavic languages and literatures, UCLA; and assistant professor of Russian and linguistics, Pomona College. Areas of publication include Slavic linguistics and philology, world language learning, and investigating violations of international humanitarian law. arcrmc@gmail.com

Reem Dababneh studied in Jordan and Britain, earning a PhD in literature. She worked at the Defense Language Institute Foreign Language Center as a teacher and administrator for longer than a decade before moving into a different career field. reem.dababneh@dliflc.edu

Olga Dobrunoff (PhD, Moscow State Linguistic University) currently works at the Defense Language Institute Foreign Language Center. Her doctorate is in philology and second language acquisition. She has worked at Columbia University, US Naval Academy, US Military Academy, and in intensive programs. She is an alumna of the Alexander von Humboldt Foundation/Germany. Her research interests are language pedagogy, instructional technology, intercultural communication, and cognitive and psycholinguistics.

Joshua Alma Enslen (PhD, romance languages, University of Georgia) is professor of Portuguese at West Point. He holds a postdoctoral certificate of studies from the Materialities of Literature Program at the University of Coimbra. joshua.enslen@westpoint.edu

Luca Giupponi (EdD, Indiana University) is the head of technology at the National LCTL Resource Center and an educational technology specialist at the Center for Language Teaching Advancement at Michigan State University. His work focuses on faculty development, technology integration, and program evaluation.

E. John Gregory (PhD, Georgetown University) is deputy head of the Department of Foreign Languages, US Military Academy, West Point, and previously Chinese Program director (West Point). He holds a PhD, Chinese history (Georgetown); JD (University of Florida); and BS, Chinese/French (West Point) and is a Fulbright Fellow, Academia Sinica, Taiwan (2013–14). His recent work includes discursive analysis of PRC legal rhetoric. eugene.gregory@westpoint.edu

Emily Heidrich Uebel (PhD, University of Wisconsin–Madison) is an academic specialist at the Center for Language Teaching Advancement and the associate executive director of the National Less Commonly Taught Languages Resource Center (NLRC) at Michigan State University. Additional information and recent research can be found on her website, emilyheidrichuebel.com. heidric6@msu.edu

Kassema Jones (MATFL, Monterey Institute of International Studies) has spent almost thirty years in the language learning field as an administrator and teacher of Modern

Standard Arabic (MSA) and Egyptian dialect at the Defense Language Institute Foreign Language Center (DLIFLC) and at the George Marshall Center. At DLIFLC, she also served as oral proficiency tester, MSA. kassema@hotmail.com

Irene Krasner has more than thirty years of experience in education, with twenty-five years at the Defense Language Institute Foreign Language Center. There she has served as chairperson, academic specialist, project manager, Chairs' Council president, Academic Specialists' Council chairperson, Faculty Advisory Council president, test developer, OPI tester, faculty developer, team leader, and teacher. irene.krasner@dliflc.edu

Betty Lou Leaver (PhD, Pushkin Institute) is former provost of the Defense Language Institute Foreign Language Center, where her programs earned the American Association of University Administrators' Khaladjian Award for International Innovation in Higher Education. She has also administered language programs for NASA, New York Institute of Technology/Jordan, and the Foreign Service Institute. Leaver@aol.com

Jae Sun Lee (PhD, Korean linguistics, University of Hawai'i at Mānoa) is associate professor at DLIFLC, where she has taught Korean language courses since 2008. Her research focuses on South and North Korean languages in the sociolinguistic context. jaesunhi@gmail.com

Sherry A. Maggin (PhD, University of North Carolina at Chapel Hill) is associate professor of Spanish at West Point. She earned an MA in Hispanic literature and a doctoral degree in romance languages and literatures. Her research includes the use of technology in language teaching and the soldier-scholar figure in medieval and early modern literature. sherry.maggin@westpoint.edu

Zachary F. Miller (PhD, Michigan State University) is associate professor of Portuguese at West Point. He earned an MA in Portuguese and a PhD in second language studies. His research interests include second language (L2) acquisition in a military context and the effects of emotion on L2 learning. zachary.miller@westpoint.edu

Ilknur Oded (PhD, Maryland University) is dean of the DLIFLC, having previously served as assistant dean, faculty development specialist, chairperson, and teacher. Her PhD is in linguistics, and she holds an MA in linguistics from Bogazici University and an MSc in instructional science and technology from CSU Monterey Bay. ilknur.oded@dliflc.edu

Yaniv Oded (EdD, Indiana University) is senior instructional systems technology specialist at DLIFLC, having previously served as chairperson, faculty development specialist for educational technology, and teacher. His EdD is in instructional systems technology, and he holds an MSc in instructional science and technology from California State University, Monterey Bay. yaniv.oded@dliflc.edu

John Pendergast (PhD, City University of New York) is associate professor of Russian at West Point. With a BA in music, MA in Russian language and literature, and doctoral degree and MA in comparative literature, his research focuses on Russian language pedagogy and music and letters of nineteenth-and twentieth-century Russia and Germany. john.pendergast@westpoint.edu

Rossina Soyan (PhD, Carnegie Mellon University) is an assistant professor of Russian at the School of International Letters and Cultures, Arizona State University. Her research interests include second language acquisition, reading development, biliteracy, and intergenerational transmission of vulnerable and endangered languages.

Koen Van Gorp (PhD, KU Leuven) is assistant professor of second language studies and TESOL at Michigan State University. His research interests are task-based language teaching and assessment, and critical multilingual awareness in teacher education. He is founding coeditor of *TASK. Journal on Task-Based Language Teaching and Learning*. vangorpk@msu.edu

Jeff Watson (PhD, sociocultural theory and second language acquisition, Bryn Mawr College) is associate professor of Russian and is the chair of linguistics and language acquisition in the Center for Languages, Cultures, and Regional Studies at the US Military Academy, West Point. jeffrey.watson@westpoint.edu

Daniel Wang (MS, instructional science and technology, CSU Monterey Bay) is a thirty-three-year veteran world languages associate professor and a trainer of teachers. He has served with distinction as Faculty Advisory Council president and academic specialist, with specialization in optimizing proficiency-centric integration of world language teaching with data analytics. He was an early advocate of open architecture curricular design and is the inventor of the Learner Data Panel. daniel.wang1@dliflc.edu

Rong Yuan (PhD, instructional systems design, University of Central Florida) is professor at the Defense Language Institute, Foreign Language Center. She has published articles and book chapters in the field of teacher education and technology-enhanced language teaching and learning. rong.yuan@dliflc.edu

Index

Note: *Italicized* and **bold** page numbers refer to figures and tables. Page numbers followed by "n" refer to notes.

1987 (2017), 170

academe: early OACD in, 12
accountability, 6, 53, 209, 229
accreditation, 207–8, 210–13, 215
ACTFL. *See* American Council on the Teaching of Foreign Languages
ADDIE (Analyze, Design, Develop, Implement, Evaluate), 231n5
Advanced Language Academy (ALA), 3, 13–14
advanced learners, 103, 165–70
advanced proficiency, 35
advisor/advising: teacher role. *See* mentor/mentoring
ALA. *See* Advanced Language Academy
Aleinikov, Andrei, 47
Alsufieva, Anna, 160
alternative assessments, 142, 144, 146–47
ambient noise, 8, 70, 173
American Council of Teachers of Russian webinar (2022), 20
American Council on the Teaching of Foreign Languages (ACTFL), 4, 50n2, 53, 98, 147, 194; Proficiency Guidelines, 50n2, 145; Writing Proficiency Test (WPT), 99, 104–5
Andrew W. Mellon Foundation, 139
Arabic, 13, 58, 67–69, 71, 73, 76n2, 109, 196, 201; Egyptian, 67–77; Modern Standard Arabic, 58, 67, 69, 196

Armstrong, P., 38
Aronoff Preschool, 20
assessment: alternative, 142, 144, 146–47; formative (*see* formative assessment); summative (*see* summative assessment)
Association of Departments of Foreign Languages, 212–13
Atwell, S., 10
Aubrey, R., 19–20
authenticity, 49, 146; cultural, 58; linguistic, 58; material, 80
authentic materials, 6, 8, 11–12, 18, 20–21, 34, 39, 42–43, 45, 48, 55, 69, 70–72, 74, 79–80, 83, 97, 99, 101–3, 105–6, 119, 124, 127, 142, 145, 147, 171–72, 178, 186, 222, 224; unadapted, 8, 11, 69–73, 101–103, 105, 170–71

Bachman, L. F., 194–95, 196
Balfour Declaration of 1917, 73
Baralt, M., 110
Barsch Learning Style Inventory, 199
Beckett, G. H., 171
behaviorist language teaching, 209
Bernhardt, E., 200
bicultural competence, 4, 29, 38
Big Ten Academic Alliance, 31, 139, 141, 142
bilingual competence, 4, 29, 38
Black, P., 194, 195
Blackboard, 35

237

Bloom, B. S., 194
Bloom's taxonomy, 31, *31*, 38
Bondarenko, M., 54, 180
Book Creator, 110
bottom-up processing, 8, 70, 173
Boyer, N. R., 109
Brinton, D. M., 166
Buck Institute for Education, 146
Byrnes, H., 122

Campbell, C., 7, 14, 108, 177–78
Carroll, J. B., 9
CBI. *See* content-based instruction
Chaiklin, S., 127
change in perspective, 38
Chinese, 97–105, 196; Chinese Mandarin, 20, 53–64, 79–88, 196
Clementi, D., 194
Clifford, R., 17, 44
CLIL. *See* content and language integrated learning
coach/coaching: teacher role. *See* mentor/mentoring
cognate, 18, 45–48, **46**, 50n4, 70, 71, 111, 179, 181, 183
cognitive L2 pedagogy, 23, 177, 178–79, 231
cognitive style, 5, 16, 179, 199
cognitivist language teaching, 209
collaborative learning, 8, 31, 34–35, 44–45, 47, 54, 120, 157, 170–71, 176, 221
collaborative problem-solving, 121–22, 124–25, 127
collaborative teaching, 221
colloquial language, 172
Comer, W. J., 45, 160
community-based learning, 3–4, 8
comparative linguistic analysis, 46
competitive orientation, 227–28, 230, 231
comprehensible input hypothesis, 21, 179
Concordia Language Villages, 19, 64n4; "Language Training Center General Course Description," 59–60; two-week immersions at, 58–59, 60, **61**, 62, 63
constructivist/constructivism, 6, 9, 18, 80, 207–8, 210; social 80, 195
constructivist language teaching, 209
content and language integrated learning (CLIL), 12

content-based approach to using authentic materials, 71–72
content-based instruction (CBI), 10, 12, 18, 154, 159, 166, 174–75, 177; spiral-like design to facilitate OACD-enabled, for novice learners, 179–80; supported by inter-task, 182–86, *184*, *185*
continuous formative assessment, 5, 196, 198
continuous improvement, 208, 226
conversation, 59, 62, 75, 110, 120–21, 128, 132–33, 142, 147, 153, 181, 184, 207
Corin, A. R., 7, 12, 128, 178, 199, 203n5
course design, 6, 9, 98, 102, 108–9, 152–53, 158, 207
Covey, S., 231n4
creativity, 6–7, 42, 49, 55, 108, 127, 170
critical discourse analysis, 33–34, 38, 39n2, 39n3, 97, 101–4, 105n2, 106n3
critical language studies, 58, 230
critical reflection, 8, 29–30, 107–8, 113–15
critical thinking, 35, 166, 197; skills, 32–34, 49, 167, 169, 171–72, 174–76
Critical Thinking Skills Project, 167, 169, 171, 175, 176
culminating task, 82–84, 86, 88, 90, 153, 157
cultural awareness, 29, 31–37, 122
cultural governance, 100
cultural proficiency, 41–42
Czech, 11, 178

daily operations, 228–29
DA. *See* diagnostic assessment
Dababneh, R., 74, 203n5
data analytics, 79, 90–91, 236
Davidson, D. E., 7
debate, 11, 60, 69, 83–84, 90, 167–72, 175–76, 198
Defense Language and National Security Education Office, 58–59
Defense Language Institute Foreign Language Center (DLIFLC), 3, 7, 15, 22, 41–42, 53, 199; basic course, 53–54, 63, 68; Basic Czech Program, 11; Directorate of Continuing Education, 41, 68, 193, 196, 200, 203, 210, 212, 216n1; early OACD at, 11–12; Evaluation and Standards Division, 210; Hebrew Basic Program, 54, 222; Hebrew Department, 222, 226, 230, 231;

Index

immersion facility, one-day and two-day immersions at, 55–58; Korean course, for previously achieved Advanced Koreans, 30–31; OACD framework, emergence of, 12–14; OACD introduction in DLIFLC Chinese Mandarin courses, 80–83, *82*; Office of Standardization and Academic Excellence, 211; Public Affairs Office, 38n1, 50n1, 64n1, 76n1, 92n1, 203n1, 231n1; Russian Basic Program, 11, 18, 48–49, 54; School of Distance Learning, 80; School of Resident Education, 80, 196, 199–200, 202, 203n2, 203n5, 204n6; textbook-based Chinese Mandarin Basic Program, 54–55; "Turbo-Serbian" immersion-conversion courses, 11–12
Defense Language Proficiency Test (DLPT), 75, 76n6, 81, 98, 104, 222–23, 225
defossilization. *See* fossilization
Department of Defense, US, 30, 39n1, 50n1, 64n1, 76n1, 92n1, 203n1, 231n1
Department of Foreign Languages, West Point, 109
Department of the Army, US, 39n1, 50n1, 64n1, 76n1, 92n1, 203n1, 231n1
Derderian, A., 111
diagnostic assessment (DA), 60, **61**, 62–63, 74, 175, 193, 195, 197, 199–202, 203n3, 203n4; online, 62, 196, 200
diagnostic instruction: OCAD as enabler for, 193–202; preparatory activities, 197–98; scenarios, 197; through formalized formative assessment, 199–201; through informal formative assessment, 196–97; translation and writing, 198–99
discourse, 32–34, 70, 84, 88, 90, 100–1, 103–4, 152, 156, 169, 209
disposition toward change, 229
distance learning, 81, 83, 88, 200, 215, 216n1
distance learning immersion course, 107–15; critical reflection, 108–9; individualization, 108–9; modular flexibility, 110–11; objectives and description, 109–10; personalized flexibility, 111–13; sequential flexibility, 113–14; for study abroad students, 107; transformative growth, 108–9
DLIFLC. *See* Defense Language Institute Foreign Language Center

DLPT. *See* Defense Language Proficiency Test
Donato, R., 120
Dutch, 9

E&L Cognitive Style Construct, 16, 199
Edney, K., 100
educational leadership, 227–28
Egyptian Dialect Program, 67–76; assessments, 69; authentic materials, early introduction of, 71; content-based approach to using authentic materials, 71–72; curriculum of, 68–69; delivery of course content, 74; flipped classrooms, 74; formative assessment, 74; learner involvement, 69; learner selection, 74; materials, 69; project-based instruction, 73; task-based instruction, 72–73; use of unadapted authentic materials, integrating, 69–73
elective learning object, 81, 83, 85–86, 88, 91
enabler for transformative learning, 29–39
engagement, 6, 12, 18, 49, 59, 99, 102–3, 105, 108, 119, 171, 223
English (ESL/EFL), 213
Entis, S., 199
error correction, 172; error patterns, 82, 90–91; errors, 35, 37, 73–74, 82, 86, **89**, 91, 111, 183, 186, 199
Esmantova, T., 46
experiential learning, 99, 107–9, 113–14

facilitator/facilitation: teacher role, 4, 7, 30, 56, 168–69, 173, 195
faculty empowerment. *See* teacher empowerment
Farrell, K., 100, 106n2
features of OACD, 8 (complete list), 41, 45–6, 48–9, 64, 81, 105, 142
film, 12, 69, 71, 103, 125, 165–76. *See also* media
first-generation educational program evaluation, 209
Fisher, D., 43, 47, 50n3
flipped classroom, 74, 147, 166, 170–71
flipped learning, 19, 31–32, 35–36
Flipped Learning Network, 31
Florida State University: Center for Educational Technology, 231n5
force multiplier, 6, 22n4

Foreign Service Institute (FSI): Advanced Russian Course, 41–42; early OACD at, 10–11; Russian Department, 68
formal language, 172
formative assessment, 19–20, 35–37, 62, 68, 74, 81, 91, 146–47, 175, 193–204; formalized, 193, 196, 199–202; informal, 74, 170, 193, 195–98, 202; performance-based, 4, 7–8; proficiency-based, 4, 7–8
fossilization, 8, 35, 37, 90, 108, 120, 198, 201
foundational learning object, 81, 83–85
fourth-generation educational program evaluation, 210
fractals, 21, 221, 227–28
French, 11, 58, 101, 109, 140
French War College, 7
Frey, N., 43, 47, 50n3
Froelich, J., 12
FSI. *See* Foreign Service Institute

Gallagher, M. C., 43
Garza, T. J., 194
general education, OACD in, 14–15
German, 109, 140, 200
Gilbert, T. F., 226
Gillette, B., 120–21
Giroux, H., 15
Glickman, C. D., 221, 228
Gold Standard Project, 146
Gordon, S. P., 221, 228
grading, 153, 155, 157, 161, 170, 209
gradual release of responsibility (GRR), 18, 41–50, 54, 159, 178, 212; effective strategies to recognize cognates, teaching, 46; gradual transition from fixed, linear scope and sequence to OACD through, 43–45, *44*; learners with choice of materials, tasks, and activities, 48–49; OACD at level 0/0+, features of, 46–48; sound representations of Cyrillic letters, teaching, 45–46, **46**
gradual transition to OACD, 18, 43–45, 178
grammar, 8, 11, 18, 37, 43, 69, 76, 103, 111, 120–22, 129, 132, 155, 157, 167, 178, 194, 230–31
Grigorenko, E., 203n4
GRR. *See* gradual release of responsibility
guided design, 14

Halliday, M. A. K., 122
Hebrew, 17, 20, 54, 68, 221–23
highly inflected languages, 177–79
Hindi, 19, 142–44
holistic sociocognitive imperative, 187
human performance improvement and technology (HPI/HPT), 226–28

$i + 1$ rule, 21–22
ILR. *See* Interagency Language Roundtable (ILR) scale
immersion, 11, 13, 19–20, 53–64, 69–70, 91, 98, 107–15, 127, 171, 200, 225; inside and outside of country, 63
immersive learning, 107–15
individual differences, 42, 59, 60, 119–21, 126
informal formative assessment, 74, 170, 193, 195–98, 202
institutional culture, 21
instructional-curricular initiatives, 222–25
instructional design, 226–27
instructor workload, 20–21
intensive courses *versus* non-intensive courses, 19
Interagency Language Roundtable (ILR) scale, 42
inter-institutional collaboration, in curriculum development, 130–48; alternative assessments, 146–47; changes in enrollment, 140; flexible, textbook-free curriculum, 142–44; professional development needs, 141; proficiency-oriented, OACD-enabled OER modules, 141–42; project-based language learning, 146; reverse design, 144–45; task-based language teaching, 145–46
International Society for Exploring Teaching Alternatives (ISETA), 14
International Society for Exploring Teaching and Learning (ISETL), 14
interpretation, 59–60, 103, 111, 147, 153
Interstate New Teacher Assessment and Support Consortium, 213
inter-tasks, 19; content-based instruction supported by, 182–86, *184*, *185*
intonation, **89**, 155, 173
Isabelli-García, C., 98
ISETA. *See* International Society for Exploring Teaching Alternatives

Index

ISETL. *See* International Society for Exploring Teaching and Learning
iso-immersions, 54–59, **61**, 63–64
isolated immersion, 30, 147
Italian, 20

James, C., 200
Japanese, 140
Johnson, P., 76n3
Joint Security Area (2000), 168, 170, 174
Juan-Garau, M., 98
Juche (self-reliance) belief, 32–34, 39n23
Jung, C. G., 199

Kaplan, M. M., 178
K-8 Irvine Hebrew Day School, 20
Kegan, R., 227
Kelian, L. L., 14–15
Kim Jong Un, 39n23; 2019 New Year's Address, 33
Kinginger, C., 100, 106n2
Kirkman, S., 109
Klein, G. S., 5
Kogan, V. V., 187n1
Korean, 29–39, 58, 140, 165–76, 196; North Korean, 30–34, 38–39
Krasner, I., 18, 32, 47, 54, 146, 178, 224
Kroll, J. F., 98
K-12 education, 14, 16–19
Kumaravadivelu, B., 120

L'Allier, J. J., 81
Language Flagship, The: domestic and overseas, 9, 15, 151; Korean Language Flagship Program (at the University of Hawai'i at Mānoa) 165–76; Russian Language Flagship Program (at Portland State University) 151–60
language proficiency, 4, 9, 50n2, 57, 82, 97, 105, 141–42, 148, 166, 194, 199–200, 224; development, 145; growth, 178; testing, 109
languages across the curriculum programs, 12
Lantolf, J. P., 194, 203n4
Lash, A., 195
LCTLs. *See* less commonly taught languages
learner autonomy, 4, 7, 18, 21, 29, 38, 49, 80, 86, 97–99, 102, 105, 108–10, 113–14, 120, 124, 126, 176, 197, 221, 223, 228
learner awareness, 125

learner-centered instruction, 29, 36; proficiency-oriented, 4, 8, 170
Learner Data Panel, 79, 80, 82–84, 90–91, *91*, 92n2
learner empowerment, 8, 38, 80, 99, 144, 201
learner feedback, 32, 61–62, 75, 126, 128, 173, 175, 230
learner individuality, 79–80
learner interaction, 124–25
learner introspection, 125
learner involvement in selection, design, and delivery of content: ongoing, 4, 7, 21, 30, 38, 68, 73, 74, 120–22, 125–26, 128, 152–53, 170, 207, 210
learner likes/dislikes, **126**
learner needs, 79–80
learner negotiation, 124
learner profile survey, 130–32
learner responses, 134–35
learner retrospection, 125
learner self-awareness, 120–21, 126
learner self-efficacy, 80
learner strategy, 123
learner-teacher collaboration, 42, 79, 83, 91, 103, 105n1, 108
learner variation, OACD and, 16
learning affordances, 121, 127
learning by teaching, 35
learning efficiency, 6, 9, 22n2, 81
learning plan, 123–24, 132–33; tailored, 201
learning style, 5
Leaver, B. L., 7, 10–11, 41–42, 45, **46**, 177–78, 195
less commonly taught languages (LCTLs), 19, 22, 31, 139–48, 200
Less Commonly Taught Languages and Indigenous Languages Partnership Project, 139–48
lexicon. *See* vocabulary
lingua franca, 69
listening, 8, 11–13, 17, 21, 31, 34, 45, 48, 55, 58–61, 63–64, 67, 70–73, 75–76, 81, 84–86, **87**, 88, 98, 102, 104, 124, 127, 131, 147, 157, 166–68, **169**, **170**, 172–76, 178, 196, 199–201, 222, 230
Little, D., 228
living curriculum, 79
Llanes, À., 98
Lyashevskaya, O., 43

Machin, D., 33–34
macrostrategies, 119–29
Maher, P. A., 109
May 18 (2007), 170
Mayr, A., 33–34
McCormick, D., 120
McLaren, P., 15
McVee, M. B., 43
media, 8, 30, 32–34, 71, 88, 97, 99–105, 110, 114, 151–55, 157, 159, 160n1, 167, 172–73
mediated learning, 119
mentor/mentoring: teacher role, 4, 7, 17, 21, 30–31, 35
Merage Jewish Community Center, Irvine, California, 20
Merrill, M. D.: "First Principles of Instruction," 80
metapragmatic awareness, 99–101, 105, 106n2
Mezirow, J., 5, 29, 109, 227
Michigan State University, 139–41, 143–45, 147, 234
Microsoft Teams, 35
Middlebury Institute of International Studies, 18–19, 54
Miller, J. P., 22n3
Modern Language Association Census, 140, 213
modular flexibility, 110–11
Monolingual Language Training Program (MOLT), 10
morphological complexity, 43
Moscow City Council, 153
Motivated Strategies for Learning Questionnaire, 199
movies. *See* film
multidimensional language awareness, 122, 127
multisection courses, 16–17
Murao, R., 152
Murphy, L., 108
Murphy-Lee, M., 45
music, 59, 69, 125, 133

National Council on the Accreditation of Teacher Educators, 213
National Standards in Foreign Language Education Project, 213

news, 30, 59, 151–60
Nikonova (Thompson), S. M., 9

OAPE. *See* open architecture program evaluation
Ode to My Father (2014), 170
OERs. *See* open educational resources
online diagnostic assessment, 62, 196, 200
open architecture program evaluation (OAPE), 207–16
open educational resources (OERs), 140–48
oral presentations, 69, 151–61, 168, 224
Oral Proficiency Interview, 75, 81, 98, 104, 109, 159, 222
organic teams, fostering, 228–29

PBLL. *See* project-based language learning
Pearson, P. D., 43
peer assessment, 157, 167, 169
peer evaluation. *See* peer assessment
peer feedback, 167, 169, 198
peer mentoring, 228, 230
peer observation, 228, 230
peer reviews, 20, 185
peer teaching, 35, 74, 198
Peppermint Candy (2000), 170, 174
Pérez-Vidal., C., 98
Perry, E., 100
Persian-Farsi, 13, 109, 196
personalized flexibility, 111–13
Piagetan learning theory, 45
Poehner, M. E., 194, 203n4
Portuguese, 109–14
President's Barber, The (2004), 170
President's Last Bang, The (2005), 170
principles of OACD, 7 (complete list), 76, 108–09, 129, 144, 179, 207
professional development, 16, 17, 31, 139, 141–42, 144, 202, 216, 228, 230
proficiency, 7, 10–13; cultural, 41–42; lower levels, 18, 42, 178; novice-level, 41–40, 177–87; proficiency-based formative assessment, 7–8; proficiency-oriented, content-based instruction course, 165–76; proficiency-oriented learner-centered instruction, 4, 8, 170; semester abroad experience, 97–106; target-language, 9; upper *versus* lower levels of, 17–19
program-fair evaluation, 214

Index

project-based instruction, 20, 73, 166, 171
project-based language learning (PBLL), 140, 142, 144–47
pronunciation, 71, 89, 133,152, 155, 157, 173, 182
punctuation, 103

qualitative data, 208
quantitative data, 215

rapid prototyping design, 229
Ratushnyuk, K., 20
reading, 8, 11–13, 17, 21, 30, 33–35, 45, 47–49, 55, 58–60, **61**, 63–64, 67, 69–70, 73, 75, 76n2, 81, 84, 86, **87**, 88, 98, 103–4, 131, 147, 151–164, 166–67, **169**, **170**, 173, 176, 178, 180, 186, 199–201, 219, 217, 222, 230, 237
real-world events, 17, 21, 63, 82, 111, 145, 171
recall protocol, 175, 193, 195–202
reflection prompt, 134–35
reflective learning journals, 36–38
register, 8, 84, 103, 201
repetitive orientation, 227–28
repetitive to competitive orientation, 227–28
reverse design, 144–45
Rifkin, B., 156
Rook, J., 20
Ross-Gordon, J. M., 221, 228
rule of law (*fazhi*), 104
Russian, 9–12, 15, 18, 41–43, 45–50, 54, 58, 109–11, 114, 117–38, 133–35, 151–53, 155, 157, 177–78, 180–87, 196
Ryding, K., 76n2

San Diego State University: Language Acquisition Resource Center Language Training Center, 59; "Language Training Center General Course Description," 59–60; two-week immersions at, 59–60, 62, 63
Sandrock, P., 194
Saydee, F., 19
scaffolding, 46, 48, 71, 75, 80, 83, 86, 127, 151, 153–56, 159, 195
scenario-based instruction, 3–4, 8, 10–11, 15, 19–20, 54–58, 120–21, 124, 170, 177–78, 197, 203n5
Schlesinger, H., 5
Scriven, M., 194

SCT-L2. *See* sociocultural theory in relation to language learning
SDPs. *See* spiral-like design principles
second-generation educational program evaluation, 209
self-awareness training, 123
self-sequenced modularity, 98–99, 105n1
Seller, M., 22n3
semester abroad experience: proficiency-increasing features of, 97–106; learner autonomy, 99; metapragmatic awareness, 99–101; OACD implementation in Chinese media course sequence, 102–3; opportunities to revise activities and tasks, 99; out-of-class portion, 97–99; self-sequenced modularity, 98–99; *see also* study abroad
Senge, P. M., 226
sequential flexibility, 113–14
Serbian/Croatian, 11–12, 178
Seventh Day, The, 71
Shanahan, L. E., 43
Shanghai International Convention Center, 57
simulated immersion environment, 70, 107, 111, 171
single-section courses, 16–17
skill integrated learning, 168–69, **169**
SLA. *See* second language acquisition
Slater, T., 171
small group discussion, 168–76
Snow, M. A., 166
sociocultural theory in relation to language learning (SCT-L2), 119–29
sociolinguistic competence, 98
speaking, 11–13, 17, 34–38, 45, 55, 58–61, **61**, 61, 63–64, 67, 73, 75, 76n2, 81, 98, 104, 131, 135, 147, 151–64, 167–68, 169, **170**, 199, 210, 222
South Korean National Security Act of 1948, 32
Spanish, 11, 20, 58, 109, 110, 113–14, 140, 196
spiral-like curriculum design, 177–87
spiral-like design principles (SDPs), 179–85
STARTALK Program, 19
STEPs. *See* subtopic/theme essential to progress
Sternberg, R., 203n4
strategic self-regulation, 121

student enrollment, 215
study abroad, 7, 13, 63, 107–9, 111, 113–15, 143, 145, 152–53, 215. *See also* semester abroad experience
stylistics, 8
subtopic/theme essential to progress (STEPs), *82*
summative assessment, 8, 74, 146, 194; definition of, 194; distinguished from formative assessment, 193–94; Korean Proficiency through Film course, 170, 175
Sunderman, G., 98
super-authentic materials, 70
Swahili, 142–44, 147
Sychov, S., 160

tailored learning plans, 114, 195–97, 200, 201
tailoring: of instruction, 4, 7, 30, 37, 42, 54, 60, 63, 79, 91, 114, 144, 152–53, 166, 172, 196–97, 200–1, 207
target language: use of, 8, 11–12, 18–20, 36, 42, 57–60, 63, 75, 109–110, 121, 154, 171, 173, 178, 182, 198
target-language society, 6, 8
Tarrant, M. A., 109
task, definition of, 145
task-based instruction, 72–73, 108, 194
task-based language teaching (TBLT), 140, 142, 145–46
task-based open architecture language teaching, 111
task selection handout, 133
Taxi Driver, A (2017), 170
TBLT. *See* task-based language teaching
teacher as mentor, 86, 109
teacher autonomy, 221, 230
teacher empowerment, 4, 43
teacher-learner collaboration, 108
textbook-free, 3, 10, 14, 30, 33, 42, 142, 153
theme-based syllabus, 3–4, 7, 10, 19, 51, 54, 142, 165, 170, 175, 178, 180–81
third-generation educational program evaluation, 209

Three Gorges Project, 83, 86, 88, 90–91
TLLT. *See* transformative language learning and teaching
tolerance for failure, 229, 230
top-down processing, 8, 70, 173
transformative language learning and teaching (TLLT), 4–5, 7, 29, 38, 180; for native English-speaking learners of North Korean, relevance of, 30
transformative learning, 7–8, 108–9, 227; definition of, 29; OACD as enabler for, 29–39
translation, 10, 60, 67, 135, 185, 193, 198
Travitzki, R., 14–15
Trumbull, E., 195

Ukrainian, 12, 58
Urdu, 19

Van den Branden, K., 145
van Dijk, T. A., 101
van Lier, L., 54, 121, 124
vocabulary, 11, 18, 69, 111, 167, 174, 178–79, 183–84, 186, 194, 198, 201, 223, 225
Vygotsky, L. S., 43, 76n5, 80, 119, 121, 195, 203n4

Wesche, M. B., 166
William, D., 194–95
World-Readiness Standards for Learning Languages, 4, 6, 8, 30, 213
Wrigley, T., 15
writing, 34–38, 45–47, 59, 64, 98–99, 104–5, 111, 115, 124, 146–47, 154–57, 166–67, 169, **169, 170**, 170–72, 175, 180–81, 185, 193, 198–200, 203n3, 223

Zhu, W., 152
Zmarzly, J., 19–20
zone of proximal development (ZPD), 42–44, 47, 72, 74, 80, 108, 119, 121, 123, 127–28, 179, 195, 203n4; definition of, 76n5, 129n1